Bread of
Three Rivers

ᒫ ᒫ ᒫ

BREAD OF
THREE RIVERS
The Story of a French Loaf

ᒫ ᒫ ᒫ ᒫ

Sara Mansfield Taber

For Catharine
Here, to the French.

Sara Taber

BEACON PRESS   *Boston*

BEACON PRESS
25 Beacon Street
Boston, Massachusetts 02108-2892
www.beacon.org

Beacon Press books
are published under the auspices of
the Unitarian Universalist Association of Congregations.

Credits to reproduce previously copyrighted
material appear on page 244.

Printed in the United States of America

05 04 03 02 01   7 6 5 4 3 2 1

This book is printed on acid-free paper that meets
the uncoated paper ANSI/NISO specifications
for permanence as revised in 1992.

Text design by Melodie Wertelet / mwdesign
Composition by Wilsted & Taylor Publishing Services

Library of Congress Cataloging-in-Publication Data

Taber, Sara Mansfield
Bread of three rivers : the story of a French loaf /
Sara Mansfield Taber.
p.   cm.
ISBN 0-8070-7238-9
1. Bread.   2. Bread — History.
3. Bakers and bakeries — France.   I. Title.
TX769 .T28 2001
641.8'15 — dc21
2001001791

TO PETER, MAUD, AND FORREST

If I bear burdens
they begin to be remembered as
gifts, goods, a basket of bread
that hurts my shoulders but closes
me in fragrance. I can eat as I go.

Denise Levertov
"Stepping Westward"

There are romances and romances.
Mine was with a French loaf.

Contents

French-American Conversions

FRANCE	UNITED STATES
Liquid Volume	
1 liter	1.06 quarts/4 ⅓ cups
1 milliliter	0.03 fluid ounces
240 milliliters	1 cup
Weight	
1 kilogram* (1,000 grams)	2.2 lb.
1 gram (one-thousandth of a kilogram)	
1 milligram (one-thousandth of a gram)	
140 grams unsifted flour	1 cup unsifted flour
Linear	
1 kilometer (1,000 meters)	0.62 miles
1 meter (1,000 millimeters)	39 inches
1 centimeter (one-hundredth of a meter)	0.39 inches
1 millimeter (one-thousandth of a meter)	0.04 inches
Land	
1 hectare (10,000 square meters)	2.47 acres
Temperature	
Celsius/Centigrade	Multiply degrees Celsius by 1.8 and add 32 to get Fahrenheit

*Note: A gram, or one-thousandth of a kilogram, is equivalent to 15,432 grains. Grain is "the smallest unit of weight in most systems, originally determined by the weight of a plump grain of wheat" (*Random House College Dictionary*).

Prologue

A DREAM
OF BREAD

In the imagination of each of us exists a material image of an ideal dough, a perfect synthesis of resistance and suppleness, a marvelous balance of the forces that accept and the forces that refuse.

Gaston Bachelard
La Terre et les Reveries de la Volonté

MY AFFAIR BEGAN AT FORTY WHEN MY HUSBAND, PETER, found his dream job in Washington, D.C., and I left behind a position as an assistant professor at the University of Minnesota. Eight months after our arrival, I gave birth to our second child, Forrest. In my small, suburban cottage, temporarily jobless, and new to the area, I felt like a cave woman abandoned by her clan in a still, earthen den. All the women in our neighborhood seemed to work full-time. The hectic Washington pace was unconducive to forging easy friendships, and I found myself passing my weeks with little adult companionship. The interesting people I did meet seemed to lead runaway lives, constantly busy if never quite getting to that one thing they wanted to do most. Time seemed a crucial and scarce commodity.

On my walks through the neighborhood, there were questions, half-noticed but ever-present, that ambled with me. Why does work seem to gobble up bigger and bigger hunks of us every day? Where has community gone? Why is there no free time anymore? Life seemed to narrow, and I needed, badly, to prove fantasies were still out there for the taking. I yearned for something deeper, more satisfying, more pleasurable, tastier.

How to find delight again—that became the urgency of my long, little-varying Washington days. I chose the basic, sturdy, age-old woman's route: through the belly. I took to driving long distances for a bakery anyone mentioned. I loved the round, European-style loaves with hard crusts—loaves with names like *pain de campagne,* or *pain rustique*—the ones that looked like erupting mushrooms or chubby wands. *Pain au levain* especially captivated me. I loved the notion of bread made of soured dough that carried with it some sort of magical essence from one batch of bread to the next. Of course, I had been slowly seduced over the years by a youth spent in part in Europe; by Millet's luminous paintings of peasants peacefully working in pink-lit dawn fields; and by the crusty French bread formed into sunflowers that my dear friend Juliette, back from trips home, conjured up out of suitcases. So it was really no surprise that Forrest and I drove all over Washington to new bakeries, each bread-buying trip like a small celebration. Inexorably, subtly, French loaves came to seem like crown jewels. No, not jewels. Something more essential and wonderful, like air.

℮

For a time I took to baking as a way to bring French bread and Europe that much nearer. Four times, I attempted to make *pain au levain,* a five-day process that requires the baker to grow a starter by adding flour and water on a daily basis to a steadily souring lump of dough. The first attempt resulted in an utterly flat loaf with a nice smell, but a disappointing, dense texture, and sticky goo spread all over the kitchen. The second time around, my dough did rise but the loaf had a crust of cannonball hardness and a crumb with huge tunnels that would have made great naked mole rat habitat. The third time, I forgot about my souring dough and it went moldy, and the final time, one of my children knocked the bowl of starter on the floor and it broke. I took this as a clear sign that I should leave bread-baking to the professionals and make more frequent trips to bakeries.

One day as Forrest and my daughter, Maud, played in the background, I asked myself, What *is* it about bread? Why am I, here in the middle of my life, so enamored of French loaves? Two images kept cropping up: two French people sitting in a café for a long afternoon of eating thick hunks of bread and drinking cups of coffee, and a Frenchman on a bicycle with a loaf slung across his handlebars. These visions seemed to depict lives soaked in leisure, where there was time for the good things.

Then these thoughts presented themselves:

~ Bread is pure and unalloyed.

~ A loaf of bread is simple beauty, lovely texture, honest shape.

~ While chewing bread, a person can steal a little rest. Look out a window. Gaze. Let her mind float. One specification: it must be hard bread that takes time to chew.

~ To break into a loaf is to cultivate a sense of communion with the soil, with our fellows, with the divine, as Christians share bread in churches.

~ Bread can be taken for granted in the secure, reassuring sense of something good always there.

Then this thought ambled forth: It's the dailiness of bread, like a reliable friend. "Why not Lindt chocolate?" someone might ask. Though I love chocolate, its fleeting pleasures, like those romances of younger days, store little deep or lasting pleasure for me. I am after the trusty basics now: daisies, spring water, garden tomatoes, bread.

One day in Washington, I watch Forrest take apart a slice of good sourdough from a local European-style bakery. He sits on the floor and carefully and deliberately pulls the bread apart. He works away, fiber by fiber, until he is surrounded by shreds of bread the perfect size for ducks.

It is while watching this spectacle that it occurs to me that what I want, more than anything else, is to examine a good French loaf the way Forrest is examining his. My heart races when I realize that what I desire, with a strange ardor, is to understand bread in a deep way, beyond even the capacity of my tongue.

I decide I will find a wonderful French loaf—a product of a French village—follow it backward, track down its history, back into the oven, back through the kneading trough, and on into the beyonds of the country roads, to the fields of wheat, to the salt producers, to the yeast cultivators, and to the waters that contribute their bounty. I will talk to the farmers and all those whose toil goes into the bread, and hear about their lives. My project, as I imagine it, will be a natural history, an ecology of bread. The story of a loaf.

As I dreamed of France, I was certain about what I would find there. While I felt disconnected in my American city, the French would be nourished by community as well as good bread. The French, in contrast to my compatriots, would have balanced lives infused with a slowed-down sense of time that left many hours for family, friends, and contemplation. Whereas American food was a mash of carcinogenic chemicals and ingredients flown in from all over the world, my French loaf would be made of pure, local ingredients, by local rural people. While American bread was squishy and tasteless, the baguette, and all French bread, would be delicious and of the highest quality, due to the bakers' adherence to tried and true, age-old traditions. The country of the baguette would be the opposite of my country, which was responsible for the annihilation of well-made, quirky, and unique local products, and for the McDonaldization of the world. France, to my mind, would be the repository of quality. The grass would be quintessentially greener there.

As I set off on this lark, I suspected I might be seeing rural life, and Europe, and maybe even bread, through rose-colored glasses, but, as in any new love, I just couldn't give it up. I wanted to chase after my dream. I wanted that confirmation of something more.

And I found it.

THE LOAF

My oven is not black, it is golden! And it is a gold that is eaten! The color that I make delights the eye, but besides, it is thick, substantial, it smells good, it is warm, it nourishes.

Michel Tournier
Pierrot or *Les Secrets de la Nuit*

THE CHILDREN, PETER, AND I LANDED IN FRANCE IN
late June, lugging diapers and notebooks in lumpy luggage. We
passed a heavy-lidded day in Paris and then drove for five hours
to the western coast on the sleek French *autoroute,* the A-11.
By a series of circumstances, and over many months, I had decided to base myself in Brittany, and to search for a basic loaf—
one that used only the simplest of ingredients—so as to trace
bread at its purest. With the help of Juliette's parents and the
French Bakers' Union, I identified a Monsieur Jean-Claude
Choquet, in an obscure little village called Blain in the Western Loire valley, not far from the Breton coast. In 1986, Monsieur Choquet had been named a *Médaille d'Or Boulanger-
Meilleur Ouvrier de France,* Gold Medal Baker-Best French
Worker. I hoped he would lead me to my loaf.

For now, the broad landscapes of wheat, mustard, jelly-roll
hay bales, red-roofed barns, and sunken villages rolled out before us. They were a salve to my eyes so long restricted to vistas only as wide as city streets. We wandered the flat, hot cow
pastures that distinguish Loire-Atlantique, the *département* or
county that encompasses the Western Loire, for a long time before finally finding our *gîte,* a country house rental we picked
out of a catalogue for the region. The *gîte* was one of two properties sharing a typical long, rambling two-story barn-and-
dwellings structure. One half of the building was a crumbling,
working farmhouse that faced a reeking barn full of veal calves.
Our half, reached via a hummocky track lined with fruit trees,
and happily facing the opposite direction, was freshly stuccoed
and whitewashed, with heavily varnished dark wood doors giv-

ing way to a long and wide green lawn with sandbox and swings, rainbow-hued garden patches of flowers, and a nook for outdoor eating. The landlords, a Monsieur and Madame Pele—he was a driving school instructor—met and toasted us with a bottle of the local *cidre.* They explained, with laughs, that the portion of the building in which we would be lodged was once a pig shed. The French government, they wanted us to understand, subsidizes the conversion of farm buildings to *gîtes* and *chambres d'hôte,* or bed and breakfasts, both to maintain rural life in France and to provide holiday houses to country-starved city dwellers like us.

Our new temporary home was located about forty kilometers from Nantes at the edge of le Coudray, a sleepy village fifteen kilometers to the northwest of Blain, the small town of 7,430 in which Monsieur Choquet has his bakery. Blain would be the base of operations in my quest for the heart of French bread.

The truth is, I got hardly two hours of sleep that first night, I was so tense with nervous excitement at the thought of my meeting with Jean-Claude Choquet the next morning. I wondered if he would be the haughty Frenchman of the American stereotype, and I was keyed up with excitement, as though this were a blind date. On this first foray into the world of French baking, or *boulangerie,* I hoped to gain a basic overview of French bread and baking. If luck was with me, I might find my loaf.

I rose at dawn for my nine A.M. appointment, but then I got muddled among the interlaced two-lane country roads. I was late, and I roared along the sleepy lanes like a Washington commuter. I'd been given Monsieur Choquet's name by the bakers' syndicate in Nantes. They had informed me, in crisp, businesslike French, that he was a busy man, so I was mortified to find myself still wandering the countryside at nine-twenty. Unbeknownst to me at the time, the bakers' association's concern about Monsieur Choquet's time was a foreshadowing of the experience to come. For my visits to the Boulangerie Choquet were a kind of study in the uses of time, a time symphony.

It was close to 9:30 when I finally pulled into a parking place by the Blain church and raced down the street to the bakery.

Its door opened right onto the narrow sidewalk. The long windows, with displays of croissants and tarts and bags of candy, gleamed. Above the double-wide door, block letters spelled the word *BOULANGERIE,* and just beneath, in white script on the window glass, were the names of the proprietors: *J et JC CHOQUET.* The flaps of the maroon awnings over the four storefront windows were printed with the words *CROIS-SANTERIE, CHOCOLATS, PÂTISSERIE,* and *GLACES* in bright white lettering. From the second story of the facade hung a sign reading *"Boulanger Authentique,"* with the design of a baker holding a paddle balancing a lump of bread dough.

Inside the shallow shop, a long glass case holding *tartes aux poires,* croissants, and other pastries formed an aisle for the line of customers trailing out the door. I stayed at the shop entrance to take in the scene for a few seconds. Positioned at the end of the càse was a low table with a cash register and a bread-wrapping counter. Behind these stood a knee-to-ceiling wall of shelves holding dozens of loaves, all lined up and golden under the warm lights. The shelves held an extravagance of loaves: baguette-shaped breads with the intriguing names *pain gris, pain polka, pain de trois livres gris, pain de trois livres jaune, pain de 1 kilo gris,* and *pain de 1 kilo jaune.* There were also *pain saucisson* with a sausage cut across the top; *flûte moulée,* a very long, thin baguette twice the regular length; *ficelle,* a little, skinny baton of bread; rounds of *boule de pain; pain court gris* in two forms, round and oblong; and *pain moulée,* a squarish long loaf like an angled-off baguette. Nestled on the other shelves were *boule de pain polka;* dinner plate-size, flat round loaves; *pain rustique* shaped like shovel heads; *pain de cam-*

pagne in both baguette and oblong shapes; round *boules* of *pain de ménage* and *pain de ménage biologique;* and loaves, in baguette and small and large *bâtard* shapes, with the intriguing name *pain trois rivières.* There were also various smaller *pains spéciaux,* including a *couronne,* a beautiful, round golden circle about two inches thick; several *épi,* shaped like a stalk of wheat; and finally, a *fougasse,* another round loaf, but cut out, stenciled, like a tree.

Two women were greeting customers from behind the cash register, one young and blond woman with an elegant velvet bow holding back her ponytail, the other older with short-short brown hair, gold-rimmed tinted glasses, and tiny pearls in her ears. I soon learned she was the baker's wife. Her voice made a merry, splashing sound as it rung out in greeting to each customer.

I watched as an ever-replenishing queue of customers made their way up to the front of the line, put in their requests for baguettes and *boules* and *pain ordinaire,* received a prize— wrapped around the middle with a small, twisted square of wax paper or broken in half for a shopping bag—and proceeded out the door, departing the line like geese flushing off from a **V** in the sky.

A little girl with a floppy, orange-ribboned topknot received a slice of bread with a piece of chocolate stuck in it; a man carrying a long, plain, cotton sack was handed a baguette.

A plump twenty year-old asked, "What do you have for a small bread?"

The baker's wife held up a tiny loaf made from left over dough. "This one?"

The girl left laughing, three loaves in her arms, blue skirts flowing to her ankles.

The baker's wife greeted everyone, handed over loaves, made change fast.

"*Ça va?* This loaf will do?" she said.

"Voilà. There you go. There it is. There we are."

"Bonne journée!"

Her three-phrase litany rang out over and over again, and each customer was sent off with a singsong good-bye. *"Allez,"* she said, or *"Au revoir!"* or *"Voilà,"* her voice with the bells in it crying out every half minute.

As I stood in line now, awaiting my turn, I could feel the quiet bustle of the shop tingling through me. The ordinariness and plainness of the work and the bread, the efficient straight-forwardness of the transactions between the shopkeepers and their customers, and the sense of basic, patient goodwill and politeness that suffused the atmosphere in the shop were a contrast to the brusque and hectic interactions I sometimes experienced buying bread in Washington.

The baker's wife instantly came out from behind the counter when she heard my name, and introduced herself as Marie-Madeleine Choquet, Jean-Claude Choquet's wife and shop-keeper. Immediately, she disappeared through a door into the inner sanctum of the bakery and soon reappeared with a large shape behind her. A bear-sized man, with a composed, regal bearing, emerged from the doorway, and met me with *"Bonjour, Madame,"* and a friendly, extended hand. It was Monsieur Choquet.

I stammered out an apology for my tardiness and he assured me it had caused him no difficulty at all. With a smile and a calm sideways motion of his large hands he dismissed my concern about the hour.

He waved toward the scores of fresh loaves gleaming like gold-cast wands and moons and ushered me behind the counter, through a door, and down a little dark hall into a small, pleasantly cluttered space that obviously served as an all-purpose kitchen and family room. He offered me a seat at a wooden table, nestled in a corner that held a splay of baker's newspapers and magazines which he pushed to one side. I sat down and the gorgeous smell of bread that filled the air seemed to reach not only my nose, but my arms and legs, too.

He had just finished his night's work, Monsieur Choquet explained, as he sat down opposite me and folded his hands, ready for questions. The baker showed not a drop of fatigue, though he had been up since an hour after midnight. He was exquisitely patient and receptive, speaking slowly for me, as though he understood my challenge of speaking a once familiar language.

Monsieur Choquet—the French are formal and I never graduated to "Jean-Claude"—looked the quintessential boulanger. On the other hand, he might also have been a sailor. Tall, strong, solid, and trim, with late-graying dark hair, his middle-aged face had the vigor, smoothness, and rosy coloring of youth—a coloring that could have come as easily from a life spent in ocean breezes as in the wafting fragrances of fresh bread. He wore a white baker's apron over his clothes, and well-cushioned sneakers on his feet—signs of long hours passed on the move among sacks of flour and tables of rising dough. In the skinny light-blue stripes of the tight-fitting T-shirt he wore, though, and especially in the tiny skullcap of a baker's hat perched on his head, there was a subtle but distinct maritime cast.

In fact, the first thing Monsieur Choquet told me was that he had once sailed to my country. He had completed his military service by baking bread on a naval vessel that took him as far as the hills of San Francisco. Save for those sixteen months in the late 1960s, he had lived his entire life in Blain, first as a boy busy growing up, then as a worker in the baker's shop his father had bought just after the war.

On the first tack, Monsieur Choquet took a nose count of the kinds of breads produced at Boulangerie Choquet.

"As for the breads we make each day, well, principally we

make the baguette," he said. "That is the preferred bread of the French people today. But we also make other breads of the French tradition: *pain de ménage, pain gris, pain polka* . . ." He began listing all the breads I had seen on the shelves, "And then, of course, we make all the *pâtisserie* as well . . ." he said, spinning out rich and sugary terms for scores of pastries. Later, I counted the number of kinds of breads Monsieur Choquet had mentioned. He had named over thirty-five varieties.

"Tous les jours?" I asked.

"Oui, oui. Every day."

℮

The Boulangerie Choquet has two shops, one in Blain and another in Saint-Etienne de Montluc, a village a few kilometers away through forests and fields. All the *pains spéciaux* are baked in Blain, but most of the *pains de tradition française* are made in the other village.

The Blain shop is shut for an hour at midday and closes up for the night at eight P.M. Its hours have remained the same through all the decades that the Choquet family has owned the bakery. "My wife opens the shop to customers at six every morning," Monsieur Choquet said, beginning an accounting of the bakery's work schedule.

"Fourteen people work at the boulangerie. Let's see." He slowly enumerated them on his fingers. "There's me and my wife—we work the same as the others—and my partner and my son. My father is now retired. Then there are three apprentices in the pastry shop, and one in the bread section, and three delivery people, one of whom is my sister, and three half-time people.

"My personal schedule is from two in the morning until, I'll say, ten A.M., around there. My partner, Jean-Paul Breher, comes in at nine at night. He works from nine until two in the morning. And then he returns at six A.M. and works until midday. Jean-Paul is also a boulanger. We began our baking trades together here thirty years ago, the two of us, Jean-Paul and then me."

"How do you manage?" I asked Monsieur Choquet, thinking of the bleariness I experience if I miss even one hour of my requisite eight hours of rest. "When do you sleep?"

Again he dismissed my concern with a brush of his broad hand. "Oh, I sleep *un petit peu* from ten until midday. And then, since I am president of the Loire-Atlantique *syndicat des boulangers,* the regional bakers' association, I open that office for the afternoon. I return to sleep a little more in the night— from, say, nine to two."

It was plain. Monsieur Choquet was an ox for work who put to maximum use every second available to him. "There is an easier schedule for the young learning the trade," he said, as though that made up for the grueling schedule of the older bakers. "The young bakers begin work at five A.M. and stay until around noon."

Nowadays, Monsieur Choquet told me, the work is less killing than in the old days—the days before the *chambre froide,* or *chambre de fermentation.* This miracle of modern technology is a big, walk-in refrigerator like one you might find in a general store in Maine. A baker who uses a *chambre froide* assembles his loaves in the wee hours of the morning and then leaves them to ferment for as long as he likes in his refrigerated room. In contrast to bakers of the past who had to begin the next day's loaves as soon as the morning's bread was baked, the *chambre froide* allows the baker to take a break until evening, or early morning, when the loaves from the refrigerated rooms are baked for early morning deliveries and stockage in the shop. All of this adds up to the fact that if you step into a baker's shop where a *chambre froide* exists at, say, two A.M. on a Wednesday, the dough being assembled will actually be that for the bread to be sold on Thursday.

This delayed baking was one of the first of many surprises I was to encounter along the winding route into the heart of French bread. I had assumed that any loaf I might find in a boulangerie would be the product of the previous few hours' labor.

Monsieur Choquet's loaves typically stay in the *chambre froide* about ten to twelve hours. "*Si vous voulez,* if you wish, to make a good French bread, one considers that it takes—in principal, in normal conditions, at a temperature of twenty-three degrees Centigrade—six hours. From the moment one puts the dough to rise until the moment one takes out the baked bread. This is the normal cycle of an average fermentation. Now, if one lowers the temperature from twenty-three degrees to twelve, the fermentation time will be twelve to fourteen hours. This is the way of my work: we lower the temperature to ten to twelve degrees and we allow the bread to ferment for a long time, very slowly. This permits it to take on a little bit of acidity, and so a little bit more taste."

As he spoke, an image was growing in my head of a self-sufficient, distinct nocturnal world.

There are three bakers in the shop at two A.M., Monsieur Choquet said. The same three work every night. One begins the mixing and kneading and shaping of the loaves for the next day. One mans the oven, baking the loaves from the *chambre froide,* and the third starts the *pâtisserie.* All the pastries —croissants to *tarte aux poires* to Breton sugar cookies—are made the same day they are sold.

"The number of loaves we make varies from one night to the next. Oh, a day like today, we probably make seven bakings, but it's difficult to tell you exactly. A day like today we have made two hundred 400-gram loaves, we have made three hundred baguettes. We have made eighty *boules,* we have made seventy loaves of one kilo and one kilo-500, we have made fifty *pains ménage,* we have made fifty *pains trois rivières.* Of the *baguettes de tradition française* we have also made fifty. We have a broad range of breads, and there are varieties of which we make but four or five. The *pain aux six céréales*, the *pain 'triple alliance'*—of these we make but four to six a day."

e~

Bakeries such as the Boulangerie Choquet appeared in the last century. The professional bakers' organization in the Loire-Atlantique region, for instance, has been in existence for 110 years. In the towns, bread was made by boulangers much earlier than in the countryside. Before the war, people in the countryside made bread in their outdoor ovens. Bread made in a wood-fired village oven, Monsieur Choquet explained, is *"plus saisi, grillé."* It rises fast. It's grilled as much as baked. The typical village oven is very hot when the loaves are first inserted—this is what gives the thick crust—and the temperature of the oven falls throughout the baking.

But the use of village ovens has practically disappeared now. The mossy, stone village ovens I'd noticed in the tiny hamlets are currently used only for old-fashioned baking demonstrations, or to roast pork or bake cakes for special occasions and *fêtes.*

"During my father's early years as a baker, around the years of the war, all the wheat he used came from the immediate region." Back then, Monsieur Choquet said, a baker had an advantage in that there were a lot of small local mills still in existence. There were five or six mills just in Blain. A miller went out into the country to collect the wheat from the farmers. After milling, he delivered his flour to the boulangerie. Then the boulanger baked loaves from the flour, and delivered the bread—in those days they made only large, round *pain de deux livres.*

During the Second World War the French government imposed a regulation requiring bakers to use the entire wheat kernel, rather than husking it, in order to consume less of the country's grain. In some months, Monsieur Choquet said, as though this were very bad indeed, it was necessary to add corn to the wheat, stocks were so low. All through the war, bread was rationed and people had less bread to eat. Some baked it secretly in the countryside, but there were inspectors everywhere.

The baker's eyes seemed to darken for an instant, as he recounted the plight of the French in the early forties. Then their twinkle returned. "During the war," Monsieur Choquet said, "our bread was appreciated by the American soldiers. They traded for our local bread. American bread is more like cake bread or *brioche:* a sweet bread with a soft crumb and no crust. The soldiers loved our crusty French bread."

After the war bakers were able again to make their traditional wheaten loaves—many, in fact, with peacetime excitement, broadened their repertoires—and boulangeries thrived. During the fifties, there were 48,000 boulangeries spread across France. In the last ten years, however, the number has diminished to 34,000. Due to the proliferation of *supermarchés* and to the emptying of the countryside, many bakeries shut down because they were no longer profitable. In 1945, there were four bakeries in Blain, for instance, and two more in the little neighboring villages, making a total of six boulangeries in the Blinois area. Now there are only half that many. A baker must make a higher profit nowadays in order to survive, and he must bake a greater quantity in order to have sufficient margin.

A significant factor in the decline of the number of boulangeries in France has been the decline in bread consumption by the French. While several years ago it was 600 grams, the level of bread consumption today is down to 150 grams per inhabitant per day, Monsieur Choquet said. "Whereas bread used to be the basic food in France, nowadays people eat more sugared products. The French have adopted the American style. They eat cereal—oat flakes and such—and they also eat more meat and fish."

Monsieur Choquet carried on with his solemn accounting of a French boulanger's reality. "Supermarkets have threatened small shops of all sorts. Today the situation has declined so far that the *bouchers,* the beef butchers, and the *charcutiers,* the pork butchers, sell only fifty percent of the meat in France. The big stores also make a lot of competition for the boulangers, even though they make inferior bread—many use frozen dough," he said, clucking his lips. "Nevertheless they have had a big effect. In Blain there are now two *grandes surfaces*—hypermarkets—and very few small markets in town, though there is still a *boucherie* and a *charcuterie,* in addition to the three bakeries."

I thought of the sugary, squishy institutional bread produced by supermarkets in Washington, the impersonality of those huge stores. To hear of the proliferation of their kind in France fueled my conviction that the worst of American culture was infiltrating the world.

"It is so sad to see small shops disappear," I said. "In my country they are practically gone. The supermarket is *it.*"

"We know that in the United States people go to the supermarket once a week to buy their bread," Monsieur Choquet replied. "This is why the traditional bakers of France resist the *supermarché.*"

Monsieur Choquet has made careful calculations of what it takes for a boulanger to survive. "In France we consider that one needs 1,000 to 1,200 consumers for an artisanal bakery to thrive. With regard to this boulangerie, counting our two shops, we have from 500 to 1,000 clients per day, which corresponds to 1,500 to 3,000 customers, using an average family size of three people. Practically sixty percent of our clients come every day. And it goes up to eighty-five percent if you add those who come every two days. The one thing that hasn't changed is that people still buy their bread every day.

"Bread is very important in French culture," Monsieur Choquet told me, pride in his voice, "even though overall bread consumption has declined. *Si vous voulez,* bread has always been at the base of French nourishment, it has always been the essential food. In addition, it has always been a very important religious symbol in the Catholic Church, and a sign of sharing. Bread is very rich as a symbol. It's true that today people don't, perhaps, respect their bread anymore by making *la croix*—the sign of the cross over the loaf with their knife—as they did in the generation past. And before no one would throw out a morsel of bread. They ate it, conserved it. Nowadays they will toss bread in the rubbish bin.

"Today," he said, "people no longer respect bread, but that is not due to the fact that bread is expensive, because it is not. The evolution in the eating habits of the French toward a greater variety of foods may be the more basic reason. But in France bread still remains important." The Blain baker went on to say that he took hope from the "Coté Retour," a recent and growing preference of the French people for traditional, regional foods "of the *terroir.*"

Monsieur Choquet's hands were once again folded patiently in front of him.

"And what kinds of bread do your customers prefer?" I asked.

"I will say to you that today we sell principally white bread, of the French type. *La baguette* is what one sells today. It is 250 grams. But we also sell *pain d'un kilo-500 grammes* and *pain d'un kilo. Bon,* and then *pain de 400 grammes.* Those breads, all of the same dough but in different shapes and sizes, make up sixty-five to seventy percent of the sales. And after that there are the special breads."

"So the French mostly eat baguettes?" I wondered why they ate so much plain white bread when they had delicious options like *pain de campagne, pain de ménage,* and the others.

"The baguette became the preferred bread here, in the

country, in the 1950s, following the war. *Si vous voulez,* there has been an evolution in bread beginning in the fifties, due to the acceleration of the kneading process. During the war people ate *pain noir,* black bread, which included practically the whole wheat kernel, and during the years that followed the war, there grew in the French people a wish for a white bread which was, I'll say, a sign of social well-being.

"In the same period, there was a baker in Vendée who discovered by accident that if he made the mechanical kneading machine go faster the dough oxidized and the bread whitened." As the kneading bowl twirled faster, time acquired a new meaning, and speed came to have increased value for the French baker. "Rapid kneading also made the bread increase in volume, and people found the result, I'll say, better."

Monsieur Choquet held his hands up to form a plump circle, and then waved them to show distaste. "In truth, the process increased the volume, but to the detriment of taste. The bread produced by this method is bland. The baguette has the advantage of the hard crust, and the fact that it is good for dieting—since it is airy, one can eat more and gain less weight. But today," he said, "we are trying to effect a return so that people prefer bread that is a little bit browner, darker, less white. We want to push that because white bread has less taste, and also conserves less well."

I was surprised to learn that Monsieur Choquet considered the baguette—that emblem of Frenchness—a bland and fast-staling, inferior bread.

As he spoke I realized I had two side-by-side images of baguettes. On the one hand, there were the baguettes of my adolescence (and of the advertisers), a time when a picnic of baguette, cheese, and wine symbolized the most sublime in romance, leisure, and sophistication. On the other hand, there were the baguettes of reality: the American bland, mass-produced, chain-café baguettes bought really more for an illusion of French elegance than for taste, and the squishy baguettes stocked by grocery stores that I grabbed when I'd forgotten to buy bread for guests. In recent years, while retaining my image of the baguette as the quintessential bread, I had, without realizing it, actually been choosing to eat more substantial, heftier, higher-quality loaves. Image can truly make you take leave of your senses.

I later learned that Monsieur Choquet was in the vanguard of a small group of French bakers trying to reaccustom the French public to the taste of partial whole wheat and organic loaves, believing they are better for public health and the modern lifestyle. Monsieur Choquet was working hard, in effect, to return French bread to its full glory as the staff of life.

e⁓

Monsieur Choquet is positioned in the middle of a three-generation line of bakers. He grew up in Blain in a household devoted to the baking of bread, his father, Rogatien, having established the first Choquet bakery.

His paternal grandfather was a tailor who stitched men's clothing in a village forty kilometers from Blain, but he died when Rogatien was very young. At the age of twelve, needing to contribute to the survival of the family, Rogatien became an apprentice to a baker.

"It was not modern like now," the senior Monsieur Choquet, a man in his seventies, said of his boyhood apprenticeship. One day I sat with him in his white row house just across a narrow lane at the rear of the boulangerie. He was convalescing from a *"maladie du coeur,"* but looked elegant in a robe of rich colors.

The baker for whom Rogatien worked as a boy did have a mechanical kneading machine, but that was the extent of the automation. The oven was heated with charcoal or by fagots of poor quality, brambly wood, and it was the apprentice's job to keep the oven stocked with fuel. "It was hard for me as a boy because the opening to the oven was small, and it was hard to push the fagots in," Monsieur Choquet told me, leaning close across the surface of his dark, gleaming dining room table.

Rogatien also had the job of collecting and transporting all the fuel wood for the oven, and when it rained this was "less easy." What is more, since there was no running water, he had to haul all the boulanger's water from a well with buckets—or on a little cart when the nearest well went dry.

"All the dough was shaped by hand in those days. One by one, each loaf was shaped," the beautifully groomed but weary-looking baker said. "Back in those days, we made exclusively *gros pain.*" Two to three kilos of dough went into each loaf. With each firing of the oven, they baked about forty loaves, and they made three or four firings a day.

To make traditional *pain au levain,* Monsieur Choquet said, each morning the baker made sure to reserve a lump of the night's production of yeasty dough to act as the *levain,* to get the dough started for the next day. "Mother yeast," he called the *levain.* Yeast bread, *pain levure* or *pain direct,* on the other hand, took less than one hour of rising time. Mostly, however, Monsieur Choquet said, they made *pain au levain.*

"Mother yeast" caught me. I loved the thought of a microscopic mother catalyzing a French loaf.

When he was young, they started the bread in the evening at about six, the senior Monsieur Choquet said. First the flour, water, and salt were mixed with the *levain,* and often a little yeast as well. The dough was kneaded and then shaped into large, round loaves, in a process that took about forty-five minutes. Then, lacking a *chambre froide,* they put the loaves in a *meuble parisien*—an armoire—for fermentation. Alternatively, they let the loaves rise in round, cloth-lined *pannetons,* each loaf in its own basket. The dough was left to rest for five hours. It took six or seven hours from the beginning of the bread making to the baking. Mixing started about six, and the baking began at midnight or one A.M. "The bread of the past required much time."

As the senior Choquet spoke, I realized why his son had so immediately told me about the boulangerie's *chambre froide*. It had changed the French baker's life.

Monsieur Choquet ticked off an hour-by-hour account of the time it took to make the day's bread back when he was young.

"It took about six hours to prepare the bread for the first baking, and then it took about seven or eight hours of baking to have all the bread ready for sale early the next morning. We baked every two hours, starting the oven at 2400 hours in the morning. It took one hour to heat the oven and load it for the first round of baking. After heating the oven with wood for, say, half an hour, to the required temperature—this is reached when the bricks in the back of the oven glow white-hot—it took twenty-five minutes to load the oven, loaf by loaf, with a *grand manche*." The *grand manche* is long-handled wooden paddle. "Then the baking itself took fifty to sixty minutes. Thus, each baking required two hours of the night. After the first baking was complete, we reheated the oven for the second baking. That took half an hour. Another half hour was needed to reload the oven with loaves, and the hour of baking followed. This routine continued on through the night for three or four bakings."

Rogatien's workday, as dictated by the dough and the four rounds of baking, counted up to twelve or fifteen hours. He began work at six in the evening and finished at ten, eleven, or twelve in the morning. He rested in the afternoon. When he was a working boy, it was hard. *"C'était dur."*

C'était dur, indeed. By my reckoning, the *chambre froide* had won the baker's son at least seven hours away from the baking room.

Rogatien labored as an apprentice baker for three years. He then changed boulangeries to become an *ouvrier,* the next position above apprentice, working for this second boulanger for eight years, both baking bread and learning the art of *pâtisserie.* The young baker was employed by four different bakers, over the course of eleven years, and thus his education was formed.

In 1945, having little money but skilled hands, Rogatien looked around for a failing boulangerie to buy. He received word of a bakery in Blain owned by a woman who had trafficked with the Germans during the war and who was being forced to sell. Her boulangerie was not expensive, and Rogatien had to work hard to revive it "with good service and with good bread."

Rogatien's wife, a youthful, soft-cheeked woman, seemed to brim with health as she tended to her husband, bringing him glasses of water and patting his shoulder now and then as we talked. Her father had been a farmer. She grew up on a place of twenty hectares, where there was *"beaucoup de travail."* The family raised a little bit of everything "just for our own use": wheat, corn, rye, all sorts of cereals, cows, goats, chickens, rabbits, a horse, and an ox. They also had a vegetable garden. She worked hard on the family farm until the day she married, and then she joined her husband in the arduous work of the boulangerie. She was twenty-four when she married, and Rogatien was twenty-five.

"At the beginning it was hard," she explained. "Bakers made only *pain au levain* until after the war, so it was strenuous work.

"We baked the bread, we sold in the shop, and we made deliveries to the countryside too," her husband recounted. "My wife did those. Someone came into the shop to sell the bread and she went out into the country to deliver the bread. The four children loved the delivery trips. They were like a vacation!" I was to learn that the younger Madame Choquet still did deliveries.

As Monsieur Choquet spoke, a thought tumbled into my head: the Choquet children—both Jean-Claude and his own children after that—had had childhoods utterly different from the children of urban office workers in one key respect. They grew up seeing their fathers at work, and could locate, speak to, and observe their fathers pursuing their chosen occupation any time of day.

From their first day, Madame Choquet said, the boulangerie's shop had opened at six in the morning and shut its doors at eight in the evening, with a closing of one hour for lunch at noon.

During their early years both Marie and Rogatien "had seven days and worked seven," Monsieur Choquet, senior said. "In order to take a vacation one had to overcome sleepiness!" Then, thankfully, in 1936, *"les socialistes"* dictated that every Frenchman had the right to one day of rest per week. A little later, during the German occupation, the French were not allowed to bake or sell bread on two days a week, as the Germans took most of the wheat for their army. "Ironically," Madame Choquet explained, "this was good for the family. And after the war, the French government retained the two days of rest, and Wednesday and Sunday became free days for bakers." In 1946 a week of vacation was instituted for all French workers, now five weeks of vacation are due each Frenchman by law. The bakers in Blain, then as now, took their vacations in turns so that the town would always have a source of fresh bread. "Jean-Claude takes one week off in the winter for skiing, and four weeks in the summer to go to the sea," his father said. "And he is required to give his workers five weeks off a year."

This year, for the first time in ten years, Peter had been able to take three consecutive weeks of summer vacation in order to join me and the children for part of our stay in France. Like Peter, I had had few opportunities for extended vacations. How would life in the United States be changed, I wondered, if we all had to take the month of August off every year? Might having time to restore and recollect ourselves breed a different, deeper appreciation of both leisure and work?

The four Choquet children—including Jean-Claude—went to school in Blain, and one went on to the *lycée* in Nantes. The Choquets' two daughters worked in the bakery until they married, and one still works there, making the bread deliveries to the countryside. The Choquets see all of their children every day and their grandchildren come for a snack after school.

As I listened to Madame Choquet speak about her three-generation family with its members flowing in and out of each other's houses, an image of a deep-nested, rural, Millet family began to grow in my mind.

"It was a good life," Madame Choquet said, summing up. "A life *de famille*—and work in a *métier* that gave happiness. It was pleasing to see the clients each day. We had a lot of contact—they are our friends. Now they still come and buy our bread every day."

As of 1996 the boulangerie had stood under the name Choquet for fifty years. Rogatien—he and Marie both in their mid-seventies—was *patron* of the boulangerie for thirty-nine years, having taken up the ownership of the bakery at age thirty-one. In total, he worked for forty-eight years as a baker, from the age of twelve until the age of sixty. At the time we talked, he had been retired for about twenty years—since Jean-Claude took over the bakery in 1976. Not one for sitting around, Rogatien continued to work as his son's employee after retiring, until he had to stop due to health considerations. He speculated that his heart trouble was probably due to "too much work, too much hard work, and too much fast work."

Gathering the threads of his life, the first Choquet baker concluded, "*C'est un bon métier.* I adore my work. I have never wanted another occupation. In baking, one gets to be there for the whole process. *On assiste à la totalité du pain.* One attends to the loaf from the kneading to the fermentation to the baking. *Le pain:* it's simply water, flour, *levain,* and salt. All natural. *Pain français c'est nature.* French bread is nature."

$e\sim$

Solid, eager Jean-Claude Choquet began work at his father's bakery in 1963, when he left school at age fifteen. In 1976, he "took succession"—as the French so aptly call this turnover of a life's work from father to son—of Boulangerie Choquet.

"So you learned everything from your father?"

"Voilà!" Monsieur Choquet said to me back in his homey kitchen. "I never left home. I have worked here for my entire life, except for the sixteen or so months on the boat, for my obligatory national service."

From September 1967 to January 1969, as he had mentioned at the outset of our conversation, Jean-Claude baked his way across the Atlantic, as a French *matelot,* or enlisted man, to San Francisco, Mexico, Panama, Martinique, Madeira, and finally back to Toulons. While on the boat, he said, still delighting, "We used seawater to make the bread! When we were at sea, eh? Not while we were in port. It worked perfectly because the proportion of salt in seawater just about corresponds to the proportion of salt that we use in bread. We add thirty to thirty-three grams of salt per liter of water to make bread, and that's about the proportion of salt that there is in water from the sea!"

From Monsieur Choquet's maritime tale, I took away a simple but enchanting fact. Bread can be made from three common ingredients: ocean, yeast, and wheat.

Jean-Claude Choquet's mother told me it had always been her son's dream to be a baker, to follow in his father's floury tracks, but by the time he returned to Blain from the navy, he had discovered he had a severe allergy to flour. "He had become an asthmatic, and had to wear a mask whenever he worked around flour dust!" the baker's mother said.

The senior Monsieur Choquet continued the story. "I said to him, 'Jean-Claude, you *could* change trades,' but my son replied, *'Pas question!'* "

Unwilling to abandon the baker's life, his parents said, taking turns relaying sentences about their son, Jean-Claude Choquet just continued dipping his hands in flour. Nowadays he no longer mixes or kneads or shapes the bread dough, but he makes the pastries, oversees the baking, and—ever since his father's retirement in 1976—manages all the bread and pastry baking, and the administration of the two shops.

While the boulangerie on rue de Nantes has remained in Choquet hands for fifty years, its offerings have changed in tune with time and generation. "We have not changed the basic breads we make," Jean-Claude told me, "but we have multiplied the varieties. Now we make not only standard white breads, but *pains bis,* which contain a portion of bran and germ, and *pain complet* or *intégral,* made from flour using the whole wheat kernel." Bread has become a more festive food in recent years, and bakers have multiplied the kinds of breads they make so that customers may eat different dishes with different sorts of bread. As a diner can take *noisettes de porc aux pruneaux,* a pork dish from the Loire region, with white wine, and finish with a red wine, he can begin with a white bread and finish with a bread with a darker crumb containing a little bit of rye. "I say bread is like wine—each dish needs its own accompaniment."

To top off the steady progress of the Choquet boulangerie, Jean-Claude became a Gold Medal Baker-Best French Worker *Médaille d'Or Boulanger, Meilleur Ouvrier de France,* in 1986. Every three years in France there is a national competition for the tradesmen of the country, *le Concours des "Meilleurs Ou-*

vriers de France." It concerns not just bakers, but all the crafts-men's trades, in which baking is included. For the competition, bakers from all over France are assembled in one city. A jury made up of master bakers decides which of the bakers are the most proficient and bake the tastiest bread. Each contestant must bake, by hand, an assortment of loaves—everything from *pain au levain* and yeast bread, to rye bread—in front of the jury, at a central place, away from his shop. The year Jean-Claude competed, the contest was held in Rouen. The baker-judges on the stand give the competitors points. "It is necessary to receive an average grade of sixteen on the whole of one's work," Monsieur Choquet said. "That is to say, the baker must do *very well* on his work. And it can be that no one earns the ti-tle, or that ten do, or that two do." With great modesty, Monsieur Choquet indicated that he now serves as one of the judges of the competition.

When I asked his parents how he came to win the *Médaille d'or Boulanger,* his mother gazed at her husband and said, "He had a good *école.*"

❧

Both doers by nature, Jean-Claude Choquet and his wife Marie-Madeleine first came together to organize dances and other activities for the young people of Blain. Though both grew up in Blain, Marie-Madeleine was three years older than Jean-Claude, so they hadn't known each other in school.

When the couple was first married, Marie-Madeleine had worked as a teacher. But then, when Jean-Claude took over the boulangerie, she followed the unwritten law for bakers' wives: she left her job to help her husband in the business. She has worked in the shop for over twenty-five years.

At age eighteen, after earning his high school *baccalauréat,* Jerome, the Choquet son, started his training in *pâtisserie.* He did his ten months of army service and then worked in the bakery at the Palais de l'Elysée, the residence of the president of the republic: the French White House. There, he made *gâteaux* for the president and his guests. Afterward, he did a *stage,* or training stint, at a big *pâtisserie,* also in Paris, to further perfect his trade, and finished off with an apprenticeship in Nantes. Then he returned home to Blain to work with his father. "Jerome is a member of the bakers' association now," his father said, "he has the direction of his career."

At one point in my long conversation with the baker, a slim young man in loose, white trousers and a T-shirt to match Monsieur Choquet's peeked into the room. The baker beckoned him in. The young man had a smudge of flour on his cheek and another in his shiny, dark hair. He was carrying a pink-frosted cake topped with sugar decorations of forget-me-nots.

"Madame Taber, this is my son, Jerome."

Jerome nodded to me, with a quiet smile, and then he and his father held a brief conversation about the cake and when it would be picked up.

When Jerome left, flashing me another smile, I wondered at the simple pleasure a man must experience when he sees his own son, grown and confident, following in his footsteps.

A broad smile filled Monsieur Choquet's face.

℘

A few days later perky Marie-Madeleine Choquet and I drive to an *auberge*—inn—by the Nantes-à-Brest Canal in a tiny, white Citroen truck. We deliver bread to three restaurants, proceeding straight into their stainless steel kitchens and placing the loaves in big bins. Madame Choquet shouts out cheery greetings to the cooks as we unload our cumbersome bundles of baguettes. When the deliveries are complete Madame Choquet wipes her hands on her gingham apron and takes me back to the boulangerie, for *un petit goûter*.

The hallway going back deeper into the building from the shop front is immaculate. Ushering me into the kitchen-family room where I met with her husband, Madame Choquet remarks, "We're only clean in the afternoon. The boys who work at night have their coffee here and dribble the crumbs from their bread all over." She pokes at the bits of crust on the floor with her toe. "Look, there's the ironing I'll do later," she says, pointing to an ironing board holding a small pile of clothing.

"Upstairs we have a TV, a piano, and the bedrooms. This is our office, our living room, our dining room, our kitchen, our laundry room, *tout*. It's not enough room, but it is what it is." The room, square-shaped, is divided into quarters. One quarter is taken up by the kitchen, one holds a rocker, the third is occupied by some shelves, and then there is the eating area. The kitchen fixtures are bright and varnished. Demitasse coffee cups sit on a rack. There are baskets, a brass teapot, a ceramic duck family. There is a microwave and a shelf of liquor up high. The room possesses a sense of clean, busy disorder. She motions to me to sit down at the table in the corner to the left of the door, where I had sat with her husband.

Madame Choquet offers me a plate of five different cookies, including an American-style chocolate chip cookie. I am amazed to see it there. Now that's something worthwhile that we Americans have passed along, I think to myself. I happily munch a couple of French sugar cookies, ignoring my vow to take no sweets until after lunch.

Above the table is a carved wooden plaque of a baker's shop. On its surface, in relief, are a baker's scale and a man with bread in a sack on his back.

Joining me at the table, Madame Choquet explains that she and Marie-Claire, her assistant, do the heaviest business in the shop in the morning. There is a rush before and after morning mass, and also before and after school. At noon there is also a little push. The afternoon brings the fewest customers.

I comment that it seems like fun to serve and greet people in the shop.

"It's true. We have good relationships with people," Madame

Choquet says, considering the rhythms of her work at the boulangerie. "That is the good part. And we have the pleasure of
making decorative breads and cakes for marriages and births.

"*Oui*, the work is *très agréable*. But it is necessary to get up
early," Madame Choquet says, sighing as if that fact punctu-
ated everything. She tells me she gets up at 5:30 in order to
open the doors at 6:15. "And we don't shut at all until eight P.M.
I go to bed at nine in order to get up early again. The work is
never finished. There are always things to do.

"My work is not at all stressful, but I don't like the day when
we raise prices," she says, thinking out loud about the emo-
tional toll she had experienced earlier that day in informing
each customer that her or his bread would cost more from now
on. "I don't like this day, but it passes. The price hasn't gone up
in two years, but people complain. And the people without
work—it's *triste* for them. I would prefer to give them a gift
than to ask them for money."

"Was this life your dream?" I ask.

"I was a teacher!" she replies immediately. "I was a teacher
for twelve years. I taught math at the *collège*—children of thirteen to fifteen years. I *chose* that."

Considering again the matter of time in her life, she says
that during the course of a week, she and Jean-Claude are able
to see each other very little. To her, their weeks are oceans—
ceaseless tides of work. "*Ça c'est dur.*"

"It's not easy. I see Jean-Claude at midday sometimes. Then,
in the evening, a little, but he goes to sleep fast, before me. He
doesn't sleep much, but when he does he really sleeps . . .
That's *le problème* of the profession. When there are marriages
it's *très dur.*"

Turning to her memories of earlier years in their lives, Madame Choquet tells me, "When the children were young we
dedicated Wednesdays to them. We had a *chalet du bois,* a
wooden cabin in the forest twenty kilometers away. Tuesday

night we left, and gave all of Wednesday to the children. There was no TV there. They'd play, we'd take walks along the edge of the canal, they'd ride bicycles and horses. We did this until they were at the *lycée*—for fifteen years. Now Jean-Claude has meetings on Wednesday afternoons and I take care of the house. The last time we went to the *chalet* a lot was four years ago. It's sad not to go there, but there's always much to do instead of going to the cabin.

"If Jean-Claude didn't have so much responsibility, the work would be less," she says, looking down at the table. "These days he spends a lot of time occupied with the problems of others. . . .

"He has stomach problems," she adds. "They don't go away, except when we're on vacation." For one week in the winter, she and Jean-Claude go to the snow. "In August we try to recuperate."

The relentless nature of their lives becomes clearer and clearer to me as Madame Choquet talks. I wonder how she feels about her son being a baker.

Her tired eyes now brighten with a gleam of pride. Her son knows it's difficult but he likes the work. "He wants to be his own *petit patron*. That's the big advantage."

I realize, reluctantly, that even French villagers can have rushed, treadmill lives, and perhaps bakers most of all. Like milk produced by dairy farmers, loaves must be made, without fail, every day of the year, and on into the limitless future.

Madame Choquet pokes at her empty coffee cup. "Right now, at this moment in the summer, we have to work every day without shutting because our colleagues have gone on vacation until September. All summer two boulangeries work for three."

Madame Choquet rises from the table with a sigh and a smile that seem to summarize her life. It is time to return to her customers.

As I left the Choquets' family room that day, I noticed a

frame holding a poem on the wall to the right of the door. It was translated into French, from *The Prophet* by Kahlil Gibran. The title of the framed version was *"Vos Enfants,"* "Your Children."

As I read the poem, several lines seemed to speak of the Choquets and the way their boulangerie was like a well-built ship, holding strong and yet being shaped and reshaped with time and each passing generation.

> *Your children are not your children.*
> *They are the sons and daughters of*
> > *Life's longing for itself . . .*
>
> > *You may strive to be like them, but seek*
> *not to make them like you . . .*
>
> > *For life goes not backward nor tarries*
> *with yesterday . . .*

e~

Monsieur Choquet explained over coffee in the same snug kitchen that first day, that in the afternoons while his bread ferments slowly in his *chambre froide,* instead of resting he seizes the extra time and goes to his desk. To this dedicated, quietly confident man, the baking of bread requires much beyond the mere mixing of ocean, yeast, and wheat.

In addition to overseeing and participating in the work at the back of the bakery and acting as a judge in the national baking competition, Monsieur Choquet was serving as a president of the Confederation Nationale de la Boulangerie, not only for the *département* of Loire-Atlantique, but for the whole western region of France, which comprises twelve *départements* and approximately four thousand bakers.

From his leadership positions, Monsieur Choquet writes policy, addresses debates within the profession, and lobbies on behalf of French boulangerie in general—spending much time "occupied with the problems of others," as his wife said. As president of the western region's *syndicat,* Monsieur Choquet travels as their representative to Paris to discuss with the government such matters as the rate of bread sales and the price of bread. "It is the *syndicat's* aim to have close to the same price all over the country, to avoid competition."

I mentioned the bloody Bread Riots of the 1680s, which centered on the high price of bread, and the French government's long-standing intimate involvement in regulating the price of France's staple food.

Monsieur Choquet sat back in his chair and spoke with conviction and clarity. Although the government used to limit the price of bread, price fixing is now prohibited, and each baker determines the price of his bread. Competition does occur, but the price of a baguette or 400-gram loaf is virtually identical across the country. The average price of a baguette from Marseilles to Lille is four francs, about seventy cents U.S.

"Beyond the price of bread, the profession is concerned today with three principal axes, three orientations, *si vous voulez,*" he said, bringing me up to speed on the primary issues for French bakers. "The first is the protection of the *métier* of *boulanger.* That is, we are trying to ensure that only the people who attend to the entire production process—those who knead the dough, who conduct the fermentation, who bake, and who sell the bread—can call themselves *boulanger, boulanger-pâtissier.* There are about thirty-eight thousand artisan bakers of this kind in France."

The baker's words substantiated reports I had read in American newspapers that there had been heated controversy in France over who had the right to call himself a baker. The issue had erupted in response to the proliferating practice of supermarkets to buy frozen dough, bake it on the premises, and call their bread departments *"boulangeries."*

"And, it seems that the current government is favorable. It is helping us to take this step," the baker said, a glint of satisfaction in his eye.

"The second point on which we are working equally hard is the brawl around the prices supermarkets put on bread—the basic product of French nourishment. That is to say, the supermarkets sell bread at very low prices, since they don't need to sell bread in order to survive, and this creates competition for the artisan bakers, and puts the whole baking profession at risk.

"The loss of village boulangeries would be a grave matter," Monsieur Choquet said, his hands folded patient and solid as paperweights on the table. "Beyond the economic and nutritional role of bakers in this country, the baker plays an important social role. In France, there are thirty-six thousand communes and there are thirty-six thousand boulangers, so bakers are well planted throughout the French territory. Virtually all the communes of France have a boulanger, and boulangerie remains a very important point of animation of a neighborhood or a village or little town. Because the purchase of bread is a daily purchase, the boulangerie is a meeting place, a place where people gather. To lose the local bakery would be a significant loss."

The baker's well-framed positions and poise made his points seem watertight. As he sat across from me, he struck me again as the unflappable sailor, as if he had the winds at his back, and no sudden waves could buck him.

"The third issue on which we are working is the establishment of an obligatory day of closing for all commerce each week. Because the big enterprises or the industrial bakeries can work, by rotation of their personnel, every day of the week, this has put pressure on the artisan bakers to do the same. That is to say, if this keeps up, those who work *en croûte,* on a crust, with very few personnel, will be obliged to work seven days over seven. So, this is the third point on which we are battling—so that the artisan bakers, even if they are of a small size, can have at least one day of rest. In France, the workers' right to a day of rest is assumed, but today we are moving backward. It is a combative issue. The truth is that this policy will be rather difficult to obtain as the trend is the reverse—toward commerce every day out of seven."

"In the U.S. the stores are open every day until midnight," I said, shaking my head.

"Yes, it's true, but it's a bit of a shame," he said diplomatically. "Commerce never stops."

I asked the baker—who voluntarily works "seven over seven" in order to fight (ironically) for his colleagues' leisure time—what he did for his own enjoyment.

"These days, I bicycle quite a bit," he said. "And I like the mountains a lot. I love to ski on my vacation. . . . But, well, to tell the truth, I am in the office a lot, concerning myself a little bit with the issues of the profession. . . . So, as to leisure, I really don't have any."

This stark comment brought me to a halt. Added to Madame Choquet's comment about her husband's stress-related stomach problems, it delivered me a new awareness: the baker of Boulangerie Choquet was as overworked and leisure-deprived as any Washington, D.C., dweller. On the other hand, I could see, now that I had the Atlantic between me and my country, that he, like many of my fellow Washingtonians, adored his work. I certainly knew, myself, the pleasure of it. I could see now that a large amount of work is not always a burden to the one engaged in it. Work that is imposed feels like work, though as Monsieur Choquet's words and actions implied, work that is freely chosen can be something else: deep satisfaction.

ℰ

As Monsieur Choquet described the arduous nature of his job, his battles on behalf of the baker's trade, and the threats posed by supermarkets to boulangeries, I wondered why anyone would become a baker. How did he, as president of the bakers' association, encourage new bakers and maintain standards?

The approach of Boulanger Choquet is to tackle problems head-on.

Possessor of a strong belief in rigorous, on-the-job training of bakers, Monsieur Choquet has had a hand in setting national standards for the training of bakers and, at the bakery level, in the teaching of many apprentices. To become a certified artisan boulanger requires a considerable commitment of time. Two to three years of apprenticeship—periods of study alternating with training at the kneading table—are required in a program organized by the national syndicate and the national Chambre des Métiers. Aspirants start their apprenticeships at age sixteen, after completing their baccalaureat degree at the *lycée,* and work toward the completion of a series of required exams and diplomas—first the CAP, the *Certificat d'Aptitude Profes-sionnelle,* obtained at the end of two years, and then the *Brevet d'Enseignement Professionnel,* the BEP, earned at the end of four. To attain the level of *Brevet de Maîtrise,* or Master Baker—the level of accomplishment achieved by both Jean-Claude and Jerome, the diploma that is the icing on the cake, as it were—takes five years. At the end of these *stages,* a young person—usually a man—is a full-fledged boulanger.

Only 2 percent of French bakers are women. Monsieur Choquet explained that the baker's trade remains a physically demanding one, even though mechanization has made it easier. Also, the fact that baking work is done at night prevents women who have families from opting for his *métier.* "However, this year, in Loire-Atlantique it was a girl who received the title of *meilleur apprenti*—best apprentice."

The Blain baker clearly believes artisan bakers will never become an extinct species, despite threats afoot. "There was an *époque* when only those who couldn't complete school learned the baker's trade, but these days, there are a significant number of young people who have completed the *baccalauréat,* and the exams of an *école supérieure* at a university, who come back to learn the trade. And then there are also people nowadays who pursue a scholarly interest but don't find employment, and they come back to the boulangerie to look for professionalization. Some of them do a *baccalauréat* in management and learn the *métier* well. This is more and more frequent. This is the proof that, in the end, the manual trades continue to interest the young."

As for the employment prospects of bakers, Monsieur Choquet said, "Nowadays in boulangerie, anyone who is prepared to move will find employment relatively easily, though not always in his region of origin. There are many of us Frenchmen who resist leaving our homes. All the beach areas and mountain resorts have a need for surplus manpower, so there are some bakers who work the summer on the coast and the winter in the mountains. He who wants to work today can work."

I wanted to believe Monsieur Choquet's words. At the same time, I wondered if the conviction in his voice was just the optimism of the advocate, or a product of wishful thinking. I found myself wondering how much longer—in the face of the indisputable convenience of supermarkets and the picked-up pace of modern life—any traditional baker who wished to would be able to find viable work. A sense of dread set in my belly. I knew the difference between a town with a bakery and a town without. I knew what supermarket shopping was like, and how it contrasted to the familiar, pleasant environment of the Boulangerie Choquet. Could boulangeries become part of supermarkets, as seemed likely, and remain the same? In my heart of hearts, I didn't think so.

℮

Finally I came to my question, the question that had transported me across the Atlantic and into this tiny, obscure bakery in the sun-beaten heartland of France.

"What is the secret of good French bread?"

Monsieur Choquet's shoulders seemed to settle a notch. He was on home territory now. His words began to fly, his tone quickened, and his eyes shone. His fingers spread out on the table. "The thing that is most important in the making of bread, *chacun pour soi*—to each his own—be it the modern way or the more traditional, the more ancient, is to respect the steps of fermentation.

"There are three basic French products that issue from fermentation. These are the bread, the wine, and the cheese. All of these require care. It's the job of the boulanger to manage well the fermentation of his dough. It is from the fermentation that the bread takes its taste, and if one doesn't respect the stages of fermentation, one will not have a good bread. Each baker has his method for conducting the fermentation, and with the same flour, in the same place, two bakers are going to make two different products, because they conduct the fermentation in different ways.

"Climatic factors—humidity, air temperature—also play into and complicate the fermentation. The making of bread is like the making of wine. It must be left to rest alone from time to time. *Il faut laisser le temps au temps.* Time must be left to time."

When Monsieur Choquet made this clear, emphatic statement, I received it as a gold nugget in my palms. The baker had clearly stated that a French loaf with a rich, deep taste could only be produced through an extended period of fermentation. To produce a loaf of quality, a baker had to make a determined choice—one that required both long hours of rest for his bread and high doses of patience from himself. He had to make the courageous decision of favoring taste and quality over efficiency and speed. With regard to life itself, Monsieur Choquet's six words seemed to resolve the apparent contradiction between hard work and rest. Time for fermentation *is* the element that provides the balance, turning hard work from a draining to an enhancing part of life. Hard work—and its product, good bread—*requires* rest.

Monsieur Choquet wended on: "I believe the one essential thing for French bakers is to stay authentic. And to be authentic means we must not cheat with the fermentation. The management of the fermentation process, for the baker, I will say to you, is the quality of the professional.

"As France is an agricultural country with several types of cereals, the bakers mix in a little bit of the different sorts of grains, to obtain the tastes of the different regions, but always the essence of a good bread is respect for the fermentation."

"That's the key of French bread?" I said.

"*Voilà.*"

౿

Thinking of ocean, wheat, and yeast, I said, "What other things are essential to good bread?"

"After respect for the fermentation process," Monsieur Choquet said, "the secret of good bread is good ingredients.

"Our traditional French bread is, number one, pure flour. Not so much organic as without additives, without improvements, without ascorbic acid, without lecithin—pure, milled wheat.

"There are two essential characteristics of a good flour." Monsieur Choquet tapped a thick finger on the table. "The first is that the flour must be capable of retaining the fermentation gases. A good flour is one in which the gluten is of sufficiently good quality that it has the capacity both to stretch and to retain gases."

He tapped his finger again. "The second, of equal importance, is that the flour must be able to ferment well. *Si vous voulez,*" he said, tapping two fingers at once now, "it is the mix of these factors that makes a flour a good flour."

The boulanger explained that today millers are able to analyze and measure the quality of a particular flour in a laboratory and modify it according to their requirements. For instance, if a miller has a wheat that begins to ferment too rapidly, he can adjust it by mixing it with other particular wheats.

"So, behind the boulanger is the miller. . . . It is important to have a good miller, but it's not a problem. I think in France today we have lots of millers who are competent. I have three mills. We are lucky in our *département* to still have fourteen small mills—in certain *départements* they have only two or fewer—so I have chosen those that aid me best in my work."

Monsieur Choquet's voice resonated with fathoms-deep knowledge of his trade.

"So a good flour is important," I said. "And salt?"

"As for the salt I use in my bread," Monsieur Choquet said, "I use sea salt from here in France."

Here was the ocean in the loaf.

"After salt, bread needs an agent of fermentation. That is the microorganism, yeast. Sometimes I use wild yeast, or *levain,* sometimes I use industrial yeast, and often I use a mixture of both.

"As for the water we add to our bread," Monsieur Choquet said, "we use the municipal water from Blain, pumped from an underground water table. We take our water from the tap. . . . *Voilà.* There it is."

And there I was. I had the basics with which to begin my search for the heart of a French loaf: flour, salt, yeast, and water. Ocean. Wheat. Yeast. But there was one more bit of groundwork to lay before I would begin to track down the ingredients of a loaf.

℮

I awaken long before the ring of the alarm clock I bought to help me rise this morning. Anxious about getting to the Choquet Boulangerie by seven A.M.—Monsieur Choquet has invited me to watch the kneading, the ultimate treat in my bakery viewing—I pull on the clothes I set out the night before, wash my already tired eyes, and back the car out of the nook beside the *gîte* at 6:30. I don't yet seem able to kick the rushed pace of my life back home, even though that is one of my main purposes in coming to France.

For twenty minutes, I drive through a languid, village-dotted landscape resembling the English countryside. Pays Trois Rivières, or Land of Three Rivers, as this northwest sector of Loire-Atlantique is called, is named for the three waterways that run through it—the Isac, the Don, and the Brivet. Once known for its dairies and renowned for its cider, this rambling, partially wooded alluvial plain is an area of mixed farms mostly devoted to the production of meat, milk, and cheese. Subject to heavy winter rains, the region is rather nondescript, but I grew attached to it almost the moment we set foot on it. There is an intimacy—a manageable quality—to the land, and the area is deeply rural, which, in itself, satisfied a deep yearning. The Loire-Atlantique's very unpretentiousness may, in fact, have made attachment quicker. I've always found it easier to talk to a woman in an old sweater than a woman in high heels.

I spy old earth and wheat straw barn-houses, and pass through tiny three- or four-house hamlets, each with a round-backed communal bread oven of crumbling stone.

About ten minutes into the ride, I enter the tall quiet of the Forêt du Gavre, a *domaniale* forest—a state park of 11,000 acres. The long and carefully cultivated woodland, a vestige of the ancient Forêt de Broceliande, was owned by the Dukes of Brittany in the thirteenth century, later repossessed by the French crown, seized during the French Revolution in 1791, and has ever since remained in the hands of the state.

As I drive through the stands of tall trees, the world is still. Mine is the only car on the road.

At the center of the forest, ten empty, radial roads come together at La Belle Étoile, "The Beautiful Star." During the war —Loire-Atlantique was the site of an Allied push—the English soldiers dubbed the star in the forest "Picadilly Circus," and people say that their tent platforms can still be found, covered in moss and foliage, hidden in the trees. One of the roads that meets at the center of the star leads out of the woods and straight past fields and farmhouses toward the church spire at Blain.

Blain, an ancient Gallo-Roman town built on an old Roman crossroads, functioned at the time of the Romans as an important commercial center. Just to the west of the town's *place,* perched on a grassy hill dotted with wild hyacinth, is an ancient, wayside pilgrim stop. The chapel's namesake is Saint-Roch, the patron saint of bakers.

Emerging from the *forêt,* I drive down the arrow of a road toward Blain. Pastures, damp with dew, flank the roadway on both sides. I can see the small center of human hubbub dead ahead. It seems the town, with all its bright-faced little shops, is asleep now, close-eyed and dim, as I pull through its narrow lanes, and yet already, at quarter of seven, a line of customers trails out of Boulangerie Choquet into the cool morning air.

Madame Choquet is at her station behind the counter. Her face is shiny and clean, like her counters and showcases. She cheerily ushers me past the counters, past the family room, into a back hall, through its dimness, and into the baking rooms at the rear of the building. There she drops me off and returns to the shop front.

The baking area is divided into three main rooms set rail car fashion, one after the other. I position myself at the wide, open doorway between the first and second rooms. At a big work-table pushed against a wall in the second room, one of Monsieur Choquet's apprentices makes croissants. Soon another young man joins him, singing along to the rock music playing in the background at medium volume. The atmosphere is one of calm, pleasant busyness. The young men—they must be in their early twenties—wear white T-shirts with "Choquet" and a loaf of bread printed on them, and faintly gingham powder-blue and white jeans.

As I watch, I'm struck by the sense of playfulness in these bakery workers. Bread has a play inherent to it: the bean or the penny in the loaf, the sheer delight of my daughter as she holds a fresh round, and these young Frenchmen pressing their fingers into hunks of moist dough. Bread—both in its eating and its making—seems to offer gifts of play and time.

The two apprentices are now laying out the croissants on a pan. As they do so, they curl the pastries so that their ends teasingly almost meet.

As they finish their work, I survey the space. The first of the three rooms—the one in the corner of which I'm standing—is the kneading and shaping room. The next—the one into which I am peering and where the croissant-rolling is taking place—is the baking room. The large double doors of the *chambre froide*—which can hold four ovenloads of rising dough—lead off to the left side of the baking room, and an immense, two-story oven is set into the back wall. The caboose—beyond a door to one side of the oven—is the *pâtisserie* room. I can catch glimpses of Jerome Choquet's elbows and legs as he works back there decorating tartes and tortes.

The rooms are spotless, with white walls and mopped linoleum floors. There are several lines of rope suspended parallel to one wall of the baking room, and these are hung with ten or twenty gray *couches,* the flour-rubbed cloths used for raising dough. The oven is modern and huge—with each of the two levels about twelve feet across, nine feet deep, and two feet high—twelve meters, or 108 feet square. A window spans the front of each of the oven doors, and I can see scores of baguettes head-on, lined up obediently like soldiers, steam rising as they bake. There are several wheeled tables—they're about the size of gurneys—resting helter-skelter about the room. The tables have removable wooden boards that can be laid across them any which way—to be grabbed when needed. Three have round *boules* rising on them. There are also tall wooden shelves on wheels, one of which is filled with rising loaves.

The two young men are now taking down the *couches* from the lines, rolling them up, and placing them in a neat pile.

I am absorbed in this atmosphere of industry. There is a sense of rapid, step-wise efficiency in the men's movements. And of course I'm wooed by the smell of fresh bread.

Out of nowhere, Monsieur Choquet appears at my side to greet me, and introduces me to Jean-Paul Breher, his partner. "Pa Paul—we call him 'Pa Paul'—is our *chef boulanger,* our head bread baker." Monsieur Breher is seemingly dressed for tennis. He is wearing white shorts, a white T-shirt, and tennis shoes. I will soon find out why. His work is at least as strenuous as a tennis match. Much shorter than Monsieur Choquet, he has an athletic build, with thick, strong legs and strong biceps. His hair is rumpled above brown eyes. He wears thick glasses.

I watch Monsieur Breher making *pain ordinaire*—baguettes. As he works his body is active every instant. Remarkably light afoot, he seems to burst with energy. A fox to Monsieur Choquet's ox. He moves to a deep mixing bowl anchored to the floor in the kneading room, the first in the three-room baking train. He opens the valve to a huge sleeve and it begins shooting flour into the bowl. He turns a nearby spigot and water starts running into the bowl from a pipe. He flicks on the kneading machine. It is 7:15 A.M. From the storeroom, he fetches a cake of yeast the size of a pound of butter. He breaks it up with his beefy fingers and tosses it into the bowl. Mon-

sieur Choquet explains that Monsieur Breher is adding industrial yeast, "yeast that is industrial, but natural," he says, re-
peating his earlier words. I make a mental note to find out the
difference. All this time, the kneading hook—it looks, indeed,
like two immense Captain Hook hooks facing each other—is
turning the dough in a steady, slow swirl.

The flour, water, and yeast added, Monsieur Breher brings
in a two-foot-long tray of bouncy, buoyant dough that looks
wonderfully alive, and dumps it, flubbering, into the revolving
bowl. "That's the *levain*," Baker Choquet says, "the treasure of
the boulanger since ancient times."

As Monsieur Breher watches over the spinning bowl and the
apprentices shuffle shelves of dough about the baking room,
Monsieur Choquet explains the nature of this baker's gold. "A
levain begins with the *chef*. The *chef* is a little bit like the fire
the men of prehistory kept. They kept their basin of flames that
always served as their riches.

"Si vous voulez," Monsieur Choquet says, going more deeply
into the making of *levain,* "the *chef* is the little piece of yeast-
filled dough that the baker keeps from a batch made a day or
two before that is used as the 'inseminator,' or the 'mother' to
spur the fermentation of the next batch of bread. That is to say,
we take the *chef* of the dough saved from the previous day—say
a kilo of dough—and then we go and add a little water and a little flour, and this becomes the *levain*—that which will serve as
the foundation of the next batch of bread dough." *Levain,* in its
most ancient form, is simply dough left out in the air to be
soured by wild yeast.

"The way I start a *levain* is this," Monsieur Choquet says. "As
you know, yeast is produced through fermentation. I make the
levain for my organic breads via fermentation of an apple—via
cider. It is also possible to raise bread just with the wheat alone,
without the addition of any extra sugars, as there are naturally

occurring sugars in flour. Or, instead of using apples, you can raise bread with wine or milk, but the taste of the product will be a little different.

"To make a *levain,* a dough, this way, it is necessary to start by fermenting the apples in water. The sugars in the apples attract the wild yeast and then, once the fermentation starts, the cider can be incorporated in the dough. I capture the juice when it has fermented and add it to flour, and that multiplies the natural fermentation of the flour by wild yeast."

I am fascinated. Apples: a new, minor character in the story of my loaf.

"Making a *levain* takes several steps. For the first fermentation, the dough made with the apple juice must be left to ferment for a length of time, a little like cider or wine. Then, in stages, progressively, the quantity of dough is increased. At each stage, you add water and flour, on top of juice. Then you leave it to ferment again for a dozen hours. Then you re-add flour and water. This process lasts about three or four days.

"Once you have the *levain,* it takes, in general, between six and ten hours to make *pain au levain* itself. Between the moment when one begins kneading and the bread is baked, count ten hours. Less, when it's very hot, but otherwise ten hours. One kneads the dough. One lets it rise for the first time. One punches it down. One lets it rise another time. Then, after that, one shapes the dough, and one lets it rise once again, and after that, one puts it in the oven. That's how I make *pain au levain.*"

Monsieur Choquet has just described a laborious, time-gobbling procedure for making a loaf of bread. His hands fold together and then spread open and wide.

Boulangerie Choquet uses *levain* in practically all its breads, even to its croissants a little *levain* is added. "It is the *levain* that gives the special taste to a boulanger's bread."

Then the boulanger tells me that, most often, he uses a smidgen of industrial yeast to help his *levain* breads along. He explains that, by French law, a baker may add 0.2 percent industrial yeast to a *pain au levain* and still consider it authentic. "Save for the organic breads which are made uniquely on *levain*," Monsieur Choquet says, "we put a little *levain* and a little yeast in almost all our breads—the *levain* to bring acidity, the slightly sour taste of *levain,* and the commercial yeast for a fermentation that is a little bit more regular and less time-consuming. Our industrial yeast, produced specifically for artisan bakers and cultivated through a natural process similar to that for beer, is a great help. Fermentation on *levain* alone depends on wild ferments, which are much more difficult to measure, so the making of pure *pain au levain* is variable and risky. It is difficult to maintain quality, because one is more a *tributaire du temps*—the dough is subject, as I say, to the weather, the rain. And so, for a daily production of quantity, the use of *levain* alone is much less rational. With the industrial yeast, one has a fermentation that is more reliable."

A conversation with two officials at a yeast company I was to visit later in my French stay awakened me to the difficulties involved in producing a loaf made solely "on *levain*." One of the yeast men explained to me, "A real, natural bread with natural *levain* is very difficult to make. It requires a lot of know-how and a lot of time. Unless you have a ready-made yeast, you start from nothing. You need a minimum of four or five days—not to make the bread but just to create the *levain* for the bread. Then, once your *levain* is ready, you need at least six to eight hours to make your bread. But if you make a yeast bread, you can have a loaf in one and a half to two hours, as opposed to a minimum of five or six days!"

"One has to make *pain au levain* every day," the prize-winning baker cautions now, as we watch the kneading bowl cycle, "because it is necessary to maintain the *levain*, to keep it alive. Every day, we keep a little of our dough, we guard it to parcel out the next day."

With this remark Monsieur Choquet reaches out to touch a bowl of puffy *levain* set nearby. It bounces back in response to a press from his fingertips.

The baker moves closer to me and his hands gesture in a sort of caressing motion toward the *levain*. "These days, young bakers have less and less of this sense of touching the dough because the work has been mechanized, but they compensate for this lack of sensing their live doughs through superior technical knowledge. They may understand better than older bakers the phenomena that go on with the fermentation."

I watch the apprentices as they move about the room. Everywhere they go, they bend down to examine a lump of dough or give it a pinch. Clearly, they are still being tutored not only to be technicians but artists, like their older mentors.

I spy a basket of fragrant, crispy-looking loaves just out of the oven—loaves Monsieur Choquet identifies as *pain trois rivières*.

He explains that *pain trois rivières* is the only type of bread he makes without *levain*. The bread is made by the *poolish* method, an approach, like *pain au levain,* that takes more time than the method for the average baguette. A *poolish* is a mixture of water, a lot of water, flour, and a little yeast, and was brought to France by Polish bakers in the last years of the nineteenth century. "It's like a *crêpe* batter," the baker says. "In a sense the *poolish* replaces the *chef* of the *pain au levain*. When the watery mixture is well fermented one adds the rest of the flour and one makes the dough. *Si vous voulez,* we first take three liters of water. We mix it with three kilos of flour and we put in a little bit of yeast. We use organic flour type 65. This is a flour that is less refined than white flour, containing a part of the bran and a little bit of the wheat germ. Then we put in a little bit of yeast—depending on the duration that we want to give this fermentation. *Si vous voulez,* if we want a long fermentation of twelve hours we will put in, for three liters, six grams of yeast. The *poolish* rises then for twelve hours. Or, if we are disposed of a little bit less time, we will put in ten grams of yeast per liter of water and let it ferment but three or four hours.

"Next, when this *poolish* is sufficiently fermented, we add," he says, figuring aloud, "three more liters of water and six kilos of flour. And then we put in"—he is figuring again—"thirty grams of yeast. Now, at the dough stage, we knead this mixture for fifteen minutes, or for eight minutes with a spiral kneading machine. Then we leave it for a first fermentation of one hour. Following this first rising, we weigh out portions of the dough, shape them in *boules,* and leave them to ferment for thirty or forty minutes. At this point, we shape them into their definitive form—baguette or *bâtard.* Next, we leave them to rest—it's an hour and a half or two hours—at a temperature of twenty to twenty-three degrees—and then we bake them in a hot oven of 250 degrees. *Voilà.*

"Here you have a bread that is much less acid than *pain au levain.* Fermentation on *poolish* is much softer, gentler as a taste. The *poolish* gives a light taste of hazelnuts to the bread."

I linger a moment, savoring the fragrance of the loaves that will become the lodestar for the duration of my voyage into French bread.

ℰ

Monsieur Choquet excuses himself to attend to matters elsewhere in the boulangerie.

The hum of industry vibrating through the two rooms is the hum of bees—calm, quick, efficient, closely timed work. There is an unspoken pride in the actions of the men. They make little of me, seeming to regard themselves as high in status and engaged in vital work. And there is as well the age-old rightness of eager young men learning from experienced, wiser older men. This work is different from that spurred by compulsion or impossible deadlines. It seems in its proper proportion here.

Monsieur Breher—across from me—is brushing the sides of the large kneading bowl with a rubber scraper as the *pain ordinaire* dough continues to rotate. Using his trained eye, he adds a little more water. Satisfied by what he sees in the large bowl, he turns to its smaller neighbor. He begins mixing *pain de ménage*.

Meanwhile, at the oven in the adjoining room the two apprentices I watched earlier are removing long, skinny, golden baguettes and placing them in a tall, cylindrically shaped *panier*—basket—that has about a quarter of its upper portion open like a door in a tree stump.

Monsieur Breher is now at a new station: the cutting machine. He fetches a lump of *pain de ménage* out of a large bowl from somewhere out of sight and puts it into a big funnel positioned above his head in the kneading room. The machine drops out the dough in round, one-kilo hunks that roll off along a conveyer belt. As they come along, the baker grabs the blobs, turned *boules,* combining some of them into two-kilo hunks, and sets them on one of the boards on the rolling tables. When the cutting machine has finished this particular job, there are thirty-one hunks of dough resting peacefully. Fifteen of them are the smaller loaves, sixteen the larger. The small loaves are lovely, perfectly round domes about five inches in diameter by four inches high.

Monsieur Breher stops the big kneading bowl at 7:35, exactly twenty minutes after he started adding the flour. The *pain ordinaire* dough is now very smooth and white.

Continuing on to the next step, he cuts armfuls of flailing dough out of the mass in the big bowl and, climbing onto a chair or tossing them up, hurls them into the three-foot-high funnel. The funnel is soon full, bulging at the top. The machine again begins producing round blobs, and, transported by the conveyer belt, this time they fall onto revolving, long *couche* slings. The cloth slings are suspended in a sort of Ferris wheel. Each sling automatically moves back once six or eight evenly spaced lumps of dough are set into it, and another appears to receive the next allotment of apportioned dough. On the slings, Monsieur Breher explains, they will be left to rise—to be elongated and shaped into baguettes by another machine at the opposite end of the conveyer belt, after the rising. *Pain ordinaire,* or *pain normal,* requires half an hour of repose, the *chef boulanger* tells me.

The slings of rising *pain ordinaire*—the machine has now stopped—are sitting filled with round balls of dough lined up evenly, like eggs in a box.

All the *pain ordinaire* dough is cut into the single baguette-size lumps, but Monsieur Breher grabs up some blobs midway down the conveyer belt and combines three at a time into *gros pain*—the enormous one kilo-500 gram loaves. These he puts to rise on a shelf.

The baker explains quickly as he moves for a moment into the storeroom, that the same dough is used for *flûtes, baguettes, gros pain, boules, pain gris, pain jaune, ficelles. . . .*

$\backsim$

It is now 8:00 A.M. For a moment there is a lull, a calm in the rooms. Most of the dough is mixed and resting on shelves, trays, or slings. Big hampers of baked loaves are lined up at the door, ready to be delivered to homes in the countryside, or to the two shops.

From time to time throughout the morning, the bakers and apprentices have consulted a large book that details the types and numbers of loaves to be made for the day. Now one of the apprentices places the book on a shelf.

For a fraction of time, the busy little baking center seems to stop altogether and take a deep breath, as if the tide has receded.

Presently, the pace of work picks up again. An apprentice trolleys over a huge shelf to receive baked baguettes from the oven. He fishes out several loaves at a time with his long-handled baker's *pelle,* or peel. The oven yields four trays of *ficelles,* the skinny baguettes, and three or four of the *flûtes,* the larger ones.

Jerome, the Choquet son, runs through the workroom holding in both hands a cake with raspberry frosting.

Monsieur Breher now begins the *façonnage*—the step after one or two risings: the shaping of the dough. He works fast, bending, squatting, lifting trays of loaves, smacking balls of dough and pressing down, palms to dough, with all his weight. He starts by shaping the *boules* of *pain de ménage.* He folds each orb of dough into itself six or eight times on what will be the bottom of the loaf, and leaves the top of each loaf a lovely round dome. Once he finishes shaping the *boules,* he places them, in pairs, side by side between pleats of floured *couches.*

Now that the *pain ordinaire* has rested the required twenty minutes, the baguette shaping begins. The rounds of dough are now fed automatically from the slings into the baguette shaper. Long, squiggly snakes of dough emerge from the machine. Monsieur Breher places these in black scalloped metal forms, each holding eight baguettes. The younger men come over to help him to straighten and shape the loaves as they go in the forms. Only the baguettes are shaped by machine at the Boulangerie Choquet.

Next Monsieur Breher shapes *gros pain*—the big, fat, six-inch-thick baguettes of one kilo-500 grams and of one kilo. He mashes out the hefty gob of dough, folds it toward the center several times, mashes it down, rolls it round and long, presses the fold together and knits it closed, pinching with his fingers. Here the fold remains on top.

All the work proceeds by innate knowledge. It is constant and fast now. There are no watches in the place. The work just ticks along, step after step.

Monsieur Breher's brother, a gaunt, cheerful-faced man, comes in to hang around and chat to his baking brother and whoever else happens by. I can barely understand him. He was a technician at the Centre Nucléaire, I'm told, and it destroyed his voice. Monsieur Breher and the apprentices smile at him and rib him with their jokes.

It is 9:30 A.M. All of the loaves are now shaped for the next day. All day they will rise slowly in the *chambre froide* at ten degrees. Then, in eighteen hours, at two A.M., they will be baked.

The morning's product from the baking room is gathered at the door: hundreds of beautiful golden baguettes in a basket.

Monsieur Breher comes over to stand beside me. He says the Boulangerie Choquet uses ten tons of flour per month, a mere portion of the four million tons of wheat France uses every year.

The workers are brushing their hands against their trousers. I wipe the flour off my dark pants and stamp my shoes. I wave to the handsome young apprentices and to Monsieur Breher, thank them, and tell them, *"Vous avez un emploi merveilleux."*

The morning is yet young and I am restored. I can smell the fragrances of the breads, and am thinking that the baking men of Blain are time artisans as well.

♱

"And you like your *métier?*" I said to Monsieur Choquet as I gathered my notebooks at the end of my first morning at the boulangerie.

"Ah, oui, oui. Beaucoup." He waved his hands gently just above the tabletop, as if it went without saying,

"*Si vous voulez,* what pleases me the most is the fact that even in making the bread in the same way every day, there are the climatic factors that make each baking different. Each time one must manage the fermentation.

"Now, the bread maker's trade can appear to involve the most banal of doughs, since bread is always made with just water, flour, salt, and an agent of fermentation, but apart from putting these same four ingredients together they are not governed in the same way from one baker to the next. So it's this that one must manage well."

It seemed to me, as Monsieur Choquet spoke, that this "management" he mentioned was a deceptively straightforward term for an essential and mysterious ingredient that each good baker adds to his dough. Like the unique sensibility that an artist brings to his or her work, a baker crafts his loaves with artistry, knowledge, and a spoonful of inimitable idiosyncrasy.

I now had in my mind a multifaceted picture of Monsieur Choquet, the baker. He was a thinker, a commander, a craftsman, and also an alchemist, a presider over mysteries. Jean-Claude Choquet seemed to me a *gros pain,* a man who epitomized sturdiness—in his mind, in his physicality, and in his clear-washed eyes.

"But wait, just *un petit moment,*" the baker said as I gathered my things in preparation to say good-bye, "if you have time."

He left the room for a moment. Alone, I thought, here is a man at the apex of his life. With fifty years tucked under his belt, Monsieur Choquet seemed to be using his time to the fullest and living at the height of his potency. It seemed to me that he could go on forever.

Monsieur Choquet soon returned with an armful of loaves in his arms. He had brought me four of the organic breads he made. In his embrace were three round *boules* and one baguette. "This is the organic *pain au levain,*" he said, handing me one of the *boules,* "made of organic flour and fermentation from an apple.

"And this is *pain de ménage* with natural fermentation using yeast on top of *levain.*

"This is the *pain de campagne,* with a bit of rye inside.

"And this is *la baguette de pain trois rivières,* named for the three rivers of our region. Personally, I like this bread a lot."

Then Monsieur Choquet cut me a piece of each, and he watched me eat the best bread I'd ever tasted.

He sent me off holding the loaves in my arms like four treasured infants.

⁓

A while later, Peter, Maud, Forrest, and I drove around looking for a place for a picnic and finally came upon the park in le Coudray. There we sampled the selection of Monsieur Choquet's loaves, with cheese and salami, in dappled sunlight. Each of us tossed adjectives into the air as we tasted the four different breads. Happiness floated around us like petals drifting in spring air.

First, we tried the *pain au levain.* The loaf had a hard, chewy crust, a great sourdough taste and classic sourdough sponginess.

Eight-year-old Maud said, "It's like salt water."

The *pain de ménage,* which we sampled next, was made with the same flour as *pain au levain,* but contained a little industrial yeast along with the *levain.* It looked more organized, less left to the laws of nature, and was lighter and airier, and dryer than the rest. The *pain de campagne* was robust, very sour at first contact, with a flash of beer at the end.

Peter said of it, "The crust is like biting into the head of a match."

Finally, we tasted *pain trois rivières,* Monsieur Choquet's favorite loaf. The children passed judgment with absolute conviction in their voices:

Maud said, "It smells like spices. It smells soury and floury."
Three year-old Forrest summed it up for us: "Tastes good."

After our meal, we flopped under the trees, sunlight filtering down through branches over our sleepy faces. We drove back to the *gîte*, quiet and full. As though we all knew a secret.

❧

At our evening meal, we had eaten a whole loaf of *pain trois rivières*. It smelled like heaven and tasted a mile deep.

Afterward, I walked alone down a cow path and watched the sun turn the flat field a sharp lemon. I had a deep feeling of calm as I stood looking out into the glowing field. Monsieur Choquet worked magic, and his bread had fulfilled my dreams. I had found my loaf.

❧

At the end of my visit with Monsieur Choquet, I'd asked the baker where his ingredients came from. "The wheat," he said, "comes from a miller in Pont-James, about three hours south of here. He gets his wheat from an organic wheat cooperative that, in turn, get its wheat principally from the Poitiers area, from the *departement* of La Vienne. The yeast comes from Lesaffre, the biggest yeast company in France. I buy my salt from the *paludiers* of Guérande, when it's cheap enough, and from the big sea salt industry in the Midi when it's not. Of late, I've been forced to buy from the Midi. And as for the water, it's from the tap—from an aquifer near Nort-sur-Erdre."

❧

Perhaps it was the pull of the ocean. I decided to track down, first, the story of the salt.

SALT

The mineral that slows down the multiplication of yeast cells, regulates the fermentation process, and adds flavor to the loaf.

I saw the salt
in this shaker
in the salt flats.
I know
you
will never believe me,
but
it sings,
the salt sings. . . .

Pablo Neruda
"Ode to Salt"

THE CHILDREN, PETER, AND I MADE OUR WAY TO GUÉRANDE, a walled, hilltop village in the west of France where salt is harvested by the most basic of methods. There *paludiers,* farmers engaged in a strange and ancient task, rake salt out of the sea.

The first of our fifteen or so days on the coast, we drove down the promontory from Guérande to behold a kingdom of salt: overrun with salt farms and ruled by salt makers. It was a water maze of canals and ponds and dikes extending kilometers into the distance; a land of reflector ponds, mud, and sunlit wheat, olive, mustard, and russet grasses. A few gently curving roads threaded their way through and around the ponds, heading toward the open sea which I could just make out gleaming in the distance.

Now and then among the pools I spied a dark wooden barn, or an ancient stone one—salt barns, or *salorges.*

On a peninsula to the left of the ocean in the far western distance, I could see the church tower in Le Croisic, a small fishing and tourist town situated on a headland of the Cote d'Amour, the Love Coast.

Here and there among the oddly shaped pools, were grids of smaller, rectangular ponds, each with a single white dot at its perimeter. These dots in a row made sprints across the landscape. They could have been ancient Celtic signs.

Gazing across this glinting waterscape, I was immediately intrigued—to learn more about the salt harvest, the workers, and to bend over the ponds and peer into their salt chambers.

℮

Saillé, the salt-workers' village where I am now standing with giant, slim Michel Evain, is a tiny, mica-schist island barely above sea level set in a vastness of salt pans. Though it has existed for centuries, the village—a few streets' worth of rowhouses—seems tentative, perched as it is like a gull at the trailing edge of shore. A bell tower dominates the lines of small, whitewashed and stone houses with granite window trim and door frames. The houses—all in a row—are solid, two-story dwellings attached one to the next in long, barnlike structures. Their shutters are in blues, dark reds, and greens, with hydrangea, lavender, and geraniums in window boxes. Abundant bushes of lavender, clusters of *jaunet,* a sweet-smelling yellow bush, and poppies stand outside the houses along with trellises of roses. The houses have concrete courtyards in back with sheds for bicycles and tools and baskets and dogs, and big, open, weedy yards for growing cabbages, cauliflower, onions, and tomatoes. They are long spaces, some with salt-crusted wheelbarrows parked in them. There is a salted look to everything—the surfaces a little bleached and glittered. At the edges of the village cluster are modern, freestanding houses, in the same general style as the old, but with shiny wooden fences and swing sets out back. The church is situated in the middle of the island, with carefully tended flowers surrounding its stone faces.

The streets of Saillé are tiny, narrow, wending. From the mid-marsh causeway leading from Guérande to Le Croisic, just three or so parallel roads strike out onto the island, with a few interconnected lanes crisscrossing them, petering out finally in *salines*—salt farms—and *salorges* on all sides.

I meet Monsieur Evain in the early afternoon at the Maison des Paludiers, the small salt museum across the tiny *place* from the church. Peter and the children are off wandering among the fishing boats at Le Croisic. Monsieur Evain is the director of this small institution dedicated to educating the public about the salt-maker's life and work, a moonlighting job apart from his regular employ as a professor of technology at the Institut de Technologie in Saint-Nazaire and as a part-time *paludier*. Monsieur Evain, his wife, and children are long-term residents of Saillé. The *paludier*-professor has invited me to see the salt. Soon after I arrive, he takes me out onto the marsh.

The *paludier* stands bareheaded in the searing sun and hot wind. Over six feet, in his mid-forties or early fifties, he has a handsome face: eyes the color of honey, a mole by his sunburned nose. He is wearing a white shirt, lightweight khaki trousers, and slip-on sneakers.

We are standing in the marshland at the skirt edge of Saillé. Far away, across the seascape of glittering pools and dikes, I see the bell tower at Pradel, another village of *paludiers*. As we look out over acres and acres of indistinguishable, olive-green man-made pools, Monsieur Evain outlines the salt-making process for me. Each *paludier*, he tells me, has one or more *salines*. "An *exploitation*, the interlocking collection of pools that make up the salt farm, is the *saline*. This is how we describe it." As an Old World farmer might have several fields scattered over a mountain slope, a *paludier* may have a *saline* here, another two miles distant, and a third in between. "Behind the word *saline* is a double terminology. On one side of its meaning the *saline* is the whole *exploitation*, but the word *saline* is also used to refer just to the specific place where one gathers the salt."

Motioning toward a rough conglomerate of odd-shaped, dike-divided ponds, in the middle of which lies a grid of even, rectangular pans, each with a small salt heap at its perimeter, Monsieur Evain explains, "That is one *saline*, and those rectangular pans at the center are the *oeillets*. These are the crystallizing ponds, the place in the exploitation where we collect the salt. The *oeillet* is our unit. I farm fourteen *oeillets*. Mine is a small farm."

Monsieur Evain says that the *oeillets* are transmitted through the generations, exactly like an agricultural property. His *saline* was in his wife's family, and marriage is what brought him to Saillé. His own great-grandparents were *paludiers* in Mesquer, an area just a few kilometers to the north. "An average *exploitation* is sixty, though there are some fools who farm as many as eighty or one hundred," he says. Though he calls the big saline workers "fools," I detect a touch of envy, or admiration, in his voice.

"As for how the salt is made, the salt is formed by a process of condensation, evaporation, and crystallization." He explains that water from the sea is captured and is induced to flow through a series of interconnected, shallow evaporation pools, until it reaches the *oeillet,* where it finally crystallizes.

Monsieur Evain explains that the whole saline system is gravitational. "That is to say, in each *saline* the water moves from pool to pool with only the aid of a very weak slope." All the basins in a *saline* are inclined in coordination with one another, and the slope is so weak that the water advances at a speed so slothlike as to be almost imperceptible. "As you can see, one can hardly see the current—and the water that enters the system one day will not find itself in the form of salt until the end of two days. The slope goes like an *escargot,* and ends up at the *oeillet.*" The making of that slope, he says, is a real art. I watch the shallow, still purple water for signs of movement as it travels its snail course. For an instant, I think I detect a tiny current, a water whisper.

"Now I will show you my *saline.*"

He leads me to a trenchlike canal about six feet across that snakes its way in from the bay through the flat marshlands. Its steep sides are lush with grass. This watercourse is moving swiftly. If I were to fall in, it would carry me along. "This is the *étier,* the first link in the salt-making circuit," Monsieur Evain says, "the source of the seawater for the *saline.* The whole salt basin is irrigated by *étiers,* such as this one." This *étier,* he says, which brings in water from the sea near La Baule, supplies all the *salines* on this southeast side of the road to Le Croisic. When he turns to me his eyes shine. "This same *étier* has been used for at least five centuries!"

Every day, the ocean water in the *étiers,* he explains, rises and descends with the tide, exactly like the waves at the beach of La Baule, the nearby sunbather's paradise. The variation in the level of the water in the *étier,* like the level of the water in the bay, is due to natural cycles, to tidal rhythms and seasonal fluctuations. Like rising bread dough, a *saline* is governed by the pulses and caprices of nature. If a baker is ruled by the fermentation time required by his loaves, a *paludier* is ruled by the seasons and the weathers they blow over his *saline.*

"The whole salt-making operation is governed by the sun and the moon," Monsieur Evain remarks. It is moon and sun play.

A problem, the *paludier* tells me, is the natural wear of the water on the banks of the *étiers.* Water has a way of hollowing out the banks as the tide rises and descends. Over time, if there is no intervention, the winding *étiers* become nothing but a series of hairpins. Alluvial deposits are made on the interior of the hairpins, while the opposite side is hollowed out. This hollowing proceeds all the time, day and night. "If we want to preserve the salt basin that has been transmitted to us by our ancestors, it is necessary for us to maintain the banks. Because of this, we have to do what we call 'extraordinary actions' in the winter. We scour the *étier* in certain places, and strengthen the banks so they don't collapse. In winter, when there is no salt, we fix all the dikes and surfaces of the *saline;* we work to preserve the site."

At the edge of the *étier,* Monsieur Evain outlines more of the salt-making process, explaining that all along the *étier*'s course, there are little trap doors that feed the *vasière,* the first pond of the several *salines* along its route. He indicates a slim wedge of what looks like wood or slate, less than a foot wide, stuck in the narrow mound of turf dividing the *étier* from a wide, glinting pool.

"The first thing to comprehend about the *vasière*," he says, flashing a long hand toward the large pool, "is that it receives water only every twenty or twenty-two days." A *paludier* must have patience with time, for his ability to make salt depends on a willing sea. Monsieur Evain explains that the tide height—of the sea and of the *étier*—varies each day. Each day there is a different coefficient, a measure of the difference between the height of the low tide, which he calls "water death" and the high, or overflowing tide. The coefficient ranges from a low of 35 to a high of 115.

"When the coefficient is high enough, the water passes through the little hole in the barrier I made here, letting water into the *vasière*." Monsieur Evain's long finger is now tapping an eight-inch slate with a small notched hole in the middle of its top edge that serves as a lock or a plug between the *étier* and the *vasière*. "It is ultimately this little trap door that maintains the level of the water in the *vasière*. It's nothing but an artificial siphon."

The trap door looks like the tiny drawbridge to a castle. It amazes me that by way of simple handmade, toy-size lock-gates such as these the *paludier* controls the water of the sea.

The influx of water into the *vasière* follows the lunar cycle, Monsieur Evain says. When the sun and moon are in line and pulling together—for about four or five days and occasionally six or seven—spring tides occur, and during those days the water enters the *vasière*.

"The *saline* is really a big laboratory," Monsieur Evain says, using another metaphor as we stand with our toes just above the flowing moss-green water of his *étier*. I gaze at the smooth, undulating water, enjoying its cool swiftness. My companion's eyes reach across the salt basin toward the horizon. "To understand the process of salt-making, it is first necessary to take account of the fact that the water that comes in here is salt water. That is to say, each time a liter of water comes into the *saline,* approximately thirty-five grams of salts come with it. This is a crucial factor in the process of concentration.

"Notice, too, that I did not say 'salt,' in the singular—for 'sodium chloride.' Of the salts of the sea, eighty percent are sodium chloride. Sodium chloride is the essential salt, but there are also borates, phosphates, sulfates, and plenty of other salts."

Monsieur Evain turns into the professor that he is, and delivers a mini-lecture on the *paludier* trade. I grab the brim of my floppy gray hat, holding it on my head as I attempt to grasp his words before they fly into the hot wind. "A *paludier* is a tradesman, and his trade, above all, is subject to hygrometry." Rain is the critical factor in a salt-maker's year, he explains. If a man is given a very dry summer he will have a good harvest. "It is the rainfall, above all, that determines the year's harvest, because rainfall is crippling. When it rains all salt-making stops. Production comes to a halt."

A salt man, like a baker or another kind of farmer, must have a trunkful of patience. When the skies conspire against him, he must surrender his time. In addition, he must have a kind of internal barometer—a sixth sense for the humidity in the air, for the moods of the particular season in which he is living.

"As a *paludier,* one is in constant interrogation with the weather. In a word, a *paludier* is able to go to his saline and come back in short order, but if the *paludier* doesn't anticipate the coming rain he will lose salt, and he will lose money. So we *paludiers* are very close to the weather. We have a sole master—the weather."

Monsieur Evain breaks his gaze toward the glinting horizon and turns to me. "Now we arrive at the part that is a little bit intellectual: how to regulate the water. The *paludier*'s greatest challenge is to regulate the amount of water he allows to flow into the various ponds, so as to maximize the crystallization of the salt."

The *paludier*'s greatest challenge, more particularly, is to decide how much water to stock in his *vasière*. Ideally he stocks a quantity just sufficient to furnish his saline for twenty-two days. "For if one hasn't let in enough water, for example, the *saline* won't have enough water for making salt, and if one has let in too much, one will have poor yields. *Voilà.*

"But you see here, a little, the problem for the *paludier*: What quantity of water am I going to leave in my *vasière?* Because what weather will it be next week, in fifteen days, in three weeks? No one knows. We, like everyone, make an estimation. Obviously, we don't stock the same quantity of water in the month of May as in the month of August—so we behave on that basis—but who can really predict the weather?

"In terms of water regulation, if I get the feeling that it will rain in two days, I must stop the flow of water now. Because if I wait, in two days a quantity of water will arrive from my *vasière* and add itself to the rain and I risk overflow. So, the more the *paludier* anticipates the weather with exactitude, the more salt he will harvest."

I can hear the urgency in Monsieur Evain's voice as he relays this critical ingredient of a *paludier*'s success. His hands waver from the quick gestures that indicate a flurry of activity, such as when the *paludier* decides to open or close his traps, to the thudding hands of defeat when he fails to act at the right moment.

"The *paludier* is happy if at the end of the cycle, at the moment the high tide comes again, when the live waters arrive, he begins to see the bottom of the *vasière*. If exactly as much water evaporated as he had predicted, that means he has calculated well. *Alors,* there you see it is necessary for the *paludier* to predict the weather and this is not simple!"

Yes. I am again astonished at how vulnerable the *paludier* is. He can apply the wisdom he has gained from years of scrutinizing the sky, and decide to open or close his gates according to his informed guesses, but ultimately he is a marsh mouse trying to outrace sudden and unpredictable storms. It is a strange duty, this activity so delineated by the whims of rain and sun.

Monsieur Evain guides me across the weedy, dry ground away from the *étier* and toward a series of ponds of diminishing size. All are set in the flat, dry mudscape like so many trenched-off safety zones built by a battalion of industrious boys. I am to learn that this is literally the case. All the ponds and dikes were, at some point in history, dug and shaped by boys grown up. The dikes dividing the pans are constructed of a cracked, black-gray-blue mud, and are oddly clean, neat, and bare of vegetation. Each dike is only wide enough for a single foot—perhaps a foot wide at most. Monsieur Evain issues a warning to walk carefully, as the dikes are delicate, handmade constructions.

"Here is a place that is a little bit privileged," Monsieur Evain says, motioning to me to halt. "From here, one can see the three primary basins that form the *exploitation.* Here, closest, is the large basin, the *vasière.*" He is pointing toward a pond approximately the size of a neighborhood pool and about the depth of the shallow end of a swimming pool. "That is the first reservoir. Beyond is the second basin, the one we call the *cobier,* in which one diminishes the depth of the water to accelerate evaporation. And then there's the third basin with the lowest water level, the place where one gathers the salt."

Monsieur Evain is indicating a network of salt pans that, to the untutored eye, looks like a maze of haphazardly placed, undifferentiated pools. The tiny, subtle, and critical differences between the pools of this third basin are hidden until Monsieur Evain spells them out.

As Monsieur Evain speaks, though, I am beginning to gain a general comprehension. My mind suddenly flashes on the series of rusted troughs outside my brother-in-law's house in the New Hampshire woods. It strikes me that this salt-making process exactly replicates that used by Bill to make maple syrup each spring. One product is sweet, the other salt, but both are jewels cast up after long, hot toil.

Monsieur Evain now ushers me up to the labyrinthine pond network of the third basin, the salt collection basin proper. Small, shallow ponds of varied, lopsided, oblong, rectangular, and squarish shapes, all divided by low, foot-wide dikes, frame and abut a neat, central, official-looking area divided into two rows of six rectangular ponds about ten meters long by five to seven meters wide—the *oeillets*. The odd-shaped outer ponds, of which there are twenty-five or so, are almost completely separated by their low mud walls, save for a small break in the perimeter of each one that allows the water to flow in a long, slow slalom from one to the next, and finally arrive at the business end of the operation, the rectangular ponds.

"Here, we are at the *saline,* in its narrower sense," Monsieur Evain says, "the place where the salt is gathered. In the *saline,* you have three types of compartments. First you have the *fares.* The *fares* can take any shape." He indicates the odd-shaped ponds situated all around the central rectangles.

"When one puts them end to end, the *fares* represent the essential surface of the saline," Monsieur Evain says. "As the water travels through the *fares* its level declines. It starts at a depth of about six to ten centimeters, and by the last pond in the sequence, only four or five centimeters remain."

Monsieur Evain bends his long, thin, egretlike limbs, and pulls up a board at the edge of one of the *fares,* showing me a couple of other methods by which the water in the *saline* is regulated. "The water advances always via one of these traps," he says, "a wedge of wood with holes that can be opened or closed like the plugs of a barrel, or with a little corner of wood that one raises according to the weather." He gestures onward in the *saline* where I can see a couple of wooden traps lying along the top of a dike. "Here I have unplugged one," he says. "There I have raised two. It's these drains that act to regulate the water that enters in the *fares*."

Monsieur Evain is now pointing out three larger shallow ponds at the end of the *fares'* course. These are the *adernes,* the second type of compartment in the central *saline*—to which the *fares* lead. The *adernes* are the reservoirs for the *oeillets* in the same way that the *vasière* is the reserve for the *cobiers* and the *fares*. The *adernes* look so like the *fares* that I have not taken note of them until this moment. Only their slightly larger size, and their proximity to the *oeillets,* distinguishes them.

"The *oeillets* are over there," Monsieur Evain says, motioning beyond the *adernes* toward the very shallow rectangular pools—the last stop in the water's long journey through the *saline*. "The *oeillet* is the crystallizing pool, the place where the *paludier* gathers the salt. *Oeillets* are grouped by lots, or groups, if you wish, and a group is called a *lotie d'oeillets*. The *oeillet* is the place that is shallowest in the *saline*."

We are now standing on a cracked dike about two feet high, looking out over two rows of rectangular pools, separated one from the other by low mud dividers. At the far edge of each pool is a small, low semicircle of mud extending from the dike into the pool. This, my guide tells me, is the *ladure,* or salt-collecting platform. The *ladures* are glittery, white, half-moon shapes against the tawny mudscape. Each *oeillet* is reminiscent of the free-throw zone of a basketball court.

"Now look over there," he says, extending his arm toward one of the farthest pans in the *saline*. A corner of the pan is completely dry. "See that *oeillet* there that shows its back? That says that last night, when I fed the *oeillets* something to drink I didn't give them enough water, because that one shouldn't show its back. It should be under a shallow layer of water like the others. So I didn't give it enough. I made an error. That is the problem in this *métier*. It's not a big thing, but I have maybe two meters square that aren't covered with water. And two square meters that are not covered with water is like having a two-meter-square rock in your garden. That area of the garden, or the *saline*, doesn't bring back anything. It's an error. I have been mistaken in my water regulation. Now, inversely, if I had left too much water, that too would be an error. So the *paludier* passes his time bawling himself out. Ah, one is always in error. The problem is that one must be in the least possible error. The *paludier*'s is a trade where perfection does not exist."

Monsieur Evain stands with his nose raised to the wind for a moment. It is a wind that is so warm and beats at me so briskly that, if I were not fascinated by the *salines*, I would seek shelter. "You see the breeze is coming from over there. West is over there, so these are east winds, northeast. These are the winds that absorb water, the dry winds. These are the good winds for the *paludier*. The winds that come from America, on the other hand, have traveled four thousand kilometers over water. When they arrive here they are already full of water, so when they arrive these west winds take up very little water for us. On the other hand, the winds that come to us from Russia have traveled four thousand kilometers over earth, and they don't have water in them. So, when they come they caress the surface. These are the good winds! *Vive l'est!*"

Monsieur Evain grins at teasing his North American visitor, then says, "Now I am going to show you, with that *oeillet* over there, how one takes the salt." We tiptoe along the dikes, Monsieur Evain moving like an astronaut on the moon.

"Attention there. Because these are long handles." Monsieur Evain has taken up his *las*. The *paludier*'s tool is a five-meter shaft meeting a flat perpendicular board about five feet across. The toothless span of the rake is secured to the handle by metal wires. The *las* looks like something the giant in "Jack and the Beanstalk" might use, it is so oversized. "The *las* has one side— a flat side—that serves to pull. And then, the other side—the beveled one—serves for pushing."

"Now, see here what has happened in the *saline*," the *paludier* says, squatting on his haunches. I squat too, and squint into Monsieur Evain's magic pool. "I filled the oeillet yesterday and, as you see, with the effect of the sun and wind, the concentration has been sufficient that the salt has crystallized and settled itself here in the *oeillet*. You can't see the *gros sel*, but the *fleur de sel* is what is floating over there—a little bit on the surface."

The *oeillet* is a clean rectangle of rosy-brown water about an inch deep. Here and there sudsy-looking clumps of white are floating on and just under the surface. Monsieur Evain tells me those floating clumps are the finest salt in the world: the salt flower, the *fleur de sel.* He cautions me as I lean toward the salt and the carefully hewn mud dike begins to crumble a little bit. "Watch out. It's tender there. . . . You can walk, but pay attention. It's soft."

He tells me the *fleur de sel* is a salt that has rapidly crystallized under the effect of the wind. It comes from a species of microstratum across the surface of the *saline* from which the water has evaporated so as to crystallize the sodium chloride just beneath the surface of the water. Since this produces salt crystals that are both tiny and very fine, their density is light, and they float. On the other hand, by contrast, the heavier *gros sel* rests on the bottom. Monsieur Evain expounds on the virtues of the floating salt. "This *fleur de sel* is fascinating because it is just at the limit of crystallization: at the point when it passes from the liquid state to the solid state, but just! As soon as you put it on a leaf of salad, *poof!* It disappears right away.

Impossible to see the salt. There's no need to grind this salt. It's because of this that the *paludiers* have never had a machine for grinding salt. If you wish, the *fleur de sel* is a table salt. Because you never sense it under the teeth."

He scoops some of the *fleur de sel* onto the flat of his *las* and presents it to me with the flourish of a king offering a chunk of gold from one of his mines. The *fleur de sel* is so moist and so fine—like the tiniest snow crystals—that it seems to disappear as I cup it in my hand. It does melt, like snow, on my tongue, giving up a flash of silky liquid salt.

"You see here that there are scarcely two centimeters of water. These waters are the crystallizing waters, what we call the *eaux mères*," he says, caressing the words. The mother waters.

"Now, when one takes the salt," Monsieur Evain says, "the *oeillets* look almost dry, but in fact a little water remains—a very little. This water is important. It's the water that transports the salt. Without water I couldn't take the salt. . . . I will take the *gros sel* in front of you in this *oeillet*," he says, pointing to the nearest pool.

I am about to witness the birth of the salt used in Monsieur Choquet's *pain trois rivières*.

Monsieur Evain walks to different points at the perimeter of the basin and draws his *las* through the water across its flat bottom surface toward the middle of the pan. Leaning over his *oeillet* with the grace of a dancer, he is careful that his *las* strokes the bottom of each section of the basin.

Now he makes a second sweep, going around the edges of the *oeillet* again, bringing the invisible contents of the pan into the center of the pool.

Now he is standing in the middle of the *ladure*, the mud semicircle at the end of the *oeillet*, and there, with a flick of the wrist and a SHOOSH!, like magic, like the tide itself, he draws from the pan a pile of salt about four to five feet across and perhaps a foot high. After making this extraction, he pulls the water immediately surrounding the hillock toward him another time, and brings in a third as much again.

Time stops as I watch a mound of salt suddenly appear out of the water—out of nothing. What I have just seen, even though I have seen it with my own eyes, seems unfathomable. The salt to which Monsieur Evain has just given birth is more than enough to last my family the rest of our lives.

"That's the harvest of the day," Monsieur Evain says, coming up beside me. "A good day is fifty kilograms. This is a small, small harvest."

"It's salt?" I say stupidly.

He laughs. "It's salt, yes!"

"And you don't do anything more?"

"Nothing, nothing. It's water from the sea, the sun, the wind. That's all."

"It's fabulous," I say.

"The returns are small, but that's nature."

He is holding a half-cup of salt in his hand and I take some of it in my fingers and let it slide down into my palm. I am holding a tiny avalanche of squarish salt crystals. Some of them are the size of periods on a page, but most are larger clumps of angular crystals—up to the size of a grape nut, a tear, the tiniest Lego block. The salt is wonderfully coarse, firm, and chunky. It has an off-white color, a definite gray cast. It's not that eye-breaking white of most table salt. Monsieur Evain's salt is to Morton's what wheat berries are to commercial flour. Pure, unbroken, plain. Finally I place some of the crystals on my tongue. The salt has a delightful crunch—perhaps there is even a splash of water as I bite—and it tastes, well, like salt.

While I am marveling, Monsieur Evain's technical mind is flashing on. "You can see from the color that I have taken in a little tiny bit of clay with the salt. It's this that we measure to judge the quality of the salt. See the square cubes? It is because it's so angular that it stays in crystals. There is a capillary effect that makes it stay in that form. Moreover, when it dries, it forms a carapace. This encloses the water inside. When I extract one hundred grams of salt it contains almost ten grams of water." That was the wet flash on my tongue.

Monsieur Evain goes on to comment on the rose color of the water in the *oeillet*. He tells me that Guérande salt contains bacteria—a lot of bacteria—that actually add taste to the salt. "The *vasière* is a nest of microbes," he says. As the water flows through the *saline*'s circuit and becomes further and further concentrated, different sorts of bacteria spring up and flower and affect the coloration in the pans along the route. By the time the water reaches the *oeillet,* it is crawling with bacteria that turn it dusky rose.

"The interesting thing about our salt, to make it simple, is that it is not all salt. This seems bizarre, but it is true. In the salt we collect there is a certain proportion of the water that contains bacteria and there are also minerals: among others, magnesium chloride. That is the interest of our salt. If our salt were nothing but sodium chloride, it would be without interest. It would be nil."

I am silent now, trying to comprehend this pink world within the salt marsh.

"I see that you are surprised by my talk about bacteria," he says. He goes on to convince me that the bacteria are wonderful. "The excess bacteria in the *saline* serve as nourishment for small artemias, and these artemias serve as food for the shrimps we saw earlier. The shrimps, in turn, serve as food for the mullets that you could have seen in the *vasière,* and those mullets serve as food for man, among others. This is all to say that there is, in fact, life in the *saline!*" he says, triumphant. "*Il y a de la vie!* It is bacteriological life, because one can't see these unicellular links, but there is life. It's this that proves the *saline* to be a rich laboratory."

I imagine all the little beasts in this *oeillet,* in this *saline,* in this salt: the pinkish bacteria, the trace minerals, the bits of whale food. When I eat a chunk of Guérande salt, with faint traces of blue clay and minerals in it, I am eating a whole life cycle. And this life cycle is plunked, by the handful, into Monsieur Choquet's doughs.

I lean down and swish the water with my fingers. It is the temperature of a Japanese bath.

"Yes, it's very hot," Monsieur Evain says. "Right now we are at the beginning of the season, but it can go up to thirty, thirty-three degrees! With nothing but the sun! Without a photovoltaic battery, without anything! Nothing but nature. *Rien que la nature!*"

Monsieur Evain puts his hands in his pockets and looks out over his beloved marsh. "The *saline* is a big laboratory, but there is also a part that is alchemy.

"But the thing you must know about the *paludier* trade," Monsieur Evain says, turning toward me, "is how ancient it is. The salt farming of Guérande has changed virtually not at all since the time of the Romans!"

I stand gazing across the marsh, breathing in the hot, salty scent, wondering at the sudden appearance of this product of sea and sun and trying to imagine a tall Roman hauling up a heap of salt in this same spot over a thousand years ago.

 ⌒

"White Country" is the French translation of Guérande's Breton name, Gwenn-Rann. Dwelling in a land named for salt, the people of the Guérande peninsula such as Michel Evain, and of the Bay of Brittany to the south, have hatched white gold out of this vast, wheaty-green, estuarine seascape for at least fifteen hundred years.

Over the past two millennia, on its way to the formation of its glittering salt pans, the Guérande region has undergone great coastal transformations. Originally, the hectares of salt pans now such a dominant feature of the landscape were deep under water. By the year 1000, islands had emerged in the bay of 4,000 hectares that had long swirled beneath the skirts of the hill on which the walled town of Guérande is perched. As the sea retreated, landforms, separated by sounds, which came to be called Batz, Le Croisic, Piriac, Saillé, appeared. By the Middle Ages, the Guérande peninsula had assumed the shape it holds today. The sea had withdrawn, leaving just a couple of strips of itself in an otherwise more or less dry mud land. Pans of salt remained as footprints of the former bay.

Over the centuries, the enterprising peoples of the area mastered the movements of the tide, devised salt-production techniques, and created of themselves a new kind of farmer: the *paludier,* the "salt worker" or "salt maker."

Mud was key: a thick, strangely blue clay, deposited during the Flandrian portion of the present Quaternary Era, around eight thousand years ago. "It is necessary to talk about the nature of this blue clay," Monsieur Evain told me. "You see, it's bizarre. It is clay, but it is clay that contains a lot of water, and it is, in fact, the water within it that makes this clay insulative and watertight. The clay is a sort of sponge, and once the sponge is full of water, water rests on top. Because the 'floor' between the dikes—the *oeillet*—is made of this Flandrian mud—this particular kind of clay—it holds water in and forms an excellent salt collection surface. *Voilà.*" Thus mud—used by early *paludiers* and contemporary ones alike to construct the dikes and salt-collection pans—is the foundation on which the whole salt-making enterprise rests.

Along with the mud, the *traits* left by the departing sea have permitted the *paludiers* to carry out their work. Named by the Romans *tractus,* for "trajectory" or "route," the *traits* are interior seas, or gulfs, from which issue the seven *étiers,* or channels, that lead into and irrigate the salt basin of this sector of the west coast of France.

"This *étier* that comes to our feet here is the longest of them all," Monsieur Evain said as we stood on one of the fragile dikes of his *saline*. "Seven kilometers long—taking its source by the ports of Le Pouliguen and La Baule, at the mouth, passing by the village of Saillé here, and going on to the coast of Escoublac over there at the bottom—this *étier* brings water to *salines* all along the way. It is the sea, very simply.

"The origin of salt farming here is lost in the darkness of the times even before the Romans came to conquer us," Monsieur Evain stated again. "This is because when the Romans came to turn us to *pâté*—they routed us here in the year 52—they encountered a population that was already extracting salt. The inhabitants at that time used a totally different technique from that we see today, the 'Angers technique,' but the Romans saw this and they called this place le Bourg du Sel, Saliacum, which, Frenchified, has become today Saillé."

Historic remains show that salt was collected and commercialized in Brittany in proto-historic times. Salt kilns existed at the end of the Bronze Age, and during the Iron Age, the Guérande dwellers made salt through evaporation over a wood fire. There is some evidence of salt works operated as well by the Celts in the first century. The word "saline," from the Latin word *salina,* comes from the old Breton *siline,* and from the Breton *salin.* Salt pans certainly existed in the third century, right after the Roman conquest, and Breton ships may even have carried salt to northern regions during that time.

"It is certainly our fellow man who developed this salt-farming technique," Monsieur Evain told me, with awe in his voice. The first *étiers,* and the first extensive salt farms, were dug by the British nobles who came to install themselves on the deserted northwest French coast at the time of the Breton immigration during the fifth to seventh centuries. "While the first *salines* were constructed by the early Bretons, the wholesale, and largest development of the salt basin occurred during a second era, in the Middle Ages, under the impulse of the Dukes of Brittany."

By the seventh and eighth centuries, merchants were traveling to Brittany from Ireland to buy salt. During the tenth century, Normans established settlements to exploit the salt marshes of the Bay of Bourgneuf, and when the Normans departed, abbeys and priories established themselves all around the Bay of Brittany to gain control of the "white gold."

The Middle Ages, when the Breton duchy held sway, were the golden age for the two main salt production centers of Guérande and the Bay of Brittany. François 1 declared at the time, "Brittany is the Peru of France," and salt's role in the Middle Ages has been compared to that of coal in the industrial era of the nineteenth century. Monsieur Evain said of this period, "Anne de Bretagne, along with the other dukes and duchesses of Brittany, oversaw a huge expansion of the exploitation in the salt basin. The lords and the clergy possessed the *salines* and developed them because salt was an indispensable product for Brittany, and for France in particular, and in this way it was the key to all her riches at the time." Business-minded abbots, nobles, and castelans, tradesmen, and army captains lay claim to the salt lands, levied high taxes, and employed hundreds of salt workers who were left with just enough to make a bare living. By the ninth century, a group of salt-making monks from the Abbey of Saint-Saveur de Redon had established a stronghold in the area, and the Benedictines had laid claim in Batz, the village just down the road from Saillé. Guérande was appropriately named the Salt Capital of France.

The brisk maritime salt trade was critical to Brittany's prosperity during the Middle Ages. Wheat production fed only one-sixth of the population, so commerce was absolutely essential. From the twelfth to fourteenth centuries salt was widely sought both for domestic consumption—the salting of meat—and for the fishing trade, the salting of fish. A ton of salt was required to conserve four tons of herring.

In addition to domestic commerce, international trade was at the heart of Guérande's existence during the fourteenth and fifteenth centuries. A document from the archives of Loire-Atlantique entitled "Droit et Issue du Terroir de Peri" (Laws of the Land), which covers laws for the sale of wheat, salt, and other products, reports that in the year and three months from October 1384 to February 1386, 453 ships moved in and out of Guérande's harbor. Monsieur Evain found reports of two ships docked at Saillé in 1385 whose connecting port was London. To the salt basin in tiny Saillé where Monsieur Evain and I had stood in the blistered wind, a Captain Cramford had come to fetch fifty tons of salt six hundred and ten years before.

In the mid-fifteenth century, Breton salt—that from the Bay of Bourgneuf as well as of Guérande—supplied 80 percent of London's needs, despite unfriendly relations. Trade with the southwest of England, Spain, and the Hanse of North Germany was also important.

Vigorous shipping trade continued until the end of the fourteenth century. At that time, the Hanse shippers came to favor the more profitable products of cloth and wine over heavy, cheap salt, and at the same time, the Bay of Bourgneuf, to the south, began to silt up. The deforestation of the Loire, increased alluvial deposits in the Bay, and changes in tidal patterns worked together to shrink the Guérande ports very rapidly. As Monsieur Evain said, "Now there is nothing left of the port of Guérande." By the sixteenth century all the ports had pulled back to Le Pouliguen and Le Croisic, and the port of Guérande was finished. The result was that international commerce no longer came to Guérande.

As Guérande shipping was falling at the end of the Middle Ages, toward the Renaissance, the area's *paludiers* switched to coastal navigation. At that point, the *paludiers* of Guérande who had little, flat-bottomed *gabares* took their salt and delivered it to Nantes, which had become a big port. The Spanish brought wine and the Hanseatic fleet brought cloth for offloading in Nantes, and both took on salt for their return trips. The paludiers continued to transport their salt to Nantes all through the seventeenth and eighteenth centuries, and even into the nineteenth. In this way, Guérande's international salt commerce continued to endure, while that of the Bay disappeared.

The development of salt farming by Breton nobles, clergy, and dukes gave birth to a salt tax famous in France: *la gabelle*. This tax, briefly done away with during the French Revolution and reinstated by Napoleon to finance his wars, was not abolished until 1945. It remains a vivid memory for all in the area.

The *gabelle*—a word hailing from the Arab *kabala*, for tax—was created in 1340 by King Philippe VI de Valois. At that time tariffs on products such as wine, cloth, and salt were the principal bases of taxation of regional rulers. During the time of the *gabelle*, in the words of Lucien Gaspard, a salty *paludier* old-timer and friend of Michel Evain, "Guérande was surrounded by customs officials." Guérande was a designated free-trade zone in which residents could produce all the salt they wished, but they couldn't convey the salt from Saillé to Guérande without stopping at customs. Salt was taxed on passage from one region to another. "At the time of the *gabelle*, the time of the kings, if a *paludier* was caught in possession of salt in passing through customs, he was condemned to the galleys."

Michel Evain also reported that a large part of the coastal population lived from smuggling, and repression was severe from the fourteenth century on. A 1781 report showed 3,000 men, 2,000 women, and 6,000 children arrested for smuggling in one year. Hollow cart shafts, double-bottomed casks, and loads of sticks or seaweed were all excellent spots for caches.

A third expansion in the salt basin took place in the eighteenth century. At that time the herring and sardine fisheries increased, in synchrony with the increased use of small coastal boats, and with this new fishery came an increased demand for salt to be used for the conservation of the catch.

"The salt basin existed at that time," Monsieur Evain said, "but, no matter what you do, you can't make twice as much sunshine, so they couldn't produce twice as much salt to meet the new demand. So what they did was enlarge the salt basin. That is what explains the twenty-seven kilometers of dikes that exist on the coast of Croisic. They took in the sea there, to install *salines*.

"This was the last period of the extension of the salt basin. The salt pans that exist now are only a small part of the salt-bearing surface that existed in those prosperous times. The salt territories have declined in recent years, in part, due to abandonment. But in the end, one can say that it is man and only man who has given the final contour to the coastline of this region."

e

Lucien Gaspard—I have given him this name since he is a private man—lives in a narrow, tidy Saillé row house just down the lane from the Maison des Paludiers. The entry hall to his compact dwelling is furnished with a large armoire painted *sang de boeuf*, oxblood red—the preferred color of the nineteenth-century *paludiers*. Upon the shelves of the wardrobe sits a row of pitchers used by old-time *paludiers* as they sweated on the marsh. Other than these few tributes to the past, Lucien Gaspard's home is plain and practical.

The *paludier* in his seventies, with playful blue eyes above ruddy cheeks—and the product of a long line of *paludiers*—relayed to me the story of paludier life at the beginning of the century.

"The first salt pans were made by the bourgeoisie and the

clergy," Monsieur Gaspard said by way of introduction. "And still, at the beginning of this century, Saillé's *paludiers* worked as employees of the clergy because we were part of priory Sainte-Claire, of l'Abbaye de Saint-Aubin d'Angers. The *paludiers* here didn't become property owners of their own *salines* until after the 1914 to 1918 war, or almost after this war, 1939 to '45!

"I bought la Saline-aux-Moines—the Saline of the Monks —in what year? About '53. At the time, it belonged to the family, David de Dresille. It was a Monsieur 'de,' David *de* Dresille. At that time, the harvest was divided as two-thirds of the salt for the owner and just a third for the *paludier*. After, it became half for the owner, half for the *paludier*. Now it's become tenancy. A *paludier* gives so much per *oeillet*, say one hundred kilos of salt per *oeillet* of the *marais salant*. Now we also give a part to the organization of *paludiers*.

"In those days before the *paludiers* owned their *salines*, there weren't enough marshes for everyone, *hein!* And if you didn't please the owner, he had the right to throw you out of the *marais salant*. You had nothing more but to go fishing for mussels!"

Monsieur Gaspard's paths have wound solely back and forth from the marsh throughout his long life. He began working in the *salines* at the slight age of seven, when he first began to go with his grandfather "to pull the salt"; at age twelve, he left school to "make salt" on a steady basis. If you count his work life as beginning at that point, he has worked the salt for over sixty years. "I learned to make salt from my father. We didn't have theory back then. One learned naturally." All the children of the region worked on the salt marsh whenever they weren't in school. Lucien's wife, Madeleine, a cheerful-faced woman with practical short gray hair, bought her first bicycle at age ten, with the money she made from the *fleur de sel* she collected from her family's *saline*. As a child, she, like all the girls and women of the era, helped to transport the salt from the *oeillet* to the *trémet,* the main salt stack of the *saline.* To carry the salt, she used a *gède,* a flat basket which she supported on her head. Once she married Lucien, Madeleine continued to help with the harvest, but was pleased to give up the bulk transport work. Some women have continued to help their husbands with the haulage, "but that is more the business of men," Madame Gaspard says now. "It is too hard."

Her husband verified her perspective. "The *métier* of *paludier* is hard work. It demands physical effort."

Despite the toil involved, Monsieur Gaspard, like Monsieur Evain, marvels at the miraculous reappearance of salt every year, and every sunny summer day, even after his sixty years on the marsh. "The salt comes with just the sun and the wind!" he said, training his bright eyes on my face to make sure I understood. "It all happens just naturally. Look, even if you don't have the sun but you have the wind, there is still evaporation. If you put the washing out to dry, it will dry with the wind. With the evaporation of the water in the *saline,* it is the same thing! We say to the water: 'You have to go back to heaven. You must leave and you must leave us the salt!'"

Sitting at the table in the couple's bare, spotless kitchen, taking a small cup of wine, Monsieur Gaspard looked back upon the routines of his early years of marriage. "When I was in full operation, when we were young, we still worked the earth," he explained. In addition to the cultivation of the marsh, Monsieur and Madame Gaspard planted onions and potatoes. Like their neighbors, they always had one or two cows. They had a few vines. They had their wine. They put in a hundred or a hundred and twenty furrows of wheat. When the wheat was ripe, they hauled it to the mill. From the mill, they took the ground wheat to a local baker, where they arranged an exchange of flour for bread. The boulanger then delivered, over the year, the equivalent kiloage of bread back to them by horse cart. "In the old days we lived a lot on ourselves, you see. We ate dishes that were poor, not as rich as now, but that made fewer problems for the stomach. We ate buckwheat crepes, porridge, potatoes with milk, a little meat, a little fish. We ate healthier stuff back then, you see.

"In the past, it was sometimes hard, but we cultivated the salt and at the same time we cultivated a little earth. We had all this. *On mettait pas tous les oeufs tout dans le même panier!* We didn't put all our eggs in the same basket!"

Monsieur Gaspard's thoughts meandered along the roads of his past. "It is not the same kind of life anymore," he said. "In my childhood, one took the time to do everything tranquilly. One took more time to live. People were more sociable then . . . but now people are in a hurry. In the past, we walked. We had bicycles. We hitched up a cart for going to the market in Guérande, but we took our time. We passed our childhood like this. But now you, with your cars, you must always go faster and faster. You are always rushed! *Vous êtes toujours pressés!* When you run across a traffic jam you grumble! A *bien, Dame,* it's not at all the same! People have changed, truly.

"Now, mind you," the older man looked me again in the eye, "we had misery because, all the same, we suffered the war, we had restrictions. And then, we did not have all that was necessary . . . but I still wouldn't trade my life for the life nowadays." With these words, the *paludier* brushed broad, bright strokes onto my romantic canvas of traditional rural life.

Before Monsieur Gaspard retired, at age seventy-two, the Gaspards worked eighty-two *oeillets,* each day passing through their back door at four A.M. "in the coolness of the morning" to transport the previous day's harvest of salt from the *ladure,* the salt-collection platform at the *oeillet,* to the *trémet,* the salt stack. "By seven o'clock, when the sun had risen, all the salt had been hauled to the *talus,* the embankment of the pan. Just by the two of us." At the end of the season the couple transported the salt from the *trémet* to the *salorge,* the salt barn.

"During the war and before the war, we transported salt on our heads. As soon as the war was finished, we had wheelbarrows, but before the war, in the past, salt was carried on the head, or in *paniers* hung from a yoke. Me, I always carried it on the head, for twenty-six, twenty-seven years," the *paludier* said.

When he was in full-time operation, Monsieur Gaspard and his wife packed the salt in sacks of five, ten, and fifty kilos. Twenty-two tons of sacks of fifty kilos went to Belgium and to an industrial bakery in Paris. When that business discontinued, Monsieur Gaspard delivered directly to the producers group. The cooperative would come in with a tractor and loader and take his salt away. Each month, when salt was sold from the huge *salorges* at the cooperative, he would receive a certain sum, according to his contribution to the stockpile, or his "declaration of salt." Since he produces relatively little salt now, he delivers directly to his clients. "I have a boulangerie or two. I have some little clients. Clients like you, who buy five kilos, let's say, things like that."

These days, in his retirement, Monsieur Gaspard still walks out to the *saline* every afternoon about three-thirty or four to rake in the day's salt, but he only cultivates eight *oeillets* now. "In the past my wife and I made eighty-two *oeillets*," he told me again. "*On avait du travail!* We had work! But now my *saline* is not so beautiful because so many of the pans are uncultivated. Before my *saline* was beautiful, because every pan was worked. Everything was impeccable!"

Pride of work resounded like a drumbeat in Monsieur Gaspard's words.

"I don't grow wheat anymore," the man said, a firmness in his voice now. "At seventy-two years old, it is necessary to know how to stop yourself. But I want to continue with the *saline,* as much as I can, *quoi.* As long as I have my health. I like the air of the salt marsh. I am very tranquil in my marsh, over there. The air of the *marais* makes one long-lived. One can live up to one hundred years!"

He handed me a page from a file folder. "This is not by me," he said. The sheet held a quote from Arnaud de Villeneuve:

Celui qui connait le sel et sa préparation, possède le secret caché des anciens sages. Nous admirons en même temps les ingénieurs inconnus et lointains qui ont réalisé cette chose admirable et complexe, les marais salants.

He who knows the salt and its preparation possesses the hidden secret of the ancient sages. We admire the unknown and distant engineers that made this admirable and complex thing, the salt pans.

"You see?"

"It's a very mysterious thing," I said.

"Ah bien, Dame, oui."

As I left the Gaspards' house—through the front hall decorated with the wine pitchers that quenched the thirsts of *paludiers* of generations before—it occurred to me that I had never before encountered a trade that required so fully a sense of romance in its practitioners.

❧

As I stand beside the salt stack at Monsieur Evain's *saline,* the late afternoon sun is crisping my nose and beating down on my crown. Monsieur Evain stands unperturbed, taking the time to bring me up to date on the current status of Guérande *paludiers.*

The Guérande salt basin is approximately 1,500 to 1,800 hectares in size, the *paludier*-professor says—which incorporates something fewer than 500 *exploitations,* and around 8,000 *oeillets.* These days about two hundred Guérande-area families make their living from salt-making and together produce an average of 10,000 tons of gray salt per year.

The figures roll off his tongue like salt from a *las.* By contrast, he says, the production of salt from mines in France is about five million tons. With Guérande's production representing only between 3 and 6 percent of France's food salt, the Atlantic salt producers can't begin to compete with the enormous sea salt industry of the Mediterranean, which produces 90 percent of French sea salt.

Today, Monsieur Evain muses, in contrast to Monsieur Gaspard's day, only half of the *paludiers* of the basin live entirely from salt production. Other jobs held by the *paludiers* are primarily in industry, in manual work. Les Chantiers de l'Atlantique, the Atlantic shipyards in Saint-Nazaire, account for much of this. The building trade takes second place. There are also a lot of masons, carpenters, and painters, and some *paludiers* are in the professions as well.

Monsieur Evain describes a revival of interest in the Guérande salt pans over the last twenty years. In the early 1980s, a professional training program for salt makers was opened in Guérande. Unlike Monsieur Gaspard, who picked up the trade by working alongside his father and grandfather out on the marsh, young people now can apprentice through this training program. The trainees attend courses at the Lycée d'Enseignement Professionnel, a special high school in Guérande, in the mornings and work afternoons on the *salines* with experienced *paludiers*. They spend the entire month of July on the salt farm with their mentors. "We give them a little *lotie* to make the salt themselves," as Monsieur Gaspard said. "They learn by watching me and then do it themselves."

Young people who have not inherited salt pans but who wish to take up the *paludier* trade may arrange to resurrect abandoned salt pans through the Lands Office. The harvest taken by this arrangement is shared: one-third for the landowner and two-thirds for the producer. Pans may also be rented for one-sixth the value of the harvest.

Breton salt, which contains magnesium, calcium, and trace

minerals, is now used mainly for cooking and the salting of meat. Monsieur Gaspard reflected on how the use of salt has changed with time. "Now salt is not for conservation. It's for the table. The refrigerators, *la chambre froide,* the freezers, all these have changed everything. Now one can eat meat three or five months after it was killed, with the cold chambers and all this. Before, the butcher killed the beasts according to need. There were little slaughterhouses all through the region. Now all this is finished. Nowadays the salt from here is sold all over Europe. We even have outlets as far away as America. Because our salt is very renowned."

As Monsieur Evain gazes over the marsh, today's glinting pans melt into the gleaming pans of the past. "Just think," he marvels. "For several dozen generations, since the Romans, there has not been any change in the *salines.* The only change has been the wheelbarrow, that caught on after the war. There was also the introduction of the fiberglass handle for the *las,* but this was not real progress because a handle is always a handle, whereas the wheelbarrow did away with the women's work, so that was a true change.

"Before the war, women always worked in the *salines* alongside the men. But now, although the *paludiers* have gained wheelbarrows, they have lost their women. And you cannot chat with a wheelbarrow! It's because of this that I am not sure the introduction of the wheelbarrow was real progress, but the women haven't asked to stay! *Voilà.*

"Now we use the wheelbarrow to transport the salt from the *ladure,* the collection mound of the oeillet, to the big heap of salt, the *trémet.* And agricultural tractors transport it from there. . . . But just think of it, the wheelbarrow is the only change in this trade since the time of the Romans."

"Alors," Monsieur Evain says, *"voilà,* a little bit of history."

e͜

The *paludier* and I stroll back to the museum, the Maison des Paludiers, with nature beating down on our crowns and whipping at our faces. I am walking on air, or on water, buoyant with new knowledge. In the airy, chapel-size museum, Monsieur Evain—determined to give me a head-to-toe understanding of his trade—shows me a panel detailing yearly salt harvests.

"I collect twenty tons," he explains. "The average harvest of an *oeillet* is about one ton, three hundred kilos per year, but it is extremely variable."

Next my tall guide shows me a *chromamètre,* an instrument used since 1987 to classify salt according to its purity. A beam of light is sent through a sample of salt and a calculator yields a "percent of the insoluble." The higher the percentage of insolubles—the insolubles in the clay mixed in with the salt—the grayer and less pure the salt, and the lower the quality. The higher the classification, the whiter the salt. "At the end of the year, we take a decision. All the salt that is less than sixty-three, for instance, we send to the agricultural sector—to use in livestock feed. Contrarily, all the salt that is superior to seventy-two, for example, goes to dietetic shops, organic shops, etc."

The bulk of Guérande salt is sold through the cooperative, the Groupement des Producteurs de Sel, whose motto is "Mari, Sole, et Vento," Sea, Sun, and Wind. The vast majority—about 137 of the 200 *paludiers*—are in the cooperative, and 82 percent of the salt sold in the area is sold by the cooperative. Aside from selling the members' salt, a major function of the cooperative is to find new clients. The cooperative works at this "without cease." About thirty paludiers belong to an organization called Les Paludiers Indépendants, and a third, tiny group of paludiers work on an individual basis for specific wholesalers and dealers. A portion of the harvest is also offered for sale at roadside stands, along with onions, garlic, and fruit. This local marketry has enhanced its reputation as an authentic, natural product.

The salt season is relatively short, Monsieur Evain reminds me as we stand surrounded by the framed graphs and photographs of the museum, so a *paludier* must take advantage of every sunny day. In his twenty years of salt-making he has only once begun to make salt in May. Most usual is for the salt-making to begin at the end of June. "You know the French have many proverbs," he says. "I don't know if the Americans also have them, but one of ours says, 'By Saint-Jean-Baptiste, the summer solstice, you must prepare your salt pans.'

"After mid-August the days are so short and the nights so long that it takes two days to have enough heat, so one harvests salt only every two days. By the beginning of September, one takes it every three or four days, and at the end of September, one takes it once a week, and finally the dissolution arrives. So by the twenty-ninth of September, it's finished. There is no more salt.

"The *paludiers* try to take the salt as fast as they can, because he who takes the salt the most quickly will have one, two, three harvests more than a colleague. And he will have two and a half to seven percent more annual salary. This is not negligible. It is for this that one tries to make salt as fast as possible."

I ask him if a family can be supported nowadays by work on the marsh. Monsieur Evain shrugs, as if to say, Of course! "There are those who make their lives on just the work in the *saline*. Others, like me, have other work as well. It's a choice, you see.

"The great advantage of the *paludier* trade is that one is one's own *patron*. Today one goes to the *saline*, or one doesn't. One does what one wants. One has relative liberty. It's the weather that commands, but one is still one's own boss, so that pleases a lot of the young." I am reminded of Jerome Choquet's appreciation of the independence inherent to the *boulanger* trade. "It's an individual choice, and even if there are ultimately constraints, a lot of the young don't see them. There is no boss: this is the principal advantage. The second phenomenon is that it is a *métier* that is close to nature and the young like this a lot. On the other hand there is an inconvenience. A *paludier's* work is not just making salt. It is necessary to sell it, and now that is another thing altogether.

"For me, this work is *formidable*." The tall man's arms stretch wide. "Other professors have their boats or they travel for vacation, but I have my salt."

Contentment shone in the *paludier*-professor's eyes, words, and carriage. As he strode along in the open air of his *saline* he seemed to brim with well-being. He enjoys living in the small community of Saillé, and the life he has fashioned out of determination, hard work, and passion suits him; as he told me, he sees his life as luxurious. On the practical level, he does consider it fortunate that he is an engineer at the University of Saint-Nazaire and doesn't rely on the salt to survive. But most important, he feels privileged to be able to do work—both at the university and in the marsh—that brings him deep satisfaction, while being able to afford his wife working only at home. As for Monsieur Choquet, life's answer is satisfying work.

The only fly in the ointment of Monsieur Evain's life is the threat of the *paludier* trade's being lost to the winds of progress. While we were on the tour of Michel Evain's *saline*, he halted by a cracked *saline* bed covered in weeds. "Now this is a *saline* that is abandoned," he said. "I like to show this *saline* because it is quite representative of today's *saline*. You should know that about a third are abandoned but maintained in water, a third are abandoned but dry, and a third are cultivated. Sometimes people come to the *saline* and think that because this *saline* is clean, it is functioning while the actual active *salines,* which are messier, are abandoned. This one is neat and tidy, but it has the neatness of a desert. It's dead. Nothing grows because man doesn't work it anymore."

He then told me he was looking after the *saline* of a ninety-three-year-old man, "a *grand-père*," who couldn't tend to it any longer. "I told him I would maintain his *exploitation* in water, because, to make it simple, an *oeillet* must never see the sun. If *oeillets* are allowed to go dry, they will develop cracks and the water won't evaporate. It will seep into the cracks and then the system has had it. So, to maintain an *exploitation* that is sleeping, it suffices to maintain it in water. So, I maintain his *oeillets* in water for him. As for letting *salines* go dry, nature—which, contrary to what one thinks, is hostile—brings the glassworts, she brings the marsh grasses, she brings the other plants that come to occupy the land."

Monsieur Gaspard's words carried the same dismay at the appearance of more and more abandoned *salines*. As he and I had walked back from a tour of his Saline aux Moines along the sleepy, marsh-edged Saillé street, we passed the back lots of houses. Some were strewn with workaday *paludier* tools and others sported neat, clipped lawns. The gray-haired *paludier* in his jaunty cap began to reminisce about the Saillé of his childhood.

"Back then, Saillé was a village that was uniquely *paludier!*" he said, motioning broadly toward the dwellings we were passing. "All this, you see, used to be *paludier* houses. Now they've all been purchased by tourists, as secondary homes. Even in 1950, there were still seventy-five to eighty *paludiers* in the village here—between the forty-seven professionals and the twenty-eight who were workers and made salt half time. In the past it was uniquely *paludiers*—except for the blacksmith, and the carpenter who made the salt marsh tools, and the coffin to conduct us to our last residence! Then, when La Baule began to grow into a beach town, a few workers came to live here. Then, later, carpenters came to make boats for the shipyards of Saint-Nazaire. Little by little. Before the village was all *paludiers*. But now the *paludiers* have disappeared. One by one, they've died, they've left, *quoi.*

"Now," he went on with his accounting of life's unexpected twists, "there are maybe a dozen *paludier* families here in Saillé, in our village. You can take it road by road and there are not many." He thought aloud: "Ten, is already a good estimate . . . but not more than ten. Me, I knew a uniquely *paludier* village. Now one doesn't know the people anymore."

"It's sad."

"Ah, *Dame*, life has changed, *hein?*"

Monsieur Gaspard expressed grave doubts about the future of the *paludier* trade. "It is very difficult for a young man to take it up now. One reason is that he will make the salt this year, but it will only be marketed two years from now. And in those two years he can't live on just love and fresh water! He needs to have subsidies or to receive payment for the salt in advance—he needs another source of support. Nowadays there are *paludiers* that have wives who work outside the salt. That makes a support for some.

"It is also difficult for the young to start," the old-time *paludier* went on, "because it demands a lot of physical effort. When the salt gives, there are no weekends, there are no Saturdays or Sundays. And then, one must like nature. It is necessary to like the open air, nature, and being one's own boss. One depends on oneself."

Every year, he said, there are a few who, despite the disadvantages, want to enter the *métier*. About ten a year are taught. He, for example, has trained four apprentices. But only one of them stuck with the work on the pans, even for a short time. And the new *paludiers* don't compensate for the departures into retirement of the experienced ones like himself. "Every year the number of *oeillets* that are cultivated go down. This is the trouble. The *oeillets* that are cultivated may diminish still more, and the number of cultivated *oeillets* must not diminish."

Monsieur Gaspard went on thinking aloud. "I have a trainee now, my last trainee, who makes me thirty of my *oeillets* on the side. And then, as for me, I have fifty-two more *oeillets* in the *saline* but I only do eight now.

His words were salted with grief. I tried to imagine what it would be like to be of an age when I couldn't fully continue the work I loved. I found it almost unthinkable.

This year, since he was just making eight *oeillets,* he said, he planned to transport it himself to the *salorge.* "This will perhaps be my last year. *Ça sera peut-être la dernière année.*"

Monsieur Gaspard paused. "If I had had a son, he could have continued, *hein?*"

"It's sad," I said, gulping down a sense of loss. "And who will continue?"

"Ah, well, Madame, this is the question!"

With those simple, poignant words ringing in my head—time pressing at my back—I had to leave him.

℮

Monsieur Evain and I sat on the low stone wall outside the Maison des Paludiers and talked next to the lavender bushes for a while the day before I left Guérande.

The future of the *paludiers* was uppermost in Monsieur Evain's mind. Competition from sea salt produced by other countries and via other salt collection methods was an enormous issue for the *paludiers* of Guérande, he said, another threat to their very survival.

Salt is obtained via three methods: salt mines, brine wells, and the sea. In salt mining, shafts are sunk to salt beds—ancient, dried-up seabeds—deep in the earth. The salt is blasted loose by means of explosives, and the rock salt is ferried to the surface on small cars or conveyer belts. To obtain salt from brine wells, two concentric pipes are driven into a salt deposit in the earth. Fresh water is pumped through the inner pipe into the salt bed where it dissolves some of the salt into brine. The brine is then pumped to the surface through the outer pipe, where it is evaporated in vacuum pans to form solid salt. Sea salt comes, originally, from rock. The salt in rock is continually dissolved by the water trickling through the earth, and carried to the sea in the waters of streams. These sea salts may be obtained via the age-old method of the *paludiers* or with highly mechanized approaches such as those used in the south of France. The latter pose the greatest threat to the *paludiers* of Guérande.

The salt-workers and their cooperative have sought to defend themselves against these competitors in a variety of ways, Monsieur Evain explained, mulling it over as he stretched his long legs.

The *paludier* cited, as a first instance, the recent successful campaign by the cooperative to obtain the *label rouge* for Guérande salt. The "red label" is a stamp of approval given by the French equivalent of the Food and Drug Administration to food that has been inspected and found in accord with strict standards and regulations. "One sees chickens with the *label rouge,* cauliflowers with the *label rouge,* because it's an inspection label. The red label has allowed the salt of Guérande to stand nose to nose with the other big salt countries and say to all of Europe—because nowadays we are required to take account of Europe—'Attention! This salt is not Italian salt. It is not Spanish salt. It is the salt of *Guérande.*'"

Although, in Monsieur Evain's view, Guérande salt will never be able to fully compete against Spain and Italy because of their cheaper workforces, the *label rouge* has augmented sales all over Europe. "The Germans, for example, envy us because—contrary to what one might think, as they are a very regulated country—they don't have this system. The Belgians also envy us. And in Italy and Spain, they don't have any sort of system like this. So this is one way that we are confronting Europe: with this *label rouge.*"

Monsieur Evain complained that the *paludiers* of Guérande suffered from unfair competition from the *salines* of the Midi.

These *salines* on the south coast of France use a totally different technique and produce enormous and lucrative quantities of dry sea salt.

The sea salt of the south is obtained via a three-step process analogous to that practiced in Guérande, but on a much larger scale and via a mechanized process. The *salines* of the Mediterranean consist of a huge, flat, 10,000-hectare expanse that produces over a million tons of salt a year. Immense rectangular basins permit the salt to crystallize, over the sunny months of May through August, to form a bed of salt ten centimeters thick. In the month of September, the entire year's harvest is collected in one fell swoop. Rather than being raked by hand, the southern harvest is completely mechanized. Giant harvesters collect 30,000 tons of salt spread over a ten-hectare surface in a single day. That is three times the amount of salt the *paludiers* of Guérande harvest through backbreaking toil, day by day, over the entire season. The resulting stock heaps of salt are called *les camelles,* probably because they resemble a series of humps.

Publicity campaigns have made a big difference for the salt of Guérande, though. "Among all the important chefs, there is not one *grand cuisinier* who would use salt from the Mediterranean. Not one important chef uses anything other than the salt of Guérande."

Packaging plays an important role in the future of Guérande salt. Monsieur Evain told me that the 500-gram packets of salt, with a delicate pencil sketch of a *paludier* on their fronts, which I had seen in the shops of Guérande, had been around for only a short time. "But they represent big progress for us." The lanky man leaned closer to me, his voice turned low, as though he were revealing a shameful secret. "I am one of those who fought this in the beginning, and I was wrong. I was in combat against this kind of packaging, but, in the end, I have recognized that I am with them. When one is very proud of one's product one sometimes commits stupidities.

"It is like the time a woman came to buy salt from me, a rich woman. I remember her because, you know, we here in Saillé don't drive on a golden road. But the woman came here in her big BMW and wanted to buy ten kilos of salt to put in her bath. Me, I refused to sell her any salt because I told her, 'My salt doesn't go in the bath. You can buy it if you put it in your soup, but if you tell me you're going to put it in your bath, I refuse.' Honestly, I used to be like that. But I wouldn't refuse to sell to her now—not because I have gotten older but because I know now that I was wrong."

At first, Monsieur Evain also opposed the sale of Guérande salt to Vie Claire, a commercial chain that sells dietetic, natural, and organic products. The chain was selling sea salt in a fancy box made of jute. "I remember, at that moment, we were selling salt at eighty centimes per kilo, and the man from Vie Claire was asking eight francs. The box was very pretty, but in fact what were they selling? They were selling a *box* with a semblance of salt inside. One year we refused to sell them the salt and the year after, the salt was still here in stockage. After that the old ones said, 'Now, you shut up because we need a sale, and afterward we'll see.'"

Monsieur Evain's comments reminded me of my own stance as a young field biologist against the commercialization of whale watching. I didn't want *my* whales disturbed by boatfuls of tourists, even though they might ultimately save them from extinction.

Since Monsieur Evain's early days, the cooperative has packaged its salt in ever more carefully designed and decorative boxes, and the range of sales has expanded, in tandem, each year. Monsieur Evain comforts himself with his new, wiser understanding. He told me, "It was necessary to make a step toward the women, because women are the ones who go to the market to buy salt. A woman needs a small packet and she needs a powder, and she needs a spout on the box, so we had to offer that. I am in favor of those who consume *gros* salt, rather than powder, because when one grinds salt, some of the components of the salt break up, but we are obliged to give women what they want."

Another measure of effort on behalf of Guérande salt has gone into the marketing of *fleur de sel,* the fine, melt-on-the-tongue salt that floats on the surface of the *saline. "Fleur de sel* is the last word in salt," Monsieur Evain said. "But since we collect only forty tons, it doesn't exist on the national market. We are trying to develop it as a novelty item for people who make the effort to come down to our region." A testament to the success of this approach: I recently saw *fleur de sel* from Guérande advertised, in rapturous phrases, in an American baking catalogue.

Another route the Guérande *paludiers* have taken to insure the future of their product has been to embrace "le Coté Retour," mentioned by Monsieur Choquet, to take advantage of the new and fashionable passion for the old ways, for *choses à l'ancienne* now touted all over France. Monsieur Evain was clearly torn about the Coté Retour. On the one hand, I think he believed the Coté Retour was the route to saving the *salines* and the *paludier's* way of life. On the other, he thought it was absurd. He pointed to examples of the new, positive uses to which salt was being put by connoisseurs of the Coté Retour. Newly organic farmers had begun to salt their hays in the old fashion, and breeders had begun offering rock salt to their livestock.

Monsieur Evain clearly lifted his nose, though, at the man from a branch of Christian Dior who arrived in Guérande one day to buy a *vasière.* He wanted to excavate the clays of the *vasière* to make regenerative facial masks for women. "You should have seen the stupefaction of the municipal council. They op-

posed him because it was viewed as an attack on the Plan d'Occupation des Sols, and he failed to buy his *vasière*. But then
Christian Dior went on to collect the clays of the Yangtse by
plane! That cost him the skin of his buttocks! That is one cun-
ning man. His reasoning was, 'Those clays have been there for
two hundred years and they are loaded with magnesium, potassium, calcium.'

"You know, in a way, the Christian Dior people were right.
Because people from the Centre National de la Recherche Sci-
entifique have come here, and a Monsieur Denis, a dean of the
Sorbonne, has done a thesis on skin. The professor noted that
the salt of Guérande is loaded with trace elements and the
body is usually out of equilibrium, and that, through putting
salts in one's bath, a person can restore the balance of the body.
He wrote a 430-page book on this. Now, I will certainly not buy
a book to take a bath, but his argument is well justified. And to
think that, without any scientific information, women have
made mud masks since ancient Egypt! Feminine intuition is
incredible. Tremendous. *Formidable*."

In relaying his stories about le Coté Retour and his youthful
resistance to the active marketing of Guérande's salt, Monsieur
Evain handed me the baton of the lesson he himself had
learned. Having been viscerally antibusiness—they're all out
for themselves, after all!—I, like Monsieur Evain, now had
to admit the utility of a business perspective when it came to
salt. Clever marketing, it appeared, could save the *paludiers*.
Dreams, magic, the perpetuation of high-quality, age-old products required a shrewd business sense along with a sense of romance. Both Monsieur Evain and Monsieur Gaspard, I saw
now, were both businessmen and mystics, simultaneously salts
of the earth and men of commerce.

At the end of this last talk with Monsieur Evain, he took me
to a little market down the street from the Maison des Paludiers. The shop mistress, a woman with a sleek, city-style hair-

cut who had moved to Brittany from another part of France, showed us her wares.

The simple, sparkling shop was stocked entirely of home-made products grown or produced on local farms: raspberry jam, orange marmalade, honeys of all hues, cheeses, wood-baked *pain au levain,* pickled marsh salicornes in bottles, Guérande salt in plastic bags of various sizes stamped with a line drawing of a paludier at work, tiny jars of *fleur de sel.* The shop mistress encouraged me to leaf through a book by a German showing luminous photos of Guérande and the *paludiers* along with Breton recipes. The shop was living evidence of all Monsieur Evain had told me about the fashionableness of le Coté Retour in France. I succumbed to the packaging and bought some homegrown honey, kitchen-concocted jams, and the hand-kneaded bread, as well as three bags of hand-raked salt.

The shop woman served us chilled rosé in tulip-shaped glasses, and we exchanged cordial chat for a few moments about bread and salt. She told us that the bread she sold—made of wheat grown on the baker's own land, and then hand-kneaded and baked in his ancient stone oven—was a rarity. To-day in France, she said, only people truly interested in good food bought non-supermarket bread. Dismay, first aroused in me when I heard Monsieur Choquet utter similar words, now appeared again. Resistant to having my bubble popped, I still wanted to believe that here, in Europe, people continued to eat only fresh bread baked in a neighborhood bakery. In spite of my hard-line romanticism I was being told, clearly, that the Europeans were following in my country's footsteps. Fresh bread and the time to seek it is increasingly becoming a luxury even here.

I was struck in another way during the conversation at the shop. When I first landed in France and my friend Juliette's father, who met us at the airport, told me I should greet people on the street not with just a simple "Bonjour," but with the more polite "Bonjour Madame," or "Bonjour Monsieur," I felt a deep inner resistance. I found the formality off-putting and I couldn't stand being called "Madame." But as time went on, I found the formality comforting and reassuring, a kind of safety net of civility that wouldn't let people fall. Monsieur Evain's and the shop woman's cordiality, as well as that of the Choquets, seemed to me respectful and considerate. It left people their dignity. It was never intrusive or false the way American friendliness can sometimes be. Another characteristic of the shop mistress that impressed me was that she and the other Bretons I met had time to be cordial and talk to one another. Casual human intercourse sometimes seems as rare as good bread in Washington.

As we walked back to the museum, Monsieur Evain told me about a McDonald's that had just appeared in a nearby town. Then he rode away on his bike, gawky and jaunty as a camel on wheels, saying "I'm ecological!"

❧

At the end of my visits with the *paludiers*, I felt as though I'd just finished a well-seasoned meal.

A proud, old-style, hardworking *paludier*, Monsieur Gaspard seemed not a romantic but a man whose seventy-plus years of knowledge were registered in his back and his hands. Monsieur Evain seemed a different sack of salt altogether. He was the modern *paludier*, the full-time professional, part-time *paludier*, the hobbyist with a faraway look in his eye and his knowledge in his head. In many ways, Monsieur Evain was more familiar to me than Monsieur Gaspard. He seemed cut of the same mold as my more contented American friends, those who had found a way to integrate profession and passion.

❧

Before leaving Saillé, I stand for a moment gazing across the salt marsh, breathing in the hot, salty scent. For several hours, I have been lost in a fascinating world. Washington, the children, my husband have dropped away as I have feasted on looking, listening, tasting. For a few stunned moments now, here on the marsh, the sea, the sun, Monsieur Evain's salt, Monsieur Choquet's bread all seem magnificent—like magic, like music, like miracles.

The *paludier* trade seems to me the most beautiful and strangest kind of farming in the world. Its ancientness, its adherence to the rules of the sun and moon, its alchemical transformations fill me with wonder. And the *paludiers,* its practitioners, are a fascinating, odd conglomerate of skills: mud architects, lock-keepers, weather-guessers, rakers, their days a rhythm of hauling and raking under a beating sun. The paludier trade is the ultimate lesson in the ephemerality and capriciousness of life. Utterly subject to the moods of the skies and to their own mistakes, the salt farmers pass their hours watching the clouds, adjusting their traps and plugs, never knowing except in hindsight if they've made the right decision. While the *paludier's* work is literally built on supports of clay—it is not the job for a person who needs a sense of control over his fate—it offers steady, physically satisfying work, close to the ground. And the *paludier's* is a trade that doesn't obfuscate. The human being's aloneness under the sky is, after all is said and done, the ultimate truth. Exposed, alone, out in the open, with egrets and blue herons and the great dome of sky for companionship, the *paludier* makes a humble and straightforward bid for his living. His salt stacks glitter and shine in little testaments to the effort of the individual.

As Monsieur Evain said of the marsh, "It is a world a little apart."

Even at the end of the story, and taking in the stark realities of their world, the *paludiers* shine in a romantic light. Perhaps some of the few such people left in the world, the salt farmers of Guérande, seem holders of mysteries. And yet, like the sea that ebbs and flows, like the salt and its makers, we can't live without either the old or the new.

ℰ

Back at the *gîte* in le Coudray, two sets of bells chimed the hour across the fields, one set two minutes after the other. When I first heard the two peals, I thought of them as warring bells. Now I hear them as the two tones of the world.

> . . . *Dust of the sea, the tongue*
> *receives a kiss*
> *of the night sea from you:*
> *taste recognizes*
> *the ocean in each salted morsel.*
> *And therefore the smallest,*
> *the tiniest*
> *wave of the shaker*
> *brings home to us*
> *not only your domestic whiteness*
> *but the inward flavor of the infinite.*
> —Pablo Neruda, "Ode to Salt"

⤿ ⤿ ⤿

WHEAT

⤿ ⤿ ⤿ ⤿ ⤿

The only cereal containing gluten, an elastic complex of
starch and proteins that can retain carbon dioxide gas and
stretch under pressure to form a structured loaf.

In a small field grows good wheat.

French adage from the sixteenth century

The Miller

A young man in a pressed plaid shirt stands at the top of an enormous, open truckful of wheat the sultry July day I drive into the parking lot of Moulin de Pont-James. He is holding a thick suction hose which extends from inside the towering mill into the wheat hill in the bed of the truck, and talking to a group of men gathered below. At first glance, he has the contented, king-of-the-mountain stance of a farmer perched at the apex of his hay wagon—but on closer examination, his face is tense with impatience.

The young man—he is about thirty-five and wearing intellectual-style horn-rimmed glasses and flour-dusted but creased French blue workmen's trousers in addition to his bright plaid shirt—glances down at me as I explain that I am seeking the miller.

He sighs, instructs the three other men attending the truck to proceed, then climbs down the ladder at the side of the vehicle, wiping his brow and looking hassled. Extending his hand, he introduces himself as Christophe Giraudineau, the miller of Moulin de Pont-James. With his neat, dark looks and well-fitting clothes, Christophe Giraudineau could be a D.C. lawyer stepping out of his BMW.

The next thing he tells me, briskly, is that he is very busy, since this is harvest time. I quickly say that I will try to be brief.

℮

Jean-Claude Choquet had directed me to Moulin de Pont-James—located about two and a half hours south of Blain, still in the *département* of Loire-Atlantique—and the mill that provides the organic flour for his *pain trois rivières*. He knew I would enjoy seeing the process, and was sure the miller could help me locate a wheat farmer. He himself had never met a farmer whose wheat he kneaded into his bread—a fact that startled me, as I had assumed a French village baker would hold close links with all the producers of his ingredients.

The mill, as I beheld it that mid-July day, resembled in its location—beside a bridge at the edge of a country town, next to a languid, shaded stream—and in its family-based operation, the romanticized nineteenth-century New England mill of my American imagination. But there the similarity ended. Instead of old bricks, it was composed of a pair of hulking, tacked-together, white rectangular boxes about four double stories high, flanked by a trio of silos. The roaring of electric motors filled the air. And matching their plant for practicality, the millers of Moulin de Pont-James themselves—Christophe Giraudineau, the young miller; his mother, the administrator and laboratory director for the mill; and his semi-retired father. About the whole complex on the sleepy country road hung an atmosphere of efficiency and haste to rival that of any U.S. company.

℮↷

The busy young miller led me across the lane up to a modern, angular house that shone white in its crisp newness. The well-appointed kitchen, into which the young miller led me, sparkled too—it was painted and tiled in whites and tans, the clean, pure colors of wheat flours.

He introduced me to his mother, Marie-Thérèse Giraudineau, an eager, bright-faced woman. Madame Giraudineau, who had about her a cordial, efficient air, served coffee in demitasse with a tiny bowl of brown cane sugar crystals. The young Monsieur Giraudineau seemed anxious, knotting his hands as he stood beside his mother. She patted his arm and said, "It's all right. Take a little time." At that, his hands and shoulders seemed to relax, and he seated himself at the small kitchen table. As we talked he quickly became friendly and open, eager to help.

Christophe's father, Daniel, a rake-thin dapper man with wispy, snow-feather hair, joined us presently. His son and wife did most of the talking, but he spoke up now and again, slowly motioning with his narrow hands.

As three pairs of Giraudineau eyes focused intently on my face, I explained that I was writing a book about Jean-Claude Choquet's *pain trois rivières,* that I was interested in tracing the elements of the most basic version of our most basic food—and that I was interested in organic flour for the same reason—because it made up the bulk of Monsieur Choquet's loaf.

Father and son delineated the compass of their milling operation for me. They sell twenty-five kinds of flour, producing both organic flour and ordinary, nonorganic white flour for *pain ordinaire.* "For both organic and nonorganic flours we make all the types of extraction possible."

The young miller was referring to a flour categorization system used all over Europe. "Type" refers to the proportion of bran and wheat germ that remains in a particular flour at the conclusion of the milling process, the higher the type number, the more bran and germ in the flour. In simplest terms, type follows color, with the whitest flour designated type 45, and whole wheat flour, using the entire wheat kernel, called type 150, and with types 55, 65, 80, and 110 in between. This six-type French flour categorization system, used by supermarkets as well as millers, explains in part the difference between French flour—available in a wide range and variety—and our bipartite white-whole wheat American supermarket flour. It also goes partway to explain the subtle differences in the lightness and taste of Monsieur Choquet's various loaves, which possess delicate differences in their contents of bran and germ.

"Do all the flours come from the same wheat?" I asked.

"Yes," Madame Giraudineau said, "it's simply the way one makes the extraction."

"We make bread flour, and then we make *la farine de gruaux*," Christophe Giraudineau began. And then, without so much of a blink of an eye, the French miller said something that startled this American Europhile. "This is a type 45 pastry flour made of pure American wheat."

The *gruaux*, he explained calmly, as though his words should cause no disturbance in his listener, are the finest, purest wheat grains—the intermediary products of grinding that make the very best flour. *La farine de gruau* is used in the composition of *brioches* and other *pâtisserie,* because, unique among flours, this type of flour swells. He explained that the best baking flours are the strongest flours, those made of hard wheats. These wheats make strong, high-gluten flours that hydrate easily, and possess the high-absorption capacity necessary for doughing. Their doughs offer an elastic, cohesive structure, good handling properties, and large volume with good crumb. "One puts a lot of butter into *brioches,* so it is necessary to have strong flours. American wheat is very strong. It is because of this that we use American wheat."

After making this announcement, Christophe Giraudineau went on to relay the even more stunning fact that many French millers, such as he, fortified their ordinary bread flours with American wheat as well. "We incorporate American wheat at a rate of ten percent in our ordinary flours." The most important difference between American and French wheat, he explained, is that French wheat, winter wheat—wheat that is planted in the fall, grows a few inches, lies dormant over the winter, and resumes its growth in the spring—is mostly starch, while spring wheats grown in cold zones like the Dakotas and Canada are suppler and have a higher protein content. In France there is little spring wheat—wheat planted in the spring—

while in the United States, where winters are colder, spring wheat is grown in many regions.

"We get American North Dakota spring wheat from an importer in the Parisian region—from the company Dark Northern Spring," the senior Monsieur Giraudineau said. "There's just one importer."

As if sensing the strong impression his information had made, the young miller hastened to add, "But all of our other flour is French, and we use no American wheat in our organic flours."

Despite Monsieur Giraudineau's protests, I was shocked to learn that many French baguettes contained even a small portion of American wheat. I had assumed that the flour used in French bread and French pastries, and most especially in French baguettes, would be made wholly of French wheat. It went without saying that that most French of all things in the world—the French village baguette—would be made purely of products of the French earth. Here, in my French loaf, I assumed, I would find a nation's essence. I had thought that French bread, of all things in the world, would be sacrosanct, untouched by the giant's paw of globalization. This was one of my hard and crusty, reassuring certainties: French bread would be French.

So my mind struggled with this new fact. At first, I was disappointed to think that a baguette I might pick up at a neighborhood shop in Paris, or in a far-flung village in Burgundy, could contain North Dakota wheat. But then a notion, long-familiar to my species, came to me: the purest, simplest, and most virginal is not always the most interesting or resilient. Other national symbols, I began to see as I considered further, may be likewise adulterated or inaccurate. There are probably more bald eagles in Canada than in the United States, for instance. Much as I loved the dream of local purity, I was also beginning to love the notion of new blendings of cultures.

Back in the sparkling kitchen the millers were telling me that they bought their organic wheat from a society, a *groupement,* in Vienne, a *département* to the south of Loire-Atlantique, two or two and a half hours by truck from Pont-James. Finishing each other's thoughts, mother and son explained that the organic wheat this cooperative collects in its gigantic Anglier grain elevator converges from a scattering of farmers in Vienne, Oise, and elsewhere in western France.

"Oh no, we don't choose particular farms from which we get our wheat." The young miller sat back in his chair. "The organization does that. It would be too difficult otherwise. We couldn't occupy ourselves with the sale of organic flours, and also with the supply of wheat. It's complicated as well, because all the farmers have to be advised by and inspected by an organic certifier. We couldn't know or do all that and still conduct our milling operations."

The revelation that the Giraudineaus didn't have contact with the farmers who produced the wheat they milled ended another little fantasy in my head. How much the young miller's tale of disconnected rural trades contrasted with the stories of the senior Monsieur Choquet and Monsieur Gaspard.

The Giraudineaus started the organic side of their milling business in 1973. They took on this new kind of work because it struck them as an innovative and interesting endeavor, and because they "had conviction." As Madame Giraudineau said, smoothing her hands down her apron, "Organic farming is harder than regular farming, so people who do it, do it out of deep belief."

Organic farmers are few and far between in France, she said. Organic agriculture represents just 1 percent of France's farming—with the organic farmers sprinkled all over the country.

"One is hard put to find agriculturists to do this kind of farming. It's a matter of conversion," Madame Giraudineau said, leaning across the table toward me. "The farmer must be convinced that he nourishes his fellow citizens better by producing organic wheat. It's not in order to gain money."

"No, they don't do it for money," her son hastened to add, "because they are not richer than the others."

Organic farmers and mills that produce organic flour, like all other French producers of organic products, are inspected and recertified every year by Qualité France, the mother-son milling team told me. Each type of organic flour they produce is closely examined to assure its quality and purity. "The regulation is very important, very serious," Madame Giraudineau said. Because of the rigor of the organic certification process—only farmers who have not used any chemicals on their fields may claim to have produced organic wheat—many of the organic farmers quit the practice or their children don't continue it, Madame Giraudineau said. "It's a shame. It's a shame."

"It is more difficult to cultivate organic wheat," her son explained.

"The yield is less," Madame Giraudineau said. "Because they don't use fertilizer."

"And there are sometimes losses due to diseases, so organic producers don't have the same yields as the others. In the end, though, the wheat is bought at a more expensive price. It's practically double the price of wheat in the ordinary market," Monsieur Giraudineau said, confirming his facts with his mother as he spoke.

"It's much more expensive. Happily, that's a compensation," Madame Giraudineau said.

Speaking of the commercial side of their business, the Giraudineaus explained that they mixed wheat from various *départements*—from Indre-et-Loire, from Vienne, from Sarthe—in the making of their various flours, "to make the best flour, *quoi.*" A miller's first concern is always the quality of the wheat," the young man told me. "Bakers choose on the basis of the quality of the flour, you see. And then, also, on the basis of their rapport with the miller."

Because of the need to maintain *sympathie,* and because of the high degree of competition between mills, the Giraudineaus never sell their flour by telephone. They make a personal visit to each baker and try to convince him.

"Nowadays a miller confronts the issue of attracting and keeping his clientele, *quoi.* There is a lot more competition nowadays—a miller's clients are often visited by the competition—and so fidelity is no longer as strong as it was in the past. There is a constant need to visit the clients to maintain good relations. I don't visit bakers in the summer because I don't have time, but in the autumn I go to see my personal clients and then I try to trap others, *quoi!* But it's not easy!"

The radius of the Giraudineaus' business is quite local, as they sell their flours primarily in Loire-Atlantique and, to a lesser extent, in the Vendee and Maine-et-Loire. Moulin de Pont-James delivers flour to 150 to 200 bakers.

"There are the big ones, but there are also the little ones," as Madame Giraudineau said. She refilled my miniature white cup with dark black coffee, and tended for a moment to putting some cups away in a cupboard.

Considering his work schedule, the young miller explained, "I don't have real hours of work." He and his crew begin work around 6:30 A.M., and continue until nine at night, Monday through Saturday. Sunday is the one day the drone of the mill ceases. "The mill only turns in the daytime. We turn twelve to fourteen hours a day. But not yet at night. That will come," he said, sighing at the inevitability of the demands of commerce, of the influence of "Europe."

The work at Moulin de Pont-James is the same year-round. "Summer, autumn, winter, and spring, we do our analyses of the wheat, we mix the wheats, we fabricate the flour." During the winter, the work is identical to that carried on during other times of year, although the mill collects less wheat then. During the cold months, Moulin de Pont-James receives deliveries of ordinary wheat, as organic wheat does not begin to arrive until spring. The summer months are the busiest. During the months of harvest, the mill receives wheat at a steady rate, and that gives all the employees of the mill an increase in work. The fact that personnel also take their vacations during the summer heightens the pressure on the Giraudineaus.

The young miller commented that his countrymen's tastes in bread, and in flour, had changed considerably over time. He turned the conversation now to the evolution of French tastes in bread, explaining the Frenchman's preference for white bread over dense but nourishing *pain noir* after the war, harkening fondly back to the heavy, old-style *pain de deux livres* of the 1950s, and lamenting the recent French preference for poor-conserving, weak-tasting, lightweight loaves.

"The standard bread now is the baguette, and the baguette is not good," the miller said, plain as day, echoing Monsieur Choquet's words.

For the last five or six years, Monsieur Giraudineau said, continuing with his history of French bread, there had been a slight trend in favor of denser, less developed, longer-lasting, more flavorful bread, but it was actually easier to convince bakers to use organic flour in 1976 and 1977 than at the present time. "This is true because there were fewer varieties of bread back in the 1970s." Now French bakers sell a range of bread, and these have supplanted organic bread as the one kind of specialty bread sold.

"We always follow the Americans, ten years later. So today we are making flours with a lot of cereals—up to ten cereals— poppy, millet, all those things. As for myself, I don't like very complicated breads, like that—like those in the United States. Breads with lard, or breads with onions, for example. I like to eat nuts, but bread with the nuts on the side, not the nuts in the bread. In the end one doesn't know anymore what one is eating, *quoi.*"

As for organic loaves, not many bakers had taken up the banner, he said. Certain bakers, like Monsieur Choquet, are convinced organic bread is worth the effort, but the majority don't want to make *levain,* or bother themselves with long fermentation times, so they don't make organic bread. "It bores them. They find it too restricting."

Again I heard the bell of Time tolling. Time determines quality of bread, as it does the quality of life itself—or perhaps anything of high quality.

Monsieur Giraudineau said he liked "as much as possible" to eat organic bread. "I like type 80, which is intermediate, and also type 55. I like to eat both the white and the black. It's not so much a particular sort of bread. The quality of the bread depends on the baker's way of working."

"The work of the baker determines the quality of a bread," Madame Giraudineau commented with authority. "There are different types of bakers. There are good ones and the less good, *quoi.* Monsieur Choquet is in the category of the good ones. He works well."

"Of course one's preference depends on one's taste," the young miller said.

At this, suddenly, as if struck by a bolt of inspiration, Madame Giraudineau took the reins of the conversation and was off on a rant about other countries' bread. Nationalism would be a little goblin raising its mischievous head throughout the remainder of my time at the mill. It was as though this were the moment Madame Giraudineau had been waiting for.

"Do you make *gateaux?*" she asked me. My positive answer was a tiny seagull in the gale of her story.

"We had an American visitor, the same age as Christophe, with us during summer vacation many years ago, and he brought with him from the United States—he lived in Ohio—a box for making a cake into which one put only an egg. The flours and a little yeast and cinnamon were all inside. I told him, 'No, it's not good. Disgusting! Disgusting!'"

"Bon," her son intervened. *"Chacun à ses goûts!* Each to his own tastes."

"It's true," I said, "in the U.S. a lot of people buy cake mixes in a box, and they're not anywhere near as good as those made from scratch."

"In France it's the same," the miller said—the voice of balance and moderation. "They have them at the supermarket."

"It's the same with standard American bread," I said. "It's not good."

"No, it's not good. It's *pain de mie,* crustless bread with a lot of crumb, like the English. A lot of *pain de mie.* . . . When I was twenty-three I went on a trip to the United States. It was 1973. I had just finished my milling exams, gotten my miller's diploma, and my parents offered me three months in the United States. In the end, I worked on a farm and also in a cereals research center in Wooster, Ohio.

"During that trip, I saw that the mills in the United States tamper with their flour. They put in chlorine gas—I don't know if they still do it—to whiten and sanitize the flours, to kill the germs. It's the same thing that we put in water. They put this, in gas form, in the flour. And then the flour is totally white—it's bleached—to make type 55. That flour contains no germ."

"No vitamins," Madame Giraudineau put in.

"No parasites," her son continued. "There are no parasites but there aren't any vitamins, either! That is the defect of the Americans—excuse me for criticizing—they want to sanitize."

"They are afraid of microbes!" his mother said.

"But if one sanitizes a bakery one can't make bread," Christophe said. "The natural ferments that are in the air are removed. Then you can't make bread!"

"Fermentation is no longer possible!" Madame Giraudineau said. "It's crazy!"

The dapper, older Monsieur Giraudineau entered the conversation now, egging on his wife and son, "And what about German bread?"

His son said, "It's *schwartz Brott* there."

Madame Giraudineau said, "They make concrete."

The younger man said, "It's black bread."

"Inedible! Inedible!" his mother said. Her words were sparks spraying around the room.

"This is to say," the calm son turned to me, "that we have a way of eating in France such that we don't like to eat black bread or *pain de mie* either. We like to eat bread with a crust, but a bread that is relatively light. Not like in Germany where you have *schwartz Brott,* as they call it."

"You need a saw to cut it," his mother said.

"You can't make a French person swallow that. It will stay there on the table. We have tried offering it to our colleagues," the younger miller said.

"Even the chickens won't eat it!" Those were Madame Giraudineau's final and definitive words on the subject.

With that Christophe Giraudineau suggested that his father might take me on a tour of the mill. His countenance transformed from that of the relaxed, thoughtful country gentleman of moments before to the tensed visage of a tight-scheduled businessman. He rushed off to work, saying of his father, "He has more time to talk."

As Christophe hurried out the door toward the mill, I was struck by what a likable man he was. Like Michel Evain, Christophe Giraudineau seemed to belong to a corps of well-educated tradesmen.

Madame Giraudineau nudged me toward her husband, who thoughtfully ushered me through a tour of the streamside mill. Because the milling process depends on gravity and all operations start at the top of a mill, it was up four tall flights of stairs, to the top of the steeple-high building, that Monsieur Giraudineau led me to begin.

ℯ

Wheat milling is a delicate, complex, and challenging operation. Each of the thirty to fifty kernels on a spike of wheat is shaped like a teardrop, and each teardrop of wheat is wrapped in a protective husk. The foremost task of milling is to separate these two very differently structured parts of the wheat grain: the easily crushed and crumbly kernel and the kernel's epidermis, which resists crushing and grinding. A secondary aim of the milling process is to eliminate impurities that can cause spoilage, and so the wheat is cleaned before being processed.

Both the epidermis or bran and the kernel, which contains the crucial flour almond or endosperm, may be used. The germ is located in the tear of the wheat. The bran and germ together account for most of the fiber, oil, and B vitamins in the wheat grain, and for 25 percent of the protein. The almond, however, is the wheat kernel's treasure—the part of the wheat that turns to flour when ground. White flour is composed of only the pure, ground endosperm and emerges at the end of the milling cycle.

The process of turning wheat kernels into flour is not simple. As the Giraudineaus mentioned in their kitchen, French flours are classified according to their *taux de cendres,* or ash rate— the percentage of impurities they contain.

At a mill, the wheat is sent via pneumatic conveyers through a series of machines: grooved, intermeshed rollers that shear, open, and crunch the grain so as to scrape the endosperm from the bran and grind it into powder.

In the past, millers ended up with just two products at the end of the milling process: flour and bran. In modern milling, however, several residues other than flour, like the flour and bran extracted from the various steps in the milling process, are in themselves finished products, called the *issues.*

Each miller has his own milling diagram, depending on the varieties of wheat he mills, the layout of his mill, and the quality of the flour that he wishes to obtain with good regularity. The wheat simply follows the route of the grinding diagram, overseen by a technician who sits in front of a huge table of controls.

$\backsim$

The room in which Monsieur Giraudineau and I were standing at top of the building was an impeccably clean, ballroom-size space filled solely with a maze of intersecting and curving cream-colored pipes—the pneumatic rapid transit system that linked all the parts of the operation. A far cry from the human labor-dependent wind and water mills of old, Monsieur Giraudineau told me, the mill at Pont-James functioned almost automatically. From an instrument panel, a single employee can flick switches to transfer the wheat from the silo, set the cleaning apparatuses, and convey the grain to and from the grinding machines that transform the wheat to flour. The thin, silver-haired miller shook his head at the splendor of it all.

Like a giant, masticating cow, the mill transforms 2,000 tons, or 20,000 quintals, of grain a year into flour, an amount equal to about 170 tons a month, the weight of one huge, blubber-dense blue whale. Wheat was being gulped into the mill as the miller spoke, and a crashing sound added itself to the already overpowering drone. I had to employ full powers of concentration to catch his words.

"You can see the difference between organic and chemical wheat," Monsieur Giraudineau explained. "The grains are different. The color is different. Also, the aspect. Organic wheats all look alike because one makes fewer varieties than with chemical. There is a lot of variation in wheat grown with chemicals."

After he receives the wheat delivery and sees that it is stored, Monsieur Giraudineau said, the miller's first task is to clean the wheat.

First, the grain is drawn out of the silo and piped into *bois-seaux à blé sale,* the "dirty wheat reservoirs." From the *boisseau à blé sale* the wheat is sent into the *nettoyeur,* or *separateur-aspirateur,* an initial filter to eliminate dirt, rocks, straw, empty grains, and dust. The lighter impurities are removed by aspiration. A *trieur à graines longues,* a sieve or screen for long grains, removes such foreign matter as barley and oats that have gotten mixed with the wheat, and another *trieur à graines rondes* removes any parasites mixed with the wheat. The cleaning assures that nothing enters the grinding machinery but clean wheat grains.

Upon cleaning, the wheat is ready to be ground, Monsieur Giraudineau explained. Via three successive, meticulous operations, at Moulin de Pont-James, *le broyage, le claquage,* and *le convertissage,* the wheat almond or kernel is progressively separated from its epidermis and transformed into flour. Each operation requires several passages of the wheat through a series of similar, ever-finer grinding machines. After each pass through each machine, the wheat is sieved and separated and redirected by pipe, according to particle size.

"These are B-1, B-2, B-3, and B-4," Monsieur Giraudineau said, "which are the *broyeurs.* These accomplish the *broyage,* the first of the milling operations. I'll open one up for you." The miller explained that the grinding stones of the ancients have been replaced by these box-cased metal cylinders, about a foot in diameter and a foot and a half to a yard long, that turn in a regular rhythm. Each cylindrical apparatus—about the size of a modern domestic furnace or a hefty desk—is made of two fluted or grooved rollers that turn in opposite directions, at different speeds. As the wheat passes between their teeth, the paired rollers break and crush, flatten and crack the grains, and separate most of the bran from the endosperm.

"Here we can see the interior of the apparatus," Monsieur Giraudineau said, opening the door to one of the machines.

"You see, this is the B-4, the fourth grinding passage. You can see that the wheat comes out very crushed, very clean."

I put my fingers against the smooth cylinder as the miller showed me, and captured a fingerful of flour. I rubbed the flour between my fingertips and stroked it in my palm. It was very smooth, pure, white. It occurred to me that a miller's hands must be very fine-sensed, like a blind man's.

After the *broyage,* the wheat is transferred by the mill's monorail system to the *plansichters*—essentially a winnowing machine—to be bolted or sifted.

Monsieur Giraudineau now ushered me to a landing situated between the floor holding the *broyeurs* and the top floor with all the pipes. Here, lone and impressive, stood one huge, strange box, say eight feet by eight feet, suspended on bouncing springs, that was performing a continuous, circular, horizontal movement in a perfect imitation of the winnowing arms of a farm woman living in any crop-growing continent of the world. The springs were wiggly, shaky legs, and the machine looked like a cross between some sort of UFO and a box set on Slinkys. Pipes transport the flour up to the *plansichter* after each step in the milling process, where by way of airflow and sieves, it can separate all the products.

The *claquage,* the second process after the *broyage,* or rolling, is a matter of a reduction of the *semoules,* the large particles of the wheat almond known as semolinas or middlings. The particles thus sorted are routed through a new series of cylindrical grinding apparatuses with smoother and smoother rollers, designed to grind the particles more and more finely to their final size. The *gruau,* the treasured product of the *claquage,* are the very tiny, very fine, very white particles, 200 to 300 microns in size, produced at the beginning of the *claquage.*

From the *plansichter* (winnowing) machines, as Monsieur Giraudineau indicated, taking me to a lower level of the mill, the *finots,* or small wheat particles requiring further grinding, go to another set of machines that resemble the *broyeurs* for a third process: the *convertissage.*

"These machines are the ones that refine the flour," Monsieur Giraudineau said. "Again the flour passes through four levels of grinding, beginning with the C-1, and proceeding through the C-2, C-3, and C-4." Monsieur Giraudineau went on to tell me that with these new apparatuses the mill can process 1,500 to 1,600 kilos of flour per hour, three times the rate of the old mill, which processes only 500.

The most important product of the *convertissage* is the *farine de convertissage,* the finest flour, "an almost perfect flour," as it is described in *Le blé, la farine, le pain,* a booklet published by Espace Pain Information, a French organization devoted to the dissemination of information about bread. The other *issues* of this stage are the *rémoulages blancs,* the whiter but not completely white flours, and *la farine basse,* flour for animal feed. Everything that can be milled.

⟡

At the end of the tour, Monsieur Giraudineau led me down to a half-floor loft perched above the lobby, where the Moulin de Pont-James flours are packaged and stocked. Proudly, Monsieur Giraudineau pointed out the smooth white paper bags and cloth sacks of the twenty-five kinds of flour the mill produces and delivers to its client bakers every fifteen days.

The labels of the green and white flour sacks of the Giraudineau mill bore the inscription:

MOULIN DE PONT-JAMES

44310 ST-COLOMBAN

TEL. 40 05 80 93

The sacks of organic flour had the added trademark:

FARINE "FRANCE NATURE"

"Do you make cakes a little?" the old miller suddenly asked.

"Yes. Oh, thank you," I said as he filled two sacks with organic type 45 *farine de froment*. I knew now, after my tour, that I was receiving a gift of the mill's very finest flour.

"And do you make *galettes,* buckwheat crepes?" He grabbed two more sacks, with bright green packaging, from a shelf and placed them in my arms.

Upon our descent to the lobby level, Monsieur Giraudineau indicated, with a gesture toward the open door, that the tour was almost finished. As I looked toward the sun-lit doorway, I found myself reluctant to leave the mill, even though I could barely hear myself think. I loved the smell of the flour. I loved the look of the white powder on clean wood. I loved the clean, sanctuary-like feeling of the place. My reading had informed me that millers were required to keep their operations sparkling clean due to the volatility of flour dust. Fire and explosion are constant hazards for mills. The Giraudineau mill was as clean as a monastery.

Before we left the packaging floor I took one last taste of the Giraudineaus' product. I dipped a finger in the organic flour used for *pain trois rivières*. It was fresh, light, pure. So soft to the touch that I could hardly feel it on my fingertips. Here, in my hand, was the element I had come looking for: the flour for my loaf. My body hushed, the drone of the mill ceased for a moment. I stood alone in the world with a sweet powder poised on my tongue.

ℰ

Just as we started out the door of the mill, Monsieur Giraudineau picked up a tube lying near the door—the tube looked like what you use to fill tires at a gas station—and blew the flour dust off his pant legs. "This replaces the old brush of my childhood." He grinned.

We went outside and stood by the towering silos, overlooking the stream that used to power the mill. Just upstream, beside the parking lot, was a small dam. Below it, and beside the mill where we were standing, the water was pooled. There were lily pads and wildflowers under shady trees. Grass grew to the water's edge. A few yards downstream, the slow stream narrowed again and resumed its normal course.

Monsieur Giraudineau looked over the pond and said sadly, "There are fewer butterflies and frogs nowadays. This is due to the increase of chemicals used in the fields. There used to be butterflies in *all* colors. Now there are only yellow."

℘

A modern, two-story building set against the road and right across the lane from the mill is Madame Giraudineau's province. A narrow hall and an inner door leads into the Moulin de Pont-James laboratory, a modern and sparkling room, with shiny, compact, square and rectangular machines and instruments, with many dials and switches, set on tables and platforms. In polished technical language, the mill woman, who was dressed in a freshly laundered lab coat, explained the purpose of each.

A small apparatus she described as "very delicate," is used to measure out the small amounts of wheat used in several of the tests performed by the other machines. A larger balance is used to weigh the wheat and flour used in the apparatuses requiring less exactitude. One instrument checks the humidity and protein levels in wheat. The *mini-pétrin* is a tiny kneading machine used to evaluate the quality of a dough. This apparatus serves to evaluate the technological value of a flour, or behavior under pressure of a dough made according to predetermined conditions—with the strength of a dough defined as the work necessary to deform it under air pressure.

Another machine supplies a "falling number" for the wheat that arrives at the mill, an indicator of the quality of the unmilled grain.

Two machines set side by side measure the key obsessions of

a miller—the *taux d'extraction*, the extraction rate, and the *taux de cendres*, or ash rate, of the Moulin de Pont-James flours. The *taux d'extraction* is the quantity of flour produced for each 100 kilograms of wheat.

The *taux de cendres* is the quantity of mineral residues, principally the bran, contained in a flour. The purer the flour, the weaker the *taux de cendres* is.

"It takes us two hours to test the wheat we receive," Madame Giraudineau said. "My assistants and I analyze it and then we pay accordingly. By way of these analyses, if the boulanger says the flour was bad, or attributes a failing in his bread to the flour, we can show it was his work, and not the fault of the flour." Liability, I see, now threatens even the French village miller.

Millers, like farmers, are checked by their regulating agencies regularly, and must keep records that demonstrate the quality and characteristics of their flour. "We have exact parameters," Madame Giraudineau told me, standing proudly in her white lab coat. "In just a moment I will take you upstairs to our offices."

She issued brief instructions to her young male assistant, and then showed me two airy and well-appointed offices with large picture windows overlooking the parklike grounds. The wide, carpeted corridor that separated the two offices held a bank of phones, the latest in computer equipment, and a standing desk.

The sophistication and technicality of the milling operation was striking. I'm not sure if I envisioned a complete nineteenth-century mill—but I know I didn't expect to find laboratory efficiency, white lab coats, or a commanding older woman whose technical expertise and quickness could have made her a scientist at NIH.

Standing in the doorway of the lab of Moulin de Pont-James,

I was impressed that, tucked into the back roads of France, there are multitudinous little mills and other businesses run by sophisticated, well-educated, well-traveled, and serious-minded people.

 ᥰ

Madame Giraudineau, now about seventy, and her husband, now about seventy-six, bought Moulin de Pont-James in 1959. At that time it had stopped functioning, and they resurrected the whole operation, redesigning and rebuilding from cellar to keep. Christophe's grandfather was the owner of "a mill with electrical cylinders" in another village eight kilometers away, but Christophe's uncle was the son to take over that mill. During his grandfather's era, millers' flour porters, or *rouliers*, spent their days holed up in the village café, waiting for calls from bakers. When they were summoned, they would deliver the mills' flour by wagon, "be it twenty sacks, be it one hundred kilos," said Christophe.

The whirling blades of the wind-driven mills thrumped to a stop between 1925 and 1930. Moulin de Pont-James runs on electricity.

"In 1960, there were 120 mills in the *département,* in Loire-Atlantique," Christophe noted. "And now there are thirty or thirty-five. It's only those millers who have managed their affairs well that have managed to survive.

"The number of millers in France has gone way down," he lamented. "In 1988 there were 1,000 mills in France, but by 1995 there were but 710. While there has been an increase in larger scale mills, the mills of our size are disappearing. If there is no heir, the mill disappears. We have come to a style of life where there are no longer personal relations with merchants, with people in general. Several French mills have become multinational. It's not interesting any more!"

Christophe made it clear that the millers of Pont-James are

fighting the current. "My father ran the mill and I have followed through heredity—*'par atavisme,'* as we say."

"He is hooked by the mill," Madame Giraudineau said, smiling and patting her son's hand. "We call this *mordu.*"

၁

When I asked the Giraudineaus how I might locate a wheat farmer whose grain was processed by their mill, all three scratched their heads. Madame Giraudineau, in particular, a woman used to precision of thought and action, seemed almost annoyed by her own inability to give me an immediate response. My question, which was at face a rather obvious one, seemed to have caught them by surprise.

"Where can we find a farmer?" Madame Giraudineau said, turning to her son. "Around here there are a lot of little producers who do sales at the farm. They sell chickens, butter, but they don't grow many cereals."

"It may be that you'll need to go over near les Deux-Sèvres, or to la Vienne. But that is far. In Vendee there are some too . . ." her son said.

Here was more hard evidence that the straight country lane from farm to loaf no longer existed, for it was clear from my hosts' perplexed faces that they did not know the farmers who produced wheat for their mill. And, as it turned out, there really was no ready way to identify a single farmer whose wheat *definitely* made its way to the Giraudineaus' mill and on to the Boulangerie Choquet. The whole system, the milling family explained, had become centralized.

၁

At the end of my visit, Madame Giraudineau showed me into the living room for a rest before the long drive back to Le Coudray. "No we won't sit in the kitchen this time," she said, directing me away from the cream and sugar–colored kitchen. "This room is also nice." The parlor room was wonderfully cool and decorated in a tasteful, Victorian receiving-room manner, with lace curtains, brocade sofas, and decorative clocks. My hostess served the region's Nantais and St. Michel cookies in sugar-coated crocheted baskets made by a neighbor—they were actually coated with sugar crystals—and *jus de pomme* "without sugar" from the family's apple trees. Pride of home shone in her erect posture and satisfied mien.

"We are a united family," she said from one of the comfortable, richly clad armchairs. "Christophe lives down the road just one hundred meters. My other son lives nearby as well." This son, an architect, designed the mill, its offices, and the elegant house in which we were sitting. "And we have seven grandchildren from our two sons—three of them Christophe's. We are very lucky."

But while the anchoredness of the older Giraudineaus and of Christophe was attractive, it was also troubling. On the one hand, the young miller had all the rootedness and community ties an urban, late twentieth-century American might long for. On the other hand, what if Christophe had wanted to become a psychologist or an atomic physicist? He was clearly very bright and talented. What if he had wanted to do something else? Was a sense of stricture the other side of the security supplied by his remaining to take over his parents' business? Despite the reassurances of Christophe's situation, I caught a whiff of the disadvantages associated with sticking to the family cowpath. Unexpectedly, I found myself drawn to the fluidity of my own culture. Raised as an American, I couldn't imagine being satisfied if I were to arrive at the age of twenty with the life ahead fenced in for me.

Madame Giraudineau told me she and her husband belonged to an association, along with the mayor of Nantes, devoted to entertaining foreigners. They had enjoyed the group for the most part, though they had had one American visitor who didn't like France. "She wanted to go somewhere every day. We like to go places, but not every day."

As Madame Giraudineau spoke and a nationalism I didn't know I had reared its head, it struck me that nationalism, or competitiveness about country or home is a kind of dance that foreigners, or any people from different geographies, reflexively carry on with one another. In an encounter between two foreigners, there is in each a kind of internal negotiation between pride and openness. Nationalism is a prickly, rather unfriendly emotion, both for giver and receiver. It may be, as *New York Times* journalist Richard Bernstein has suggested, that an encounter between an American and a Frenchman is a face-off between the arrogance of the new power and the arrogance of the old.

Whatever wars of patriotism were invisibly winging in the air, the Giraudineaus' generosity, like that of so many Frenchmen I came across, pumped hope into the heart of one perplexed urban American.

Madame Giraudineau urged me to eat more, and then more cookies. They were delicious—crispy, all-butter shortbread with decorative stamps. I ate as many as I could hold, and at her urging took home two packets to my children.

~

As I drove north, passing summer's burgeoning country fields, the day in Pont-James took shape in my mind. The mill seemed, in the end, like a starched and pressed shirt—conservative and reassuring. Those fresh white sacks of flour. The flour almost too soft to sense on the fingers. The full, hearty, bulky smell of the wheat. The colors of the flours in every shade in the rainbow of white—raw yellowish cream, ethereal white azalea, white of beach-cleaned bone, dogwood petals floating in the woods—were with me.

Christophe Giraudineau and his parents turned teardrop shaped, jewel-like amber seeds into something more valuable: sweet, clean flour.

The Wheat Farmer

Although I knew, given all I had seen, that a modern wheat farm could be highly mechanized, Millet was on my mind as I anticipated my visit to the farm that produced wheat for *pain trois rivières*. His calm, quietly lit paintings of farmers at work in clumpy fields composed a dream of rural peace that held me fast.

After my visit to the Giraudineaus' mill the year before, I had had such trouble finding a wheat farmer that, in frustration and coming to the end of my time in France, I was forced to return home. The remainder of my journey into the crumb of *pain trois rivières* had to wait until the following spring. For this new stage in my quest for the heart of a French loaf, I had convinced my charming, elegant, French-speaking friend to accompany me. My husband and children stayed at home, tending to school and work.

ℯ

It had been a bad year for rain. Everyone was talking about it in April when I arrived in France: the men in the *bar-tabacs,* the checkout woman at the Super-U, the Choquets when I stopped in for a *bâtard* of *pain trois rivières* and a *pain de campagne*. Adding to the marks of the lack of rain, high winds were parching the already crusted Loire-Atlantique earth. The earth was cracked in the pastures and along the roadsides as Valerie and I headed out of Blain and turned southwest for Vallet, the village where Joseph Orieux, the wheat farmer whose name L'Union Francaise d'Agriculture Biologique gave me, has his farm. The farmland soil stretching out from the sides of the roadways looked dry and dead, like that of abandoned salt pans near Guérande.

After we left Nantes and veered east, the road wove up and

down small rises, and the landscape changed from pasturage to vineyards. I was surprised that to find my wheat farmer we were entering wine country, though in retrospect this surprise presaged the encounter to come. The vines, at this season, were small squiggles of leaves on gnarled sticks lashed to poles, the poles arranged in rows that made huge V's on the bleached, cracked earth.

We entered the narrow shopping street of the village of Vallet after about an hour's drive, and soon thereafter pulled up to an angular modern house, painted bright white, with small square windows. White wooden shutters, with triangular black iron hinges were the only ornament on the outside of the dwelling. The house had the terra-cotta rounded tile roof of all the houses in the region, but all the same, it was surprising—small and modest, with peculiarly unsoftened corners. Ancient oaks guarded the surround.

Beyond the house and to the right stood the farm buildings: some stucco, also topped by terra-cotta roofs, with decorative brick window framing; others of age-freckled gray stone.

A high step led up to the front door from the empty, unembellished yard. A woman aged sixty or so, with a gray crew cut, wearing a dark blue housedress over a skirt and a shirt buttoned at the neck, met us at the door. Madame Orieux was expecting us, but did not smile and seemed uncertain about how to receive us. I had contacted her husband, out of the blue, with the help of the French Embassy in Washington, and now two American women had materialized at her door. Madame Orieux told us her husband was meeting with some men about his wine, but would be with us soon.

Three men had been moving into the next room as we entered the house. One of them, a man with a white-laced, dark chocolate crew cut, looked us over closely with sharp blue eyes before he disappeared behind a closed door.

The room we entered seemed to be the family's dining room.

Like the kitchen in *paludier* Lucien Gaspard's house, the Orieuxs' eating space was a plain, spare, small room with scrubbed buff tile on the floor. It was unadorned and sober, like its mistress. A table, covered with a red and white gingham cloth stood square in the middle of the small space. A clock hung on the wall. Those two items, along with the tan and brown bird-flecked wallpaper, constituted the extent of the decoration in the room, save for one other object. Seeing this last heartened me in the face of this rather somber woman and her house.

We had interrupted her husband's wine selling, Madame Orieux told us. This was the season, she explained. Clients came twice a day to buy the Orieux bottled wine. Two thousand people come to the *département* Sevre during this period of the year, for free wine tasting, she said. "We get a lot of visitors."

Madame Orieux repeated that her husband would be with us soon. She seemed unsure about what to say or do, but she motioned to us to sit down. She herself would not sit down, she said, as she had to go out.

We made perfunctory, stiff conversation for a few moments.

Valerie, a person able to put anyone at ease, soon lubricated the talk with her comment to the farm woman, "This year is very dry."

"*En France, c'est ça,*" Madame Orieux said. "It is becoming very dry. The weather is beautiful, it's clear, but there isn't any rain, either. It's tiresome."

"The dirt is dust!" Valerie said.

"*C'est ça.* That's it. Already, it is necessary to water."

"And normally you water in the month of August?"

"July, or June. But *non!* This is dust."

Madame Orieux's countenance began to ease a bit.

As we were still waiting for Monsieur Orieux, I asked to wash my hands. The mistress of the farmhouse ushered me toward the hall leading straight back into the house. As I followed her, Madame Orieux closed the door to each room before I came to it. Her actions brought to mind the guarded farmers I had met in northern Spain—people who inhabited isolated patches of mountain and possessed the watchfulness of small mammals who live in burrows in the earth. It was clear that Madame Orieux's open door had to be earned. My French friend in Washington, Madeleine, had shared with me her view that a sense of deep privacy is common in French farmers. At the simplest level, many rural Frenchmen don't wish their neighbors to see what they have and dislike incursions into the activities of their small, complete worlds. Like the *paludiers* with their long memories, many other rural Frenchmen as well fear any contacts with outsiders that smack of officialdom, the king, or the taxman.

Having visited the Giraudineaus and now the Orieuxs, two different but deep-rooted rural families, a thought rose to mind: Ironically, the stronger the sense of family the less open people may sometimes be to outsiders. Everything, it seemed —even those great anchors, the strong family and the simple rural life—had another side.

By the time I returned, Madame Orieux had put on a French worker-style coverall, but was still standing by the table. Like many French I'd met, she seemed to have pressing and imminent business to conduct. She was willing to wait with us until her husband came, but was anxious to move on with her business. She reminded me of an American doctor with one foot out the door of the examining room, or of myself when a solicitor comes to the door.

The moment Monsieur Orieux came into the room, his wife immediately disappeared.

"Are you in a hurry?" he asked first of all. He was, he said.

Valerie, fluent in French politesse, told the farmer we had all the time he could give us. He said he did not have very much, but would tell us what he could. He followed this statement with the comment that he was not sure he was the best person to talk to. Then he asked what it was, exactly, that we were doing. What *were* these strange American women doing at his table during wine-selling season? I told him my story, and now overcoming his reluctance, he sat down at the head of the table and folded his hands in front of him, as if he were ready to get down to business. He had the reined-in manner of a man summoning his patience, resigning himself to attend to the task put before him. This entailed an exerted refocusing of his mind, for the truth is, the whole time that I spent with Joseph Orieux, as I asked him about his wheat, he was thinking about his vines.

A handsome man was sitting across from us: rich brush of silver-laced dark hair, a strong nose. He was wearing the French countryman's royal blue plaid shirt and French blue pants, as well as plaid felt slippers, *pantoufles.* His hands were thick, work-toughened. The farmer had, at once, the rugged, wind-carved, good looks of a Hollywood cowboy, the taciturn, cards-close-to-the-chest attitude of a Maine farmer, and startling serious blue eyes that make a listener hold close his words.

His farm, Monsieur Orieux said, was fifty-three hectares—a hectare is 2.47 acres—and as a farmer he was engaged in polyculture. Nine of his hectares were planted in vines and four in wheat. He also grew feed for his fifty head of cattle. The rest of the land was planted in grasses for nourishing the *bêtes: le foin,* hay for winter, and *céréales secondaires,* a grain mix for the cattle. They also had two milk cows—"for the house"—they made butter last year. They had chickens for the family and planted vegetables for kitchen use also. We had seen lettuce and beets growing under Quonset huts along the drive—with plastic covering to keep out the blowing dust.

Thirty years earlier Joseph Orieux had decided to become an organic wheat farmer. It was an important choice in his life. "I was young," he said, by way of explanation. He'd only come to the area, from a neighboring department, in 1965. This information claimed me for a moment as another of my simple-minded assumptions toppled: I had assumed almost all French farmers cultivated hallowed land long held by their families.

Monsieur Orieux was continuing with a description of his work. Even before he came to Vallet, he said, he had learned of the danger of chemicals. A lot of nitrogen was being used back then to grow grasses: a treatment mix of nitrogen, phosphorous, and potassium in particular. He sensed errors in the practice—*"tout le mouvement"*—and he didn't like it.

When Monsieur Orieux installed himself in the area he was the only cultivator of organic wheat. Now there are other organic farmers—"There has been a large spread"—but early on Monsieur Orieux was criticized by other farmers. They didn't like it that he didn't do things the way they did them. "But organic farming makes sense," he said, conviction in his resonant voice. "It costs less and the products sell at higher prices." The profits are the same. The Chambre d'Agriculture has now demonstrated that the two methods have the same revenues.

"The main advantages of growing organic wheat are to protect nature and not pollute the water. These are now the recognized advantages. We were forerunners," the farmer said of himself and his farm. There was no change of expression on his face, no grin, but I thought I saw a glint of satisfaction in the farmer's bright, deep eyes.

Speaking of the marketability of organic wheat in France, Monsieur Orieux said, "The time has come when France has begun to lack wheat. There are now more consumers than producers. France imports wheat now from Italy and Spain.

"And then there has been a *grand mouvement* just recently with the mad cow disease. That has given people a consciousness about organic farmers. This is an advantage."

In order to establish itself as organic, he said, a farm must pass though two years of conversion. The farmer must eliminate all the pollutants: nitrates, herbicides, pesticides, insecticides, all the chemicals. Only in the third year can the farmer begin to conduct agriculture in the new way and be recognized as organic.

"During the conversion, the land has to live," Monsieur Orieux said. "You still work it, but you modify your system of growing. It is a matter of professional conscience."

Twice a year, an inspector comes from ECOCERT, a private, state-recognized regulatory agency for organic farmers and spends half a day at his farm, Monsieur Orieux explained. At that time, the inspector surveys the whole farm, examines the family's accounts, and the farmer has to declare all his practices.

Crop rotation is an integral part of Monsieur Orieux's work on the land. He follows a three-year cycle of crop alternation. The first year, he plants wheat. The second year, he plants peas for the cows, and the third year, a clover prairie—also for the nourishment of the *bêtes*. This plant, in the same family as soy, adds nitrogen to the soil.

The cultivation of the other crops is necessary, Monsieur Orieux said, "to give the soil a rest." He lets the soil rest, and the plants replenish the soil's nitrogen, "so the soil is *bien vivant*."

If the year is not too dry—in which case nutritious grasses can die—he plants the fields in the clover mix for two years. In dry years, he is forced to plant grains for the animals in place of the clovers. "One must submit to the dryness. This year there has been a big dryness. There has been no rain since December," Monsieur Orieux said, his eyes solemn. "Usually it pours in March."

After a field has been enriched, every three years or so—following the weather—he plants a field in wheat.

Although his is a mixed farm, there are many farmers who plant only organic wheat. In Poitiers, Monsieur Orieux said, there is a relatively large number of organic wheat farmers. The region of Poitiers and the Parisian region are the bread baskets of France. "In general, organic farmers don't have big farms. Two hundred acres is about the maximum size of an organic farm. A *parcelle,* or field, of wheat can range from one to seven or eight hectares.

"One of the challenges of an organic farm is the problem of additional work. On organic farms, since herbicides are shunned, it is necessary to use mechanical machines to break up the weeds." Monsieur Orieux does this as early as possible in the spring. This machine grates the soil two to three centimeters deep. The furrow is shallow, to avoid breaking the cereal itself, but deep enough to root out the *mauvaises herbes.* "It is like passing a comb through the earth. A farmer has to be careful to do this at the right time," he explained, "when the cereal is stronger than the weeds—the wheat, say, at a height of fifteen centimeters, and the weeds at three centimeters."

"I do this weed-cutting one time only if the weather is good—one time in the spring. I can't do it now, because it's too dry. But there are no weeds now anyway, due to the lack of rain. The wheat has grown a little this spring"—he demonstrated a height of about one foot with his muscular hands—"but not as much as it should have by now."

As for diseases, there are few that affect Monsieur Orieux's wheat. Since his wheat is organic, it is less susceptible to fungi and pests than "chemical wheats." The only treatment he applies to his grain is a *traitement d'oligosel*—a treatment of trace minerals—to reinforce the plants. The minerals are pulverized into a liquid and distributed over the plants with a ten-meter sprayer.

Chemical wheat growers, on the other hand, give their wheat two or three treatments, Monsieur Orieux explained. For example, they apply a hormone that simultaneously boosts yield and prevents the plants from growing too tall. The chemical wheats yield a lot of wheat, but they tend to be very fragile. They fall over after rain, for instance. Chemical farmers also add a lot of nitrogen. The third treatment the farmers add is "at least two fungicides and two insecticides on top of the nitrogen." This load of treatments gives a high yield of 8,000 kilos per hectare.

"Weather is everything," Monsieur Orieux stated. "Ideally, wheat needs not too much rain in the winter, *pas trop,* and then in the spring it needs water from time to time." It is not possible to spray the plants in times of dryness. Not even the big farms could afford that. Fifty thousand liters of water per hectare would be needed for the water to have any effect at all.

"We are still okay here, in spite of the dryness this year. It's just April and we could still recuperate as the wheat isn't ripe until the end of July. I won't lose anything if it rains in the next two weeks," he said, thinking aloud.

"Everything depends on nature. What I'm truly worried about at the moment is my vines freezing. If the temperature goes two or three degrees lower we'll lose our vines. It was just one degree last night."

At my request, the wheat farmer-viticulturist with his mind on wine outlined the tasks of the wheat year. October and November are the planting months.

Monsieur Orieux buys his "Cyrano" seed each year from an organic supply house. Often, though, he is able to use at least some seed left over from the year before.

"I use yellow and white wheats." In choosing from the wheat varieties, Monsieur Orieux seeks types that make good bread flour. The *circuit biologique,* the organic network, informs him about the best varieties for this purpose. From seeding specialists, Monsieur Orieux looks for a wheat variety that is disease resistant and possesses optimal characteristics for baking. "But it is the miller, actually," Monsieur Orieux said, careful to give others their due, "who is most interested in types of wheats. He knows which wheats make good bread."

Turning his mind to the seasonal rhythms of a wheat farm and to the tale of growing wheat, Monsieur Orieux explained that his wheat sprigs rise above the ground before winter sets in and then rest—poised—until spring. "In the winter, we do nothing. We just leave the wheat. We can't even enter the fields because of the mud. To step in the field could destroy the plants. A truck would sink in up to the axles."

The wheat grows all through the spring and early summer—until it is the height of a tall man's knee. The actual ear of ripe wheat is from seven to twelve centimeters, the farmer said. "Then, in July, we harvest the wheat. I hire a man with a combine-harvester. I telephone him at the end of July and he does the harvesting for me.

From the farm, Monsieur Orieux's wheat is trucked directly and immediately to Biograins, an organic wheat stockage company. At the stockage center, Monsieur Orieux's wheat is mixed in the silos, or terminals, with that from other farms situated within a 100 to 200 kilometer radius of the center. Millers such as Christophe Giraudineau order their wheat from the stockage company and it is trucked to their mills, scattered all over the region.

In a mere ten minutes, Monsieur Orieux had imparted to me the story of the wheat that makes up the bulk of Monsieur Choquet's loaves. It was astonishingly simple.

ℰ

"And do you like your life?" I asked, turning the conversation from the crop to the man.

"I was born *à la terre,*" he said.

In few words, Monsieur Orieux told me that his father "had a farm like this farm," in Maine-et-Loire, one *département* to the east. He lost his father at thirteen and a half, and after that his mother worked the farm, with his help and that of his sister. He got married at age thirty-three. He stayed on with his mother until he bought his own farm thirty-four years ago.

Monsieur Orieux's summary of his childhood pointed to a faithfulness required of country people, of people of near horizons. A country boy loses his father, so he dons his father's clothes and assumes his father's duties for decades. His words brought home to me the truth that the farmer's life has always been tough, and often not a matter of choice.

"My family did not have its own farm. They farmed and worked the land without ownership. My wife and I left our home area and bought our own farm. It was our youth, so we were not afraid," he explained to himself as much as to me. "It's normal. The young want to do their own thing. *C'est la vie.*" He said all this as if this last could be assumed.

Monsieur Orieux seemed to relish, in his restrained way, the life he had fashioned with his own hands and his own grit. This, like the fact that he did not live in his family's village, contradicted my assumptions about French and European rootedness. It posed a counterpoint to Christophe Giraudineau's adherence to his family's paved roads. I was forced to remember that from time immemorial, ambitious people of little means have turned their backs on Home. Attachment to land is really the privilege of the landed—in Europe and everywhere else. Something in a human being craves choice, an occupation to which he can devote himself, work that has something to show for itself—so the landless take to the road.

"Why do you like this life?"

"I like growing wheat that is good for organic bread," Monsieur Orieux said, pride glowing in his ruddy cheeks for the first time. "*On aime notre métier.* We like our work. You get to take initiative. It's you, the sky, and *la terre.* There's not some technician behind you telling you what to do. We are more liberated, more independent, more interested, being organic." Here

was love of independence again—the outlook shared by boulangers and *paludiers.*

"And do you eat organic bread?"

"C'est sûr. For thirty years we have bought organic bread. *We
are converted!"* He laughed. For the last twenty years he and his
wife have had their bread delivered to the house. "The bread is
a *pain au levain,* without industrial yeast. It's made of flour type
65, which contains a little germ and bran." The boulanger, he
said, is seven kilometers away near Chapelle Heulin.

"I have five children and they all got their *baccalauréat,"*
Monsieur Orieux said—a fine and proud fact for any French
father. Several of the Orieux children are involved in farm-
related occupations. One of the daughters married a polyagri-
culturalist like her father. One son has a combine and tractors,
and rents out his services. Another is a *rouleur d'eau,* a water
transporter. He has a big cistern and a high-horsepower tractor.
"Right now he is using his tractor to water the roads. He wets
down the roads every day to keep the dust down." This son also
does mechanical harvesting. His work is variable and varied—
"An advantage," said his father. The third child, a son age
twenty-five, will be taking over the farm—*"Il prend la suite"*—
when Monsieur Orieux retires. "My wife is in the house," the
farmer said summing up.

"What do you like and not like about your life as a farmer?"

Monsieur Orieux held steady. "I can't answer that. There are
some things you like in life, and some you like less."

Monsieur Orieux doesn't employ anyone—except to collect
the grapes during the *vendanges manuelles* in September or
October, "depending on the weather. The vines started to grow,
and the sap to run, three weeks ahead of time this year," he
said, letting his mind run with its true preoccupations again
for a moment. "Everything is very advanced. All the vegetation
is advanced. The risk is that we'll have the *vendanges* three
weeks early.

"This year, at the beginning, it was dry. Usually we get a hundred millimeters of water. In March—not a drop. In April—not a drop. The vines aren't affected by dryness, but the coolness could kill them."

I longed to let Monsieur Orieux return to his vines and his wine-selling—but he seemed prepared to let our talk run its course.

As for his daily routine, the Vallet farmer gets up at six and takes a *petit café,* he makes his *toilette.* In the winter, he feeds the animals. Then, at about eight, he has breakfast. Afterward, if he hasn't before breakfast, he sees to the *bêtes,* then attends to clients. He works about ten hours a day. Starting work at seven in the morning, having breakfast at eight, eating lunch at one, and returning in the evening at eight. Toward ten, he goes to sleep.

"All people of *la terre* work hard."

Monsieur Orieux turned the conversation next to a concern of great weight to him. "The social taxes here are enormous. That's what kills us. Then the *primes agricoles*—the allowances of the Common Market—have caused a lowering in the price of wheat. Wheat is now tied to the Common Market. There is no way to compensate for the losses we've incurred from joining the Common Market. The subsidies are decided by the EU and everything has gone down. Compensation has been given, but it has never made up the difference. Many little farms have been destroyed as the big ones have gotten bigger. All to have money. It is getting very difficult for farmers and it will be the same for the young people coming along. In France, lots of the young are out of work. If we didn't have the *allocation* farmers wouldn't survive. It would be a complete death. There wouldn't be any farmers.

"To have a farm, you need a minimum of forty hectares—to support a family and if you're cultivating one crop," he said, showing how he manages to keep body and soul together in the face of the vast changes brought by "Europe." "I raise two crops to sell so this is more secure. One can live better with viticulture, so I devote fifteen hectares only to grapes. This makes life less risky. If one crop goes well and the other not, I'm better off.

"Our land in 1964 cost 7,000 francs per hectare, without vines. Today the value is 4 to 5,000 francs the hectare. It's gone way down. All the young have left—as a result of the devaluation of the land. People earn better elsewhere. In the area between here and the sea, all the properties are the same way. People are deserting the land. And at 3,000 francs per hectare, there are no buyers.

"The quality of the land here in Vallet is average," he explained, his brows knitted with concern. "Our shallow topsoil makes it hard. The roots of grapes grow well in clay, though. This land is good for wines. In the other direction, to the east, it's better land. It's the best land—*la terre à céréales*. In la Beauce, land goes for 20,000 francs per hectare. Over there the earth is very productive and very deep, very rich in humus. There is up to one meter of *bonne terre*. One meter of good earth and then clay underneath, so the water stops there to nourish the crops. In a wet winter, though, the wheat is ruined. The clay keeps the rain in. Poitiers is another good region of good land. Here, its mostly polyculture and vines."

The French farmers of small farms, it seemed to me, were, on the whole and for now, better off than their counterparts in many other countries. The French government and the French people value their work enough to provide substantial subsidies—to insist, damn the torpedoes, that small farms survive. But, as everywhere, more and more the torpedoes are hitting barns and cultivated fields.

Moving from land quality to water quality, Monsieur Orieux said the water today is bad. "It's full of nitrates, from nitrogen. There are as many as three hundred parts nitrates per liter now.

The water in Brittany is especially bad because there are a lot of farms—chicken and pig farms."

As we got ready to go out for a tour of the farm, Monsieur Orieux told me the best time to call, for any additional information, would be in the month of May, between eight and ten P.M., and not on Sunday—his day of rest. Here again appeared not the easygoing farmer but the busy farmer, the man with business to conduct. A man as strict in his allocation of time as a city dweller.

"Bon courage," he said as his two wine clients, who appeared from the next room, went out the door.

e~

"It was one degree this morning," Monsieur Orieux says as he leads us out to see his farm. A sharp north wind is blowing, making us double our jackets in front, battling against the chill. Spread over the farmyard are three large barns and several smaller outbuildings. I see white beehives across a scrubby field. Strolling toward one of the barns, we pass a small area of plastic-covered vegetation. I spy lettuce and radishes under the tarp.

Monsieur Orieux shows us the hay barn first, but wine is a rivulet in his mind. He tells us he produces muscadet, gamay, and a cabernet. In the barn, he shows us the railed tracks for the wagon that once trundled out the manure from the dairy cows that used to inhabit the barn. He shows us a *charrue de Brabant,* a tractor-powered plow with large wing-shaped plates for turning the soil. A five-meter-long attachment that looks like a rusted iron grid is lying in the scrub. It is used to flatten the plowed ground.

We walk through that undefined space on farms—the scrubby area between barns and between barns and fields—and turn right toward the fields. An inviting, grassy track leads off to the left, up an incline, under an arch of trees. Huge oaks stand in the fields I can see ahead. We pass a small, fenced pasture where three white Charolais and one black and white cow are grazing. The black and white cow, his wife's milker, the farmer tells us, is a Dutch cross. The Charolais is French, "a white race, a good race." These beef cows are tough, strong-looking, with long legs. To our right we pass the ends of two more large stone and stucco barns.

Monsieur Orieux has 53 hectares in all, he says. "Forty-five cultivated. The rest in woods." The earth beneath our feet as we walk is whitish like the cows. At the end of the pasture a wire gate opens to the edge of a deep, sloping hill, and suddenly we are there.

Bright green wheat plants, about a foot high, with slender fresh leaves, cover the earth for a long way, down to a row of poplars. Another slope rises up behind the copse. All the far-off fields have the dusty look of just-growing vines. I am looking at a wheat field in wine country.

Monsieur Orieux walks into the edge of the wheat field and shows me the leading leaf—from which the ear will grow. "The wheat will be eighty centimeters or a meter high eventually. Each plant sends up about twenty to fifty spikes, and each head holds thirty to fifty kernels of grain," Monsieur Orieux says, unimpressed, matter of fact.

We spend just a few moments there huddling in the wind looking out over the sloped green field. I have an unexpected response as I take in the sharp young plants. Perhaps I have been infused by Monsieur Orieux's shrug that wheat is just wheat. Whatever it is, the moment is oddly undramatic, anticlimactic. I have come so far and this is it: this is the wheat in Monsieur Choquet's *pain trois rivières.* An unassuming, unremarkable, sloping plain field of wheat.

I think of the wheat fields in Beauce, where I stopped on my last trip to France—the region Monsieur Orieux described as having a delicious, rich humus layer of topsoil a full meter deep.

My journal entry from that day:

Near Chartres the wheat fields begin. These fields are the definition of extravagant. The empires of agribusiness. Immense, yellow-white fields roll, without end, over the grand slopes of the earth. We turn off the highway and wander along tiny roads that thread their ways through the wheat kingdoms. House-high stacks of rectangular bales of wheat straw make fragments of castle walls along the roadsides. On the outskirts of a tiny village, we stop among the fields. Some have already been cut to stubble. The bleached, crew-cut lands reach to the horizon. The swathes as yet uncut are knee-high, bleached to towhead, the color of my toddler's hair. Up close, the stalks are a wonderful, bright color, crispy and dry, with bristly beards poking into the air. The dry, gold kernels crunch when I bite them with my teeth and crackle when I swish them through my fingers. Standing up from my crouch and gazing toward the horizon I am standing in Abundance: wheat plants by the hundred-billions.

I realize that wheat can have all the grandeur of "amber waves of grain," and the humbleness of a loaf of bread.

The wheat that cascades into Monsieur Giraudineau's silos and, as flour, thrumps into the Choquet boulangerie's kneading bowls, may come from a French wheat ocean, from Monsieur Orieux's quiet slope of wheat, and/or from a blond expanse of North Dakota.

I am closer to the truth now, to the flecked nature of everything on earth. Countries and their crops are so intermingled these days that there is often no longer a way to trace a particular ingredient. French millers incorporate American wheat in their flours and American bakers, in turn, use French products and techniques. This is true for everything. Regionalism is hardy, but at the same time frontiers are blurred. We've all learned a thing or two from each other and baked them into our loaves. Who can claim purity anymore? Is it still possible, if you really look hard for the truth, to have unadulterated nationalistic pride? If French bread, that symbol of nationhood, is not purely French, what *is* pure? There is no longer a way to know precisely where one's daily bread comes from.

With the system as anonymous and centralized as it is, I see now, there is no way to say, for certain, that the wheat from this particular wheat field in Vallet, France, finds itself, ultimately, baked in a loaf of *pain trois rivières,* but it is as likely to do so as the wheat from any other farm associated with the organic wheat collective that I might behold. So, to the extent that a person can trace the wheat for Monsieur Choquet's loaf, I have done so. It's a contemporary ambiguity I will have to live with.

Monsieur Orieux takes us now to the stable and the barn. These structures, from 1917, once belonged to the *châtelain* who owned the land. The farmer's step then quickens, as he leads us into *la cave,* the wine cellar, a much older building that has continuously served as a storehouse for wine.

Monsieur Orieux willingly showed me his wheat field—motioning with his arm over the small green field of half-grown wheat—but it is now, when he opens the door to his ancient *cave* that his face lights up.

The *cave* is a large wooden structure with the original, hand-hewn wood beams. In the open, dirt-floored space, there are four large, cylindrical vats of wine, each about ten feet high. There is also a round, barrel-like grape press set on its side. Two wineglasses sit on the wooden hoist for one of the vats. The tasting glasses. Monsieur Orieux the Vintner now rinses the glasses at a tap and fills them a quarter full. We taste the cabernet and then the gamay, the two reds he makes. "Women like the lighter gamay," he says. Then we taste the muscadet. Valerie, who has a refined taste for wine, tells him the muscadet is lovely. It is a quiet time. We say little and the farmer says little. There is a deep patience in him now. I settle too, full of the field of wheat and the farmer and the rich sip of his wine.

e᷈

As we drove back toward Vallet that afternoon, I said, "That was an intelligent farmer." Valerie, a woman in her fifties whose first love was a farm boy in New York state, decided that, given the chance, she would marry Joseph Orieux.

I pondered as we sped down the N-249 toward Nantes and Blain. On the one hand, I had accomplished my purpose. I had met the wheat farmer and secured an understanding of another ingredient, the bulk ingredient, of my loaf. I had gazed out over a field of wheat whose grains could well wend their way into a loaf of *pain trois rivières*. What lingered with me, somehow, was the plainness, the unadornedness, the understatement of Monsieur Orieux's wheat field. With its homeliness, its lack of glamour, its lack of self-announcement, it almost seemed to slip away the moment my eyes lit upon it. Wheat—so important—seemed almost so plain as to be invisible. Expecting to be stunned when I first beheld the wheat for my wonderful loaf, I was, instead, oddly unmoved. Then a new perspective suggested itself. The wheat's very ordinariness and humility revealed a truth about bread, about Monsieur and Madame Orieux, and even about life. The most basic, most important things are often so plain as to be nearly invisible. I had noted this in friendship: the least flamboyant people often wound up being the truest friends.

Another thought set itself in my mind after the visit. The Orieuxs had seemed serious and intelligent, but unsmiling. They presented farming as serious work. Reluctantly, I realized that what I had received from the Orieuxs was a taste of rural life as it is really lived. The *gîte* in which we stayed in le Coudray suddenly came to mind. While our end of the dwelling was a spruce vacation home, the other end of the building, which faced the opposite direction, was a muddy farm with cows wandering about, to and from which a sweaty-faced farmer drove his tractor all throughout the day. Rural life is not, in the main, the sip of the afternoon breeze on strained forearms or the sight of a sinking peach sun at the end of a day of toil. It is mostly just plain old work—with all the organizational challenges of any job. The Orieux farm was a hard place, in some ways. It was real. Its matter-of-fact work, self-protection, plainness—Jean-Claude Choquet's bread contains, in bulk measure, those ingredients too.

 ℮

When I returned to Washington I took a close look at the figures in *The Gleaners*—one of the paintings by Millet that sent me to France. The workers in the field, it seemed to me now, didn't look either happy or sad, just at work. The matter-of-factness shown in the painting, and shown to me by the Orieuxs now seemed to me, somehow, deeply durable. More satisfying, in the final reckoning, than fantasy. Perhaps this explains why, despite the frontiers between us, I felt a strong link to this couple. Because of that durable truth, and because the one other bit of decoration on the farm couple's wall, besides the clock, was a framed print of a dawn-lit scene of three women in bright kerchiefs bent over a cut field of wheat: Millet's *The Gleaners*.

∾∾∾

WATER

∾∾∾∾∾

The vital liquid that transforms starchy, powdery wheat
into a glutinous framework that stretches during fermentation
and coagulates during baking to form a loaf.

Just in front of me, water appeared from out of the darkness.

Water! . . . An immense body of water! . . . And what water! . . . Black, stagnant, so perfectly smooth that not a ripple, not a bubble, marred its surface. No spring, no source. It had been there for thousands of years and remained there, caught unawares by the rock, spread out in a single, impassive sheet. In its stone matrix, it had itself become this black, still rock, a captive of the mineral world. It had been subjected to the crushing mass, the enormous upheavals, of this oppressive world. Under this heavy weight, its very nature appeared to have been changed as it seeped through the thicknesses of the lime slabs that held its secret fast. Thus it had become the densest fluid element of the underground mountain. Its opacity and unwonted consistency made an unknown substance of it, a substance charged with phosphorescences that only appeared on the surface in occasional flashes. These electric tints, which were signs of the dark powers lying on the bottom, manifested the latent life and formidable power of this still dormant element. They made me shiver.

Henri Bosco, *L'Antiquaire*,
in Gaston Bachelard's *The Poetics of Space*

THE AFTERNOON AFTER OUR VISIT TO THE FARMER ORIEUX, Valerie and I ate an early dinner of *pain trois rivières* and *pain de campagne* from the Choquet boulangerie and various cheeses and pâtés from the Blain butcher shop, sitting by the Nantes-à-Brest Canal. As we lounged by the languorous moss green canal looking across to cow pastures, I thought that I had never been anywhere so deeply peaceful in my life.

The next morning though we were back to our hectic pace. At the crack of dawn, I had a meeting with Monsieur Choquet—a moment seized from his crushingly busy schedule—so we bolted the wonderful yogurt and croissants served at our *chambre d'hôte* and then hurried to the bakery. Here I was, hurrying again, like the American of the stereotype.

After the visit with Monsieur Choquet, we raced to Nort-sur-Erdre, where we had an appointment at ten with the water company serving the region around Blain. This visit was to quench my curiosity about the water used in *pain trois rivières.*

Suddenly Valerie poked me in the arm.

"You really mean we're going to visit a *water pumping station?*"

"Sure," I said. "I bet you've never been to one before!" And we both cracked up.

It was good to have Valerie along.

Half an hour late, we finally turned into the parking lot of a small, white concrete building with S.A.U.R. painted in crisp blue letters on its side. The letters stood for Société d'Aménagement Urbain et Rural, the Society of Urban and Rural Planning. I jumped out of the car, and almost before I did, a stocky young man opened the back door of the building and came out to greet us. He introduced himself as Jean-Claud Cruaud. His familiar tone and easy conversation gave me the curious feeling that he felt he already knew Valerie and me.

I launched into an apology for our lateness. "I *was* worried because you were late," he said. "I called Monsieur Choquet and he said you were on your way, but I was preoccupied that since you were Americans you might get lost." As he said "Americans," I had another curious sense—that that term held a special meaning to him.

Monsieur Cruaud led us in through a set of glass doors at the back of the small building. We stepped into an all-white room nearly entirely occupied by an oblong table spread with maps. The furniture was plain, modern, neat. The clutterless, dust-free surfaces looked as though they were rinsed down twice a day. Another man was standing there in greeting. Monsieur Cruaud introduced him as Marc Pautrot, who identified himself as "responsible for the sector" and his colleague as "deputy responsible for the sector."

The two men could not have been more different, though they appeared to be about the same age—in their late thirties or early forties. Jean-Marc Cruaud, plainly dressed in French blue pants, a cardigan, and blue shirt, was completely unpretentious, eager, and chock-full of goodwill. When he smiled— which he did a lot—he had laugh wrinkles around his hazel eyes, and his whole manner was marked by a sweet sincerity.

Marc Pautrot, on the other hand, was the epitome of effortless French elegance. Very handsome in the sleek, neat instance of the word, with startlingly bright light-green eyes. The wool of his sweater was exactly the mossy shade of his eyes, and his plaid shirt, too, had a strand of that woodsy hue. With his impeccable dress, he could have been a model for *GQ*, and with his crisp efficiency, he could have been a Senate staffer. A man of quick intelligence, Monsieur Pautrot spoke so New

York-fast my brain had to scramble to keep up with him. Monsieur Pautrot was at once extremely competent and precise, and deeply concerned that he not give me one drop of incorrect information. He kept saying that I must verify his words with a Monsieur Alix, a hydrologist in Nantes. I did so, though all the while I had the strong sense—confirmed later—that the man knew his facts inside and out. While Monsieur Cruaud had the sincerity of a puppy dog, Monsieur Pautrot was sincere in the serious, nervous way of a first-year college professor. The former had to work hard to get a word in between Monsieur Pautrot's machine-gun spray of words.

I don't know what I expected the men who dealt with water to be like, but I was delighted to meet these two.

The water men had prepared carefully. They had two copies of my letter—with the information I had requested highlighted in green and yellow—and a whole folder of carefully assembled information waiting for me. Chic Monsieur Pautrot launched into serious water talk almost instantly. He smoothed his hands over the big map on the table. Red lines delineated the catchment area for the water association to which this branch of S.A.U.R. belonged. The area included locations north of Blain, east to Vallet, and a couple of sectors south of Nantes. He called the surrounding regions of the map "our competitors."

Monsieur Pautrot explained that the water that flows to Blain and the Choquet Boulangerie is extracted from the water table at pumping station Le Plessis-Pas-Brunet in Nort-sur-Erdre; is pumped to a nearby hilltop *château d'eau,* or water castle, at Le Moulin des Pierres Blanches; then transported via gravity to a cousin water tower in Blain. Only the French, I thought to myself, would call a water tower a "castle." From the water tower, the water flows via a branching network of pipes to the residences and shops of Blain. "The water goes, by its own weight, by gravitation, to Blain. There is a pipe and it goes, by itself, without a pump." Blain is twenty-five kilometers from

Nort-sur-Erdre, Monsieur Pautrot explained, so Monsieur Choquet's bread receives water from the sediments of the earth that distance away.

S.A.U.R. supplies twenty-four *communes,* or 15,000 to 20,000 branches, Monsieur Pautrot explained. The *commune* is the smallest administrative unit in France; it is roughly analogous to a township—larger than a town but smaller than a county.

"This means we furnish the water needs of around thirty thousand people, starting with the principle that a home is formed of three people." In addition to the homes, the water table provisions several industries, including Blain's slaughterhouse, and farmers use the water to spray their crops. "The majority of the water that leaves our wells is not drunk. Most of it goes for baths, showers, water flushes. That which goes toward human nutrition is very small."

Monsieur Pautrot displayed a map of the water table. The aquifer from which the water company at Nort-sur-Erdre extracts its product bears the rough shape of an inverted triangle. It is about seven kilometers wide at its broadest span, with a surface area covering twenty square kilometers; it is 1,700 hectares in size, and more than 80 million meters cubed.

"The origin of the water in an aquifer is rain," Monsieur Cruaud said, offering his simple clarity to put beside Monsieur Pautrot's sophisticated, technical detail, "rain that filters down into the soil." From reserves of water, deep underground, the wells at the pumping station pull their treasure.

"On the level of topography, the lands are more or less flat," Monsieur Pautrot said, "while the earth that makes up the water table is a layer cake of sands and clays."

e∼

Yves Alix, the hydrologist at the Conseil Général, Direction de L'Espace Rural et De L'Aménagement of the Département of Loire-Atlantique to whom Monsieur Pautrot referred me, sent me a description of the geological composition of the aquifer at Nort-sur-Erdre.

The region is composed of layers of crystalline rocks: gneiss, mica-schist, and shale. "Glaciers surely passed over the area," Yves Alix wrote. "The age of the aquifer is unknown, but some of the fossil water that is present could be of glacial age, were it possible to date it. We are by no means, however, talking about an ancient water reserve isolated by glacial moraines such as those in Canada or in the French Alps."

The subterranean aquifer exploited in Nort-sur-Erdre is sand and limestone. The topmost surface layer of the aquifer is sandy. This layer originated in the Pliocene epoch of about eight million years ago. The second, deeper water table resides in a mix of clay and limestone from the Oligocene epoch of approximately fifty million years ago.

The major portion of the Nort-sur-Erdre basin sits over the Pliocene layer. To the northwest, a small portion of Oligocene strata rises to the surface, presenting its deep, underground waters to the pumps at Plessis-Pas-Brunet.

The waters of the two epochs have distinctive characters, Monsieur Alix explained. The water of the more recent, sandy aquifer contains few minerals and has nitrate levels, due to agricultural runoff, of close to forty milligrams per liter. The water table of the second aquifer, housed within Oligocene limestone, on the other hand, contains water that is mineralized, with a low nitrate content of about ten milligrams per liter. (Even this "low nitrate content" is high by United States standards where drinking water cannot exceed levels of ten milligrams per liter.) The water that is distributed by S.A.U.R. is a mix of the two.

Monsieur Alix offered a staircase and a bowl as two images to promote my understanding of the two very different water tables within the Nort-sur-Erdre aquifer.

"A theoretical drawing of the Nort-sur-Erdre aquifer shows a stair step of Oligocene epoch striations in the north of the basin, leading downward and southward toward an accumulation of Pliocene sands at the center. To the south, in another area of the aquifer, the marsh of La Blanche Noë, a layer of Pliocene sand rests above a layer of Oligocene limestone."

With regard to the Pliocene water table, the geologist explained in his letter, gravity pulls the rainwater through the topmost, solid, sandy, aerated layer above the water table proper and fills the lower, solid, sandy, saturated layer with water. "So, the aquifer takes, basically, the shape of a *cuvette,* a basin or bowl filled with sand, in which the interstices or spaces between the grains, once saturated with water, constitute the underground Pliocene water table." This, then, was the bowl.

As for the stair step water table made of Oligocene limestone, Monsieur Alix described it as an aquifer composed of fissures or cracks—as runnels or channels through rock, as opposed to chinks between grains of sand. His drawing shows a bricklike layering of rocks with water, in essence, forming the mortar between them. "The water rests in the breaks in the rock and in the canals that have dissolved their way into the rocks—what we call karsts."

On examining Monsieur Alix's drawings and explanations, I was struck that water is basically a squatter that makes its bed in any empty space it can find in the earth. Water occupies the unlabeled spaces in the ground, in a strange kind of non- or in-between existence. This perfect liquid, without which we could not live, is basically an opportunist, an interloper, a hidden cave dweller.

"How do these layers hold the water?" I asked, as I tried to envision how water resided within these bands of rock and sand and clay in such a way as to be available to be pumped up to water towers and into my favorite loaves of bread.

Monsieur Cruaud came to my rescue. "What one can say is that in fact the beds of clay are key. For example, there is a layer of sand and then there is a bed of clay that forms a bowl and the water stays captured by that."

"There is water all over," Monsieur Pautrot said. "It runs along and then it bumps into an impermeable bed of clay and stays put."

The two men patiently placed into my head a vision of layers of strata flowing within the earth—unevenly and at varying thicknesses—with watertight clay beds, sands, and limestone areas rupturing and breaking into one another. Now I could picture it. Water is stored in the niches between individual rocks and in the sandy layers above clay slabs the way water is held in a sponge, or the way water resides in the gray pebbles of a Maine beach.

Following along on the conversational current, Monsieur Pautrot stated that there was, at present, little danger of the water table being "mined" or depleted. "We currently pump in the environs of three-million cubic meters a year, while the water table must represent in the vicinity of more than twenty-million cubic meters." Furthermore, water levels are followed very carefully at a *département* level.

"To judge the quantity that is being extracted from the water table, we use piezometers. These are vertical tubes that descend into the soil at different places in the water table. The network of these tiny shafts indicates the water level. We register their readings by telephone line, to follow the water volume.

"The aquifers are continually recharged by the rain. When we look at this drawing," he said, pointing to a document on the table, "we see very well that the water level always goes back up. Fluctuation in the aquifer is weak—it is between 6.3 meters and 4.7 meters—because the surface is enormous. This indicates significant volumes of water resting beneath the soil."

I asked whether it was simply rain that accounted for the plenty underground.

He explained that only a small part of the rainwater that falls to earth is absorbed into the water table. A part is lost to evaporation, a part flows into rivers and streams, and some is drunk up by plants and crops. The rain reservoirs in the soil permit the recharging of the water table but water that is pumped out of the earth comes mostly from established reserves cached in the cracks between the deeper rocks.

The readings of the different wells and rain meters in the Pliocene sand portion of the basin show that the Nort-sur-Erdre water table is connected to the Erdre, the river to the east, and a portion of the Nantes-à-Brest Canal to the west. In the summer, the period of low water, these waterways feed the sandy water table. During periods of high water, in the winter, this reverses, and it is the Pliocene water table, fed by rains, that recharges the river and canal.

"As for the length of time rainwater stays in the aquifer—first streaming and then filtering into and replenishing the two water tables, before being pumped and consumed—one can make estimations. The curves in the pattern of rainfall, shown in the fluctuating levels of the water tables, show that there is, in effect, an annual renewal of the subterranean stocks of water. In the Pliocene water table, the length of stay ranges from some days to some months. This depends both on the place that the water is pumped and on the location that the water filters into the sands.

"As for speed of water movement in the Oligocene zone, evidence from the first year of its exploitation shows that nitrates percolating in from the soil stay in the water table a longer time than is true for the Pliocene area, but still less than a year. The fossil waters initially exploited must have been much older."

The water that pours into the kneading bowls at Boulangerie Choquet, I now understood, is essentially rain stored below the earth anywhere from a few days to a year. So *pain trois rivières* is made, in part, of rain.

The natural circulations of water within an aquifer are

termed the water table's hydrodynamics. Movement toward the edges of the basin occurs in the winter, Monsieur Alix informed me, while inverse movements toward the interior of the basin take place in the summer.

"From those niches in the earth," Monsieur Cruaud said in his clear, succinct way, "our pumps pull up the water.

"Let's go to the station now, if you wish!" he said suddenly, as if he were offering me my favorite holiday.

e⌒

My spirits rhyming with the giddy excitement of our guide, Valerie and I hurried to our car, and zoomed after Monsieur Cruaud's small white truck into the fields on the outskirts of Nort-sur-Erdre.

The pumping station was a compound of several tanks and vats and a low, white building set in a weedy field. The whole installation was fenced, and locked at the gate. Monsieur Cruaud opened the several locks with his jangling keys and held the gate open for us—the prince beckoning in two princesses.

"This pump station, le Plessis-Pas-Brunet," he said, "was built in 1974. It is owned by a *syndicat d'eau,* water commission. The station is not the property of anyone at S.A.U.R. We simply have a contract to exploit the installations and pumps that already exist."

Presently, Monsieur Cruaud led us across the weedy field away from the building to a flat, rusty, metal disc, about a foot and a half in diameter, hidden in the ground among the scruffy grasses. "This is one of the wells," he said. The well lid looked like a small manhole cover. At first it seemed not much to see for all those millions of gallons of water pulsing up through the earth toward Jean-Claude Choquet's bakery. Monsieur Cruaud motioned across the weeds toward two other nondescript spots in the grass, indicating the remaining well shafts.

Monsieur Pautrot had explained back at headquarters that two of the shafts—those into the Pliocene—were sixty meters deep, while the third—into the Oligocene—was deeper, descending to 110 meters. Each *forage,* he said, was composed of a hole and a pump. "Now there is a big difference in the water between the two. The shorter wells bring up water that is slightly acid while the other has water that is relatively basic, that is to say, at equilibrium."

Monsieur Alix sent along another beautiful, hand-drawn diagram—this one pink- and blue-highlighted—of the wells at Plessis-Pas-Brunet. The shallower wells of the Pliocene aquifer descend through an uppermost layer of solid, aerated sand where no water is retained. The water table proper consists of a band of solid, saturated sand resting on top of a layer of clay.

The deeper well that descends into the Oligocene layer at Plessis-Pas-Brunet passes through the topmost layer of soil, the Pliocene sand layer, the layer of clay, and into a region of thick limestone. Replenishing water trickles down from the surface into the limestone zone, and is captured there. It is from the limestone area that the water of this pump is extracted.

Monsieur Cruaud made sure to tell me that while the water table begins at ten meters below the soil, there are no inlet holes, or "well screens," in the well pipes until they have descended to a position several times that depth. This counterintuitive technical detail—that the wells do not just tap all the water beneath the ground—ensures that the water is collected from the lowest, and presumably purest, levels of the well. "Water is cached in the soils all around the pump and all through the sediments above the capture level," Monsieur Cruaud explained, "but that water may be more likely to contain pollutants."

From the metal disc at our feet, I looked across the weeds toward the other shafts that descended unobtrusively into the ground. I now imagined, immeasurable quantities of invisible water hidden in little drawers or pockets down inside the earth.

The water for my loaf comes not from a showy, rippling river, but from a place more mysterious and pure: a rock meadow, a mine of diamond-pure liquid—via a shaft rammed deep into the layered earth.

From the shafts, Monsieur Cruaud said, as he led us to the rear of the station building, the water is pumped to the *bâche,* a mixing tank where chlorine and lime, the two required water treatments, are applied to the water. The *bâche* is a round, aboveground, reservoir covered with a tarp holding, as Monsieur Cruaud told us, 1,000 cubic meters' worth of his company's product. Monsieur Cruaud commented nonchalantly that the *bâche* is covered due to fear of terrorist attacks, and water poisoning. The water beneath the tarp was an intriguing, clean chalky-green color, and despite its cloudy appearance, I wouldn't have minded jumping in.

Monsieur Cruaud next showed us a closet-size room at the back of the pumping station that contained two large, upright metal cylinders of pressurized chlorine gas. Pipes, he explained, transport the chlorine gas into the *bâche* where it is mixed with the groundwater.

"If the chlorine injection system ceases," Monsieur Cruaud said," the pumps of the station stop immediately."

As comfortable as an old shoe amid his wells and vats, his seriousness making me feel happy, Monsieur Cruaud showed us the lime storage silo housed within the far end of the low rectangular station. An elevator automatically shoots lime down through its wide shaft to a vat positioned below the spot where we were standing.

"From the vat here," Monsieur Cruaud explained, "the lime is pumped into the saturator." He took us then around to the rear of the silo where another outdoor vat equipped with a helicopter-like blade was mixing pumped-in groundwater and the chalky product of the lime silo to make *lait de chaux,* or lime milk. The lime-milk is sent on to the *bâche,* the standing pool of cloudy green water we saw earlier, where it is met with the second treatment, the chlorine.

⟡

Monsieur Pautrot and Monsieur Cruaud had expounded on the reasons for the two treatments applied to their basically pure groundwater in the office.

Monsieur Pautrot said, in his crisp lecturer's style, "What you need to know is that the water that comes from underground comes out perfectly potable. It's not that we do nothing, but that we *could* do nothing. The problem is that the water is lightly acid when it comes out of the soil. Why is it acid? Because the rainwater that falls on the soil is acid—charged with acidic carbon dioxide, as it is all over—and when it arrives underground there is no lime to raise its pH. To remediate that, we add lime, or chalk, to the water."

Monsieur Cruaud piped up, "It's like when you have heartburn you take bicarbonate of soda."

Monsieur Pautrot continued, "Why don't we want the water to be more acid? So it doesn't corrode the water pipes, the household pipes, the faucets, the hot water heaters, et cetera. To achieve this we raise the pH."

Monsieur Pautrot moved swiftly on. "And then we also chlorinate this water. That is to say, we add chlorine. We don't want to put in too much bleach, though, since if we add too much bleach, there are automatically important taste alterations. The chlorination rates are relatively weak here, as compared to the United States, where water is very chlorinated I believe. Our chlorine levels are weak compared to the town of Nantes, which pumps its water directly from the Loire and is obligated to treat the muddy water of the river. Here, in contrast, our water comes out of the pumps already clean. As we have water that is already of good quality at the start we don't have the need to chlorinate enormously. We chlorinate not to kill bacterias that are present, but to eliminate bacterias encountered in the piping system. We chlorinate, above all, to forestall pollution."

Monsieur Cruaud explained further, "When we have breakages in the network, when the pipes rupture, anything can come into the water from the farms. So we chlorinate—for prevention."

"For example," Monsieur Pautrot said, "the water of Nortsur-Erdre is consumed, in part, in Chateaubriand, and there are about twenty-three kilometers of marsh between here and there. Let's say there are about fifty kilometers of pipes that go to Chateaubriand. In the course of fifty kilometers of canalization the water stagnates, since it is not directly consumed, and the chlorine disappears. It evaporates. Between here and Chateaubriand there is a new pumping station, and we add in more chlorine at that station."

"It's a relay," Monsieur Cruaud broke in.

Monsieur Pautrot continued, "We add it again because for the people that live in Chateaubriand, there would no longer be enough chlorine in the water. So we re-add, but at very low levels, often fewer than 0.1 milligrams per liter. Now I know that in the United States levels are four or five more." Monsieur Pautrot paused.

Monsieur Cruaud seized the opening and said, "The French are not happy when they can smell chlorine in the water from the tap."

Eagerly, he picked up speed, grabbing the chance to wax about something he knew well. "We are in a rural milieu here, and people are not used to chlorine. During my youth, I drank well water, from the well of the house where my family lived. It was without doubt not very good water to drink. Perhaps no good at all! But we drank it because people did so during that time. In past days, in this region, in rural milieux, even in the urban areas, they had gutters, sewers that were in the roads.

Two hundred years ago all the sewers of Nantes were in the roads. People went and drew water from wells where human wastes were in the soil. In agricultural areas, there were heaps of manure at the side of the house, and wells only twenty meters off. It was important that the wells not be too far from the house since the people had to fetch water with their buckets. It was always like that! Everyplace. I don't think there were really countries where it was any different. And in Blain, *right now,* there are people who only have wells."

"It's a philosophy. It's money, and then it's a matter of liberty, of autonomy," the intellectual Monsieur Pautrot joined in. "Even though we put in very little chlorine, a lot of these people say, 'Your water is not good.' On the level of taste, simply, they say, 'Your water is not good. I prefer the water from my well.'"

Monsieur Cruaud: "Without doing analyses!"

Monsieur Pautrot: "Or they do one, one year."

Monsieur Cruaud: "Yes, or they do one during one year!"

❧

After the water is treated with the lime and chlorine, Monsieur Cruaud told us as he led us around to the front of the pump station, it flows to the three pumps in the station.

The main room of the pump house was sparkling clean, with four white walls and three free-standing, fresh-painted pumps —bulky, workmanlike machines formed of curved pipes over a foot in diameter—set geometrically in the room equidistant from each other. The pumps, the dials, the levers and controls, and the pipes were all painted in fresh, bright navy and turquoise, with red handles.

"The pumps are run by sensors. When the water level in the *château* begins to lower, for example, it arrives at this level, the lowest line, and the pumps automatically start up. And when it arrives at the higher level it stops automatically."

The pumps operate twenty-four hours a day and are fixed

with alarms in case of cessation. The station is fitted with telephones and an alarm system in town. Monsieur Cruaud comes twice a day to check their security. Another employee also visits the station every day to inspect and to clean the separator. Some days work must be done to clean the circuits, as lime has a habit of filling the pipes. Leakage checks are also conducted. "These are important public functions," Monsieur Cruaud said, "but some days there is little to be done at the station."

A meandering road took us north across the flats surrounding Nort-sur-Erdre into the trickling outskirts of the town and up a hill. The *château d'eau* at Moulin des Pierres Blanches, "The Mill of the White Stones," an imposing, massive, concrete tower shaped indeed like a turret or a thickened sherry glass, with a perfectly round stem and a funnel-shaped upper third, was enclosed in a large, perhaps two-acre yard by a high, padlocked fence.

The reservoir, Monsieur Cruaud told me, was positioned at the highest point of elevation in the area of the coalition of the syndicate's twenty-four *communes*. The tower itself had five horizontal sets of widespread tiny windows extending up its massive stem. As we stood beneath the edifice, Monsieur Cruaud explained—proprietary and proud, as if this tower were indeed his castle—that the highest of these sets of windows was placed just below the water, on the topmost landing of the inner tower. The *château* holds 3,000 cubic meters of water, each cubic meter equaling one ton. With a claustrophobic shudder, I visualized that heavy load positioned just overhead.

"The water tank starts above the last set of windows," Monsieur Cruaud assured us, "but there's a casing holding a ladder that goes up through the water so a person can inspect the level of the water."

Even more terrifying, I thought. The water man explained

that the tower had to be checked fairly frequently because birds had been known to fly up the tower shaft and die in the reservoir.

"Because our water is so crucial, the property is guarded so no one can get in," Monsieur Cruaud said.

Three or four steps up took our little trio to the *château* door. The inner chamber of the tower was frightening. Looking up, my eyes took in a huge, empty cylinder, all concrete, rising up for 120 meters, or 388 feet. A lone, thick rope hung ominously from the top of the tower. An open metal ladder ascended the vast, concrete vertical shaft. Even though I couldn't see all the way to the top—my view obstructed by the landing platforms along the ladder's ascent—I felt pent-in and awed. The fact that there was only a single exit from the tower (which I couldn't help but think about) made it the perfect setting for a thriller. The bad guy scrambles up the ladder, threatening to pour poison in the tank. With lightning wit and speed, and in the nick of time, the good guy tosses him off the ladder for a straight descent to my feet at the concrete below.

Monsieur Cruaud retrieved me from my television show. Indicating the three massive pipes at the bottom of the tower—each as thick as a teenager—Monsieur Cruaud explained that one held the water coming in from the *bâche* at the pump station. One carried the water to Blain, and one transported the overflow to a spare *château d'eau*. "A trap in the tank lets the extra water out. Otherwise the water would tip over the sides and fall inside the tower.

"Once the treated water arrives at the *château* at Pierres Blanches," Monsieur Cruaud told us, almost jubilantly, "pumping is no longer necessary. Gravity takes it to the *château* at Blain. Via gravity the water travels from castle to castle.

"You want to go up?" he asked. I didn't even pause to consider. I just shook my head, my hand, and my body, laughing.

"You sure?"

Again I begged off. A chance of a lifetime passed over.

Moving along with his tale, Monsieur Cruaud told us the Blain *château* pumps about 1,200 cubic meters of water per day into the town. Underground pipes branch and branch again. "One of them takes water to Monsieur Choquet's bakery," Monsieur Cruaud said. Even he was caught up in my bread story now.

℮〜

Back at the office, Monsieur Pautrot, Monsieur Cruaud, Valerie, and I had tossed around the threat of groundwater pollution. Thinking of my loaf, I had asked about the purity of the Blain water supply.

Monsieur Pautrot raised a well-groomed finger in affirmation. "There are potential problems of pollution, of course— quite right. The biggest problems that we have here are essentially the problems of nitrates brought by agriculture . . . by pesticides, herbicides, fertilizers meant to keep plants healthy. We currently have levels of thirty-two milligrams per liter. These levels are always rising, but still, these levels are relatively low. It is clear that we are well below the present norms, but what we also know is that this is worsening."

To prevent future pollution problems, S.A.U.R. was currently trying to establish a perimeter of protection around the Nort-sur-Erdre water table. Within that perimeter, regulations would be imposed on the farmers, private homes, and industries. "The size of the perimeter is being negotiated right now. It is a political issue also, of course.

"Those who will decide the perimeters of protection are the town halls and the prefecture. The perimeter may be in place inside of a year, but for the moment the negotiations drag along. The problem is that the water table lies beneath the best agricultural lands of the canton. So how do we do it? How do we establish the perimeter?" Concern and vehemence sent Monsieur Pautrot's sentences rushing along like a torrent. "The farmers are beginning to have big *exploitations* and then we come along and say to them, 'Monsieur, wait! Don't put any more nitrates on the soil, don't use any more pesticides, don't add more herbicides.' They say, 'We are here on this land. We have our families to support. If you say we have to lower our inputs in chemical fertilizers, our yields will go down and our revenues will drop.' They are not at all in accord."

Monsieur Cruaud put in an optimist's word. "There *is* a dialogue."

But Monsieur Pautrot persisted. "The problem is to know where we will go, in this political situation. We at S.A.U.R. are total strangers to those who will decide. We await their decision. But at the moment that we speak the pieces are not all in place. It is a very difficult problem."

Monsieur Pautrot paused before his words rained down again. "And besides the farms, there are big villages on the water table. And along with big villages come a lot of houses, and a lot of undergound sewage from dishwater, toilets, et cetera. They contribute to the pollution of the water table. While all the towns have treated their waste waters for a long time, some facilities constructed fifteen to twenty years ago no longer have the capacity to treat all their effluents.

"More and more people are thinking about water quality," Monsieur Pautrot said, now taking the broad view. "In France, there have been regions that have been strongly affected by pollution. In Brittany, they have suffered ninety to one hundred, and even beyond one hundred milligrams of nitrates, even 120 milligrams per liter. That's colossal! I think that specific pollution in certain regions has sensitized everyone. And now, whatever the place may be, everyone is interested in water quality."

"Above all at the moment we pay the water bill!" Monsieur Cruaud said, always tuned to the practical side of the matter.

Monsieur Pautrot went on to say that as of three or four years before, there had been regulation that required mayors to post on notice boards outside their town halls the results of water analyses done by the D.A.S., l'Institut Départemental D'Analyse. He explained that Nort-sur-Erdre "fortunately" has little fluctuation in water quality due to the filtering qualities of the thick layers of sand in the water table. "We may possibly have small increases of nitrates and pesticides after rains. For example, in the months of October, November, December, the rains drain these products in the soil, but on the whole there is little effect."

Monsieur Cruaud issued a warning: "These levels will increase, though, if we don't do anything, and since treatments are only beginning at this late date. There will be a slight increase in nitrate levels for the next twenty years, and after that it will diminish—if agriculture respects the need for regulation. Already, there are farmers who have made efforts. There was an *époque* when they put on a lot of fertilizers. Now they truly put on less."

Monsieur Pautrot added to his colleague's thought. "Nowadays the farmers say, 'I am now cultivating this plant. It needs so much of this, so much of that.' They estimate exactly what they need, after taking account of the photosynthesis that goes on. They try to apply to the plant only the precise amount of fertilizer that is needed. They try to plan so that if there are average rains all the products that are put on to nourish the plant will be consumed by the plant and we won't find them in the water table. It's very delicate. In years of drought the plant may very well not consume what the farmer has put on the land."

"At this moment, for instance, we are in a dry period," Monsieur Cruaud said. "Practically no rain has fallen since mid-February. That is exceptional, and there is also exceptional morning cold."

Monsieur Pautrot took up his train of thought. "We see it on the level of the water tables. Instead of the water level rising in the months of February through April, when, as I mentioned, a lot of rain usually falls, we have reached April, and instead of having risen, the level is descending. Without luck, we will go down lower and then we will continue to descend. And in summer, rains often only feed the surface."

"One must explain," Monsieur Cruaud said, always delightfully concrete, "that we can have strong rains in the summer, but since the day is longer, there is more evaporation of the rains that do fall—so they don't soak into the water table, or they are absorbed by the plants."

"Only strong rains that exceed the needs of the plants," Monsieur Pautrot clarified, "and that are not sucked into the plants, arrive in the water table. This is why February, March, April—when the days are not very long and agriculture doesn't have a lot of need for the rain that falls—are the months that the rain soaks into the water table. But this year we haven't had this, and summer may not replenish us, either."

Monsieur Cruaud cautioned further. "One must know also that with the return of the rains in the month of September, even if it rains a lot, only a very small part of the rain will arrive in the water table. If the surface of the soil is not saturated with water, the soil will not soak in the water. It will not drain into the water table beneath."

In the minds of the farmers and the villagers, and the water men too, France's drought was uppermost.

"It's a worry," Valerie said in summary.

We all shook our heads.

⌒

As we readied ourselves to go, I asked the two men about their careers as water company men. Dapper Monsieur Pautrot had worked for S.A.U.R. for over twenty-five years. He explained that the education necessary for work at S.A.U.R. depended on the job. Chemical engineers—stationed at the central office in Nantes—have a secondary school *baccalauréat* plus two additional years of training. Supervisors also have a *bac* plus two years of specialized training, and engineers a *bac* plus four. But here, in Nort-sur-Erdre, he said, they don't do anything but treatment, so they need fewer qualifications.

"There is one important thing about S.A.U.R.," Monsieur Cruaud said with pride, "We are now ready to pass the I.S.O., the International Standards Organization certification."

Monsieur Pautrot explained, "This is an international standard, an international label of quality established by an organization in Switzerland." It was interesting that this French water company aspired to meet international standards. The world is truly drawing closer.

"And you like to work here?" I asked.

Monsieur Pautrot considered this a moment. "Yes. I like it here. We have a kind of employment that is very diversified. We work in treatment, and we touch all the many aspects: water mains, pipes, and networks. We also work in management, we drive, we supervise people. And then we also have contact with the clientele. We have truly a very interesting and varied trade."

"In my job, for example," Monsieur Cruaud said, "I work only in these few designated towns. I have practically no treatment responsibility. I don't have a station. I have two water towers that I follow—I follow the quality of the water in the *château d'eaux.* I do a little supervision of the three or four people that take turns monitoring in my sector. And I have contact with clients. I deal with the outstandings, with the people who don't pay their bills, and with the people who move. I level their accounts and rectify the meters."

Monsieur Cruaud continued with his list of responsibilities. "I also work with the estimation of needed branches, with the creation of new branches, with the people who will do the construction. We go to the site, we look it over. All that touches this sector passes between my hands. Marc supervises two subsectors like mine. So he is responsible for two agents of sectors like me."

I commented that they must derive satisfaction from contributing to the provision of a basic human need.

Monsieur Pautrot looked a little quizzical. Then he said, "No. I don't think about it. Though it's true: water *is* a basic element of life. But sincerely, I don't think that we are conscious. We don't take account of that."

"It's just work?" I said.

"Yes," Monsieur Cruaud jumped in. "We put our job before all. Our internal rules make us serious. We are serious, but I don't sense it exactly as you do."

In truth I had never myself thought much until now about the pride a water man might rightfully feel for the service he was supplying. But I was glad this thought had jumped out of my mouth and given these two pause.

Our conversation waxed from the men's childhoods to their concerns about biotechnology and their thoughts on America.

Monsieur Pautrot worked his first six years with S.A.U.R. in Vallet, the wine-growing area where Joseph Orieux, the wheat farmer, lives. "My parents originated in Nantes, and when I was eight years old, we went to live in the countryside. My father made a return to agriculture at that time. He had been an industrial draftsman in Nantes. He did ten years as a mechanical engineer at the naval shipyards in Nantes and then he moved into agriculture because he desired to be a farmer. I would also say it was the *époque* for that: very 'green,' very 'hippie.' It's not that my father was a hippie but he was affected by that trend. I think my parents changed their minds later. . . ."

The little scrap of story piqued my interest; I wished I could hear more of it. I was surprised to know that this elegant man hailed from muddy roots.

Monsieur Cruaud told us that, in contrast, he was from Nort-sur-Erdre. "I was born here—150 meters away, a little farther. My father was a blacksmith. He shoed racehorses. In Nort-sur-Erdre there were a lot of race courses. There is still a hippodrome. My brother did the same thing." I wasn't surprised about Monsieur Cruaud's background. I could easily imagine him, a well-rounded, skilled, practical sort, tenderly and deftly holding a horse's hoof.

Monsieur Pautrot cast about when he tried to characterize his adopted Loire-Atlantique. "We can't say it's poor but it's not very rich here," he said, thinking it over aloud. "If you go to a nearby, richer area, it's viticulture, the muscadet." Monsieur Orieux's area. "There the revenues are more significant than here. All that is bordering Nantes, all that touches the Nantais perimeter, is richer." Monsieur Pautrot had described his area by identifying what it was not.

"The Blain region, and all that area, was known for its milk," Monsieur Cruaud put in as he iterated the gradual decline of the region. "This was once an important dairy farming area. There was a dairy in Blain and there was a buttery at Notre Dame des Landes that existed for a long time. Then all of a sudden it disappeared, because they moved the butter factory toward Heric. Then they shut that down and they moved toward Bouvron and later toward Ancenis, which is a very big town. Ancenis is the site of a big agricultural cooperative."

Having found sure footing now, Monsieur Pautrot came in. "Here in Loire-Atlantique, it's basically polyculture. One cannot say that there is one special thing. On the other hand, the agricultural *exploitations* are getting bigger and bigger. The little ones disappear and the big appear! Here in France there is significant depopulation of the countryside."

Monsieur Cruaud explained that now, unlike even so short a time as ten years before, the French government subsidizes farmers to leave their lands uncultivated, in what is called the *jachère*. "They get money from the state for leaving their lands without production! When we were at school, when we were kids, we heard people talk about fallow lands in the Middle Ages. And we are returning to that!"

Monsieur Pautrot declared, "That's all Brussels. It's Europe."

I considered for a moment a positive side of the fallow land subsidies not mentioned by the water men—a perspective presented to me by a French friend in Washington. Aside from the European Union's insistence on production quotas, the French farming subsidies issue from a firm belief in the intrinsic value of countryside. A proponent of "multifunctional agriculture," France has decided that it values the beauty of farmland to the extent that it is willing to subsidize farmers just to keep their land cleared, even if the soil is not productive in the traditional sense. The French believe all people can benefit from country relaxation, and that the quality of life is enhanced by farmland beauty, and their laws bear this out. The French government, and the French people, recognize a human need for places the eye and mind can roam. In effect, the French have legislated places of and for fantasy.

The conversation now roamed over the problems of French agriculture caused by the new markets brought on by the consolidation of the EU, an issue heating the air everywhere I went in France.

"In France, we don't buy our food at high enough prices. The products of the earth are not paid at their true value," Monsieur Pautrot said with strong feeling.

Monsieur Cruaud climbed on the bandwagon. "We now have genetically modified products that come from America. . . ."

Monsieur Pautrot went on. "Yes. This transformation of the genes of corn, for example, to make the grains fatter, or these transgenic manipulations of plants that give them autoimmunity against disease, or cause them to grow much bigger, as, for example, tomatoes—all that in France is very unpopular."

"There are demonstrations by farmers," Monsieur Cruaud

said. "Boats have been blocked in Saint-Nazaire to prevent the unloading of transgenic corn."

Monsieur Pautrot again: "France says: 'Watch. This is a degradation of those products. We don't have enough experience with those products. If we transform the genes of those plants, what will the future bring? What will it do to man in the long term?'

"One thing is sure. If we don't start paying more for our food in France, agriculture will be inexorably depopulated. One day, perhaps, we will reverse our course. We may start to remunerate farming people properly for their products. As you say, farmers work like beasts. In France, it's the same. Above all, those who have animals, and above all of them, the dairy farmers. Because they must milk the cows twice a day, morning and night. It's an enormous constraint!"

"We tell the milk producers," Monsieur Cruaud said, "to produce, to overproduce. But then when they arrive at a certain level, when they supply excess milk, they have to pay penalties. They have a tax on top. It's a bit of a contradiction to penalize them for producing too much. Because everyone starts small and everyone wants to make more. There are farmers—I have known them—who chuck out milk in the ditches to avoid paying taxes. They had a quota, a certain quantity to produce. Once they produced it, they milked their cows all the same, and that went in the ditch! It's not normal, especially when there are countries that die of hunger!"

"It would be best to pay the real price and send it to Africa or elsewhere," Monsieur Pautrot said.

He veered at this juncture and cast his eye on my country. His voice now held a sad sort of conviction. "We are in an eventful period in France. On the whole we are not unhappy. However, we in France have an 'America complex.' Whatever happens in America, we get a few years later. Each new thing that America does, we do as soon as we hear of it, we grab it up. And then the Americans do another thing. With the time difference, we do each new thing a little later. Ten, fifteen years ago, the offices in France—a lot of small places with one or two people—in a single blow, adopted the American mode: the landscaped office, with several people in a big room, with just a wardrobe to separate them. Now these businesses have realized that this arrangement doesn't work, because in America they have said that it doesn't work well, so *pouf!* We change everything! The big American brother. We have a shortage of identity!"

"And in the U.S. we want to be French!" I said, noting, among other things, that we Americans worship French food.

"But you know, we are invaded by McDonald's," Monsieur Cruaud said. "In the French culture, we like good meat, good sauces, wine. When we see the young eating nothing now but that meat sandwich with a slice of lettuce and tomato, and then the fried potatoes on the side, we don't always appreciate it. There are people who have never eaten at McDonald's. Me, I had to go two times—once because I was in Scotland. It's practical, but is it valuable as far as taste goes?"

"There are better things, it's true," Monsieur Pautrot commented. "But we can eat McDonald's and then eat in the French style also. There will be everything! There it is."

Monsieur Pautrot's perspective was a surprising new one to put beside the America bashing I had myself engaged in and had heard Europeans engage in. I had assumed all Frenchmen were simmering with anger at the United States, and I, myself, had viewed U.S. products as merely appealing to the basest of human instincts. Now it occurred to me, at Monsieur Pautrot's contention that Big Macs were acceptable, that maybe U.S. junk foods had utility, and reflected a certain kind of practical culinary genius. Maybe they were a legitimate part of the world's cookery—one inferior but legitimate choice in a marvelous array, the way rampaging purple loose strife could be an integral part of a flower arrangement containing native Maryland flox and black-eyed Susans. Or the way every tree belonged in a forest. The more the merrier, Monsieur Pautrot's words suggested.

e∽

At the end of our tour of the *château d'eau,* Monsieur Cruaud asked if we would like to come to his house for coffee. When we said that would be lovely he scurried to his car and fetched an old beige, rotary telephone with a cord wrapped around it, and plugged it into an outlet inside the *château.* The purpose was to let his wife know we had agreed to come.

Monsieur Cruaud was endearing in his boyish delight to have us visit. "It's not often we get to talk to any Americans!" he said. I knew his pleasure. When I was at home, I grabbed any chance to talk to a foreigner, too.

We followed him along the winding country roads of the gentle hills on this north side of Nort-sur-Erdre until we found ourselves on a narrow road lined on one side by an open field and on the other by a stone wall. We took the driveway leading within the wall, and parked beside a long, ancient farmhouse.

Monsieur Cruaud hastened into the house and emerged with his wife. Madame Cruaud had a fresh, pretty face, fluffy auburn curls, and sincere brown eyes like her husband's. In her leggings, she looked sporty and healthy.

We sat in the couple's small, modernized kitchen at a round table. The next room was a dining room with a loft of handhewn beams above it. Monsieur Cruaud's ten-year-old daughter and her friend—to whom we were introduced—spent their time in the dining room as we talked, listening to rock music. At one point I could hear them dancing to the music up on the loft. It occurred to me that these country girls had a much more highly developed interest in American youth culture than did my Washington, D.C.–raised daughter of about the same age who still played with dolls. Hearing the American English blasting out of the CD player here in rural France reminded me of my sixteenth summer, which I spent roaming Bornean markets to the roar of Steppenwolf. The United States *is* everywhere. But, then, *everywhere* is in the United States too. Washington is aflood with foreign products, from Camembert to Hondas.

Monsieur Cruaud told us he and his wife also had a sixteen-year-old son. "He's at the age when they're timid," he said, explaining why the boy hadn't come to greet us. The teenager's room was in a loft above the formal entrance—farther down the rambling house. His room, which we spied from below as we left, was covered with posters. Just before we left, the teenager descended his ladder to meet us. He had a sweet face like his father's and scraggly hair. In his extremely baggy jeans, he would have fit right in at Wilson High School in Washington.

The two Cruauds—she was thirty-five, she said—spoke about the great influence of the United States on France. Their curiosity about our country, it seemed, was a main reason they'd wanted to receive us. The first thing they asked was whether it was really true that we had yards without fences or walls. They had seen this on television. They found this so hard to imagine, they said—to live without privacy. The couple lives at the edge of farm fields, behind hedges and stone walls, and can see no houses from their property. Their children seldom go to other houses. The French treasure a kind of autonomy subtly different from that of Americans.

The couple leaned close to catch our words, seeming to view time for conversation as the most natural thing in the world. Openness and curiosity shone in their eyes. They seemed to exemplify the way to continue to have roots while embracing the whole world. Their way of approaching globalization was to receive it with questions and interest.

Monsieur Cruaud picked up the thread of the conversation we'd started back at S.A.U.R., as if the issue were an ongoing puzzle for him. "The French follow anything the Americans do," he said. "It's as though we have no mind of our own." He spoke again of the effects of McDonald's and of television on French life. Virtually all the entertainment enjoyed by his family and those of his contemporaries—all the movies and television programs they watch, for instance—is American. "We even listen mostly to American music on the radio, even though we don't understand the words!"

When he said this, it suddenly struck me that Monsieur Cruaud wasn't lamenting the intrusion of American culture into his life, but wondering about it, relishing it, even. So used to grousing about the spread of American television into other cultures, I was amazed to take in this jolly view of my country. The water man also had an endearing habit of dropping an American word into a phrase now and then, trying out his English.

Now I understood why Monsieur Cruaud seemed to regard us as old friends when we first stepped out of the car at the water company. To his mind, he'd met us over and over again on television.

The couple spoke about their childhoods. Dances were held in the meadows when they were young. They, in fact, had met at one. Now there are not many dances, they said, "except for those of 'the third age'—old people who didn't experience any youth during the war. They have their dances three times a week." Bicycle races were also a big thing when Monsieur Cruaud was young. Dances, bicycle races—those are what Nort-sur-Erdre kids used to do, and now they watch American television. I couldn't find it in me to view this as a positive development.

Sitting with the Cruauds in their warm kitchen, I felt my

shoulders relax and my pulse slow. The couple seemed to me the epitome of earthy, warmhearted goodness. I felt completely comfortable with them, and being in their house.

When the conversation found its way to the subject of bread, the couple told me they buy Pain Bonne-Femme, a *pain au levain* baked in Nort-sur-Erdre, pre-sliced for convenience. The family consumes two loaves a week—a far cry from the old days. "We don't eat much bread because it's fattening with the butter and everything you put on it. Older people eat a lot of bread, though. They can eat a huge *pain de deux livres.*"

The couple led us through their home, an ancient, stone dwelling added on to generation after generation. Monsieur Cruaud is able to tell by the color and type of stone when each addition was constructed. His wife gestured toward her flower garden outside, a close-tended plot with forget-me-nots, blue lobelia, and tulips. I could see beyond, but still within the Cruauds' walls, a huge green, grassy meadow and a large vegetable plot.

After the house tour, the couple took us to see the oven, or *"boulangerie,"* as they called it, next to the house. An old stone oven typical of those in the region: flat-faced, with a dirt-floor antechamber and a low baking space only a foot or so high, rounded like an igloo at the back. It housed fagots, and a baker's *pelle* leaned against a wall. The door of the hut hung with fading wisteria. Next to the oven stood the old rocky pig shed. Off in a rear corner of the acreage, I could glimpse a simple swing set cut from logs. This Nort-sur-Erdre family had all the luxuries of the good life—roots, space, land, a large, beautiful house—that compose the American dream, or any family's dream for that matter.

Just before we left, Monsieur Cruaud gave each of us a pin that read S.A.U.R. "This is a very valuable pin. Take care of it!" he said, laughing.

He and his wife came out and stood by our car to bid us good-bye, and waved numerous times before we actually pulled down the drive. They, like many of the French, seem to view each parting, even with an acquaintance, as a ritual due long and leisurely attendance. Perhaps the French are more aware of life's ephemerality than people from the New World. In any case, they wave until their visitors disappear from sight.

When we turned out of the Cruauds' long, gravel drive onto their country road, I could still see the couple standing with their hands raised in the air.

Suddenly I had a lump in my throat.

"I feel like crying, leaving them," Valerie said.

e~

As we merged onto the highway toward Blain, Valerie turned toward me.

"Can you believe we spent an hour gazing at a *château d'eau?*" she said.

"No!" I replied. We both burst into weeping, belly-clutching laughter.

"I'll never forget this day," she said. "And I'll probably never miss a *château d'eau* across a field again in my life. I think I have the eye now!"

Along the road, all the way back, we kept spying *châteaux d'eaux,* hovering like UFOs on the horizon.

e~

Later in the evening, at the bed-and-breakfast, I got myself a cup of tap water from the Nort-sur-Erdre aquifer and settled in to put down some notes.

Water is a live force. Subject to subterranean currents, it ripples beneath our feet. Running between the ribs, muscles, and organs of the earth, like earthen blood or milk, it is pumped up to feed us as though the earth were a great teat.

A flux extracted from a dark land of gems, crystals, and sediments, the water for my loaf is literally water from stone.

The capture of the water for Jean-Claude Choquet's loaf entails yet another kind of alchemy. As wheat springs up or salt blooms to the sun, quenching, essential water stores itself in and grows in darkness. Once out of its dark regions and into the baker's bowl, it turns grainy flour into the miracle of dough. Both sunshine and night-blackness mix in my loaf.

Now, when I walk across the grass, or eat a hunk of bread, I hear the water whispering.

YEAST

A fungus that consumes sugars in flour and produces
the carbon dioxide gas that makes bread rise:
the agent of fermentation for a loaf.

In all falling rain, carried from gutters to water-butts, animalcules are to be found; and . . . in all kinds of water, standing in the open air, animalcules can turn up. For these animalcules can be carried over by the wind, along with the bits of dust floating in the air.

Antonie van Leeuwenhoek
Dutch naturalist

TO FIND THE YEAST FOR JEAN-CLAUDE CHOQUET'S LOAF, I had to leave the sleepy Blain region and traverse a broad swath of France to Lille, the northern French industrial city near the Belgian border.

At Gare du Nord, I board the train to Lille. Valerie has returned to the United States and I am now on my own. The Train à Grand Vitesse is sleek and fast and filled with chicly dressed commuters from Paris to Lille, all of whom are utterly silent.

As the other passengers type into their laptops or hunch over sheaves of papers, I gaze out the window. The sky is overcast for the first time this visit. Perhaps desperate France will get its rain. As the train speeds out of Paris, we pass a sector of tall apartments, move into a neighborhood of stucco houses with tile roofs, and then into the immense cultivated tracts that extend from both sides of the train for the remainder of the journey.

Several times I see a *château d'eau* across a field. I see them everywhere. Like Valerie I have acquired the eye.

ᶜ⟋

I force myself to break my gaze from the landscape. Readying myself for a visit to a factory, as opposed to a small office or family business or farm, I take a few moments to look over my notes on yeast.

I call to mind a film that Bernard Poitrenaud, my contact at Lesaffre Yeast Company, gave to me. Made for schools, it is called *The Yeast That Lives in Your Bread*.

During the film's introduction, a cheery, ruddy-cheeked

baker holds a golden loaf to his nose and declares, "Bread without yeast, with just flour, salt, and water is *une pâte morte,* a dead dough. Yeast makes it live!

"Yeast," the baker explained, "is billions of living cells." Free-floating and ever-present in nature, in houses, and in factories, yeast cells are microorganisms, simple fungi, that reproduce via budding: the mother yeast divides in half, those offspring divide in half, and so on. . . .

A single yeast cell takes four to seven hours to reproduce, and each mother cell can give birth to twenty daughter or twin cells. The yeast species, technically known as *Saccharomyces cerevisiae,* has strains that differ like dog breeds—and yeast factories isolate varieties for different usages.

Yeast lacks the chlorophyll green plants use to make their own food, so it relies for its survival on the sugars in natural sources such as fruits, nectars, molasses, and grains. Chemicals called enzymes or ferments are produced by yeast cells, and these break down the food.

The most amazing property of yeast in baking is that it is able to transform the sugars naturally present in flour into alcohol and carbon dioxide gas.

This process causes bread dough to rise. Yeast decreases the viscous flow properties of a dough and increases elasticity. When yeast is in an oxygen-deprived state, such as when it is caught in dough, it consumes nearby sugars to sustain life. As the yeast consumes the dough's sugars, the gases it gives off are trapped in the gluten (a type of protein) present in the dough's flour. Then, as the gases expand with the heat of baking, the gluten stretches and the dough rises. From 180 grams of fructose—the sugar present in bread flour—yeast produces eighty-eight grams of carbon dioxide gas and ninety-two grams of alcohol. This transformation is at the base of bread fermentation.

In an oxygenated milieu, through a metabolic process called respiration, yeast cells consume the oxygen and sugars and nitrogenated substances around them and produce not only carbon dioxide gas, but also water and a great deal of liberal energy, an amazing twenty times more than it consumes. This quantity of energy permits the yeast to multiply abundantly.

Bread-making takes advantage of both yeast lifestyles. When, at the beginning of the process, dough is kneaded, it takes in air—it breathes—and the yeast reproduces rapidly. When kneading stops, then the yeast caught in the dough stops breathing and fermentation begins.

In commercial yeast production, such as that carried out by the Lesaffre Yeast Company, the aim is to produce a biomass of yeast as quickly as possible.

"Though yeast is a simple ingredient," the jolly baker in the company's promotional video informs us, its production requires *"beaucoup de savoir faire."*

e~

Bernard Poitrenaud, director of the "Baking Institut" of Lesaffre Yeast Company met me at Gare Marcq-en-Bareoul. The definition of dapper, in a ribbed, navy vest and a well-cut tweed jacket, this a man—of perhaps fifty—stood patiently at the platform exit, discreetly holding a sheet of paper with my name in big, crisp letters, straight from the printer.

With an amiable but businesslike greeting, and a flash of smile from his direct eyes, he led me to his car. As we drove through Lille, Monsieur Poitrenaud pointed out spots of interest and offered an account of the city. A city of one million inhabitants—"made up of the townships of Lille, Roubaix, and Tourcoing"—with Flandrian-style brick buildings and a warren-like medieval center, Lille is a highly cultured city *"très vivant, très agréable,"* my guide said. A young town, with several universities, it has attracted transplants from Paris. With the rapid TGV service, an increasing number of people now commute to Lille each day from the capital. He himself had moved to Lille from Paris twenty years before.

Monsieur Poitrenaud was a biologist, a cereals specialist in the milling industry, at the time he was offered a job at the yeast company in Marcq-en-Baroeul, he told me as he whisked me through the city streets. "Lesaffre wanted someone who knew flour," he said. "In the old days, the boulanger had to adapt to the yeast. Nowadays the yeast has to adapt to the baker. There is no longer one yeast, like there is not one flour." A great part of Monsieur Poitrenaud's job is to know the yeast needs of different markets. These needs have included those of schools, food services, and industries, as well as those of bakers in France and other cultures across the world.

When he first came to Lesaffre in 1977, the young Bernard Poitrenaud read, several times, the plaque on the wall of the cemetery across the road from the factory. The plaque read, *"Vous avez été ce que nous sommes, et nous serons ce que vous êtes,"* "You have been what we are and we will be what you are."

"It made you think," he said.

That first visit to Marcq en Baroeul, he intended to stay for three months, and then return to Paris and his family. For some reason mysterious to him, he stayed.

Monsieur Poitrenaud's family has lived in Paris for generations, but he didn't mind leaving the family seat. "The French pattern of staying where one grew up is finished." He explained this was mostly due to *le chômage,* to unemployment. A sizable percentage of the French unemployed, he said, were unemployed because they were not willing to work away from their home towns. "One has to be mobile these days." Here was another Frenchman contentedly pursuing a life far from his childhood home, like an American.

⟶

The yeast plant, Lesaffre, is set within one of Lille's residential neighborhoods, inside a gated and walled compound about two blocks long. When we turned into the compound, through the high gates, I was confronted with an inner kingdom of six-story vats; hulking, modern, white stockage buildings and ware-houses, and a maze of pipes of giant widths. Stepping out of the car, and with a sweep of his tweedy arm that took in all these grand edifices, Monsieur Poitrenaud explained that Lesaffre was the leading yeast producer in the world, with sales in 185 countries and twenty factories on five continents. "Lesaffre is commercially present in every country of the world—except Liechtenstein." He laughed.

"In the United States, Lesaffre has a small company in Do-than, Alabama, and there is also a *société* for Lesaffre products in Minnesota. Lesaffre has a large factory the size of the one we are standing in, in Mexico as well."

The company was started in 1853 as a grain alcohol factory, by a family of agriculturists and millers. The business, a *société familiale* built on the family's own capital rather than that of stockholders, produced two principal products at the outset: compressed baker's yeast for bread and malt for breweries. "Since its conception, the company has expanded its reper-toire, but its primary product remains yeast," Monsieur Poi-trenaud said as he ushered me toward a line of large, clean, rectangular buildings.

My guide led me now on a brief tour of the plant. As we walked down its paved service lanes—wide enough to ac-commodate gigantic trucks—he explained the function of each building. An immense, new-looking building about eight stories high, made of a white corrugated material, and with three enormous pipes reaching up its towering outer walls, Monsieur Poitrenaud identified as the *cuve de fermentation,* where the yeast is grown. The *cuve,* he said, is the biggest of its kind in the world, and the most powerfully automated. I felt dwarfed looking up at its nearly windowless facade. The old factory, a smaller brick building to which my guide pointed, stands empty now.

A second monstrous building was devoted to the treatment

of effluents from and residues of the yeast production process. "There are a lot of polluting by-products and so we direct large efforts toward the treatment of effluents." Some of the residues are recrystallized as animal feed; others go into treatment plants. Fully 10 percent of the company, Monsieur Poitrenaud explained, goes toward the avoidance of pollution. "This is a very important part of the factory."

A smaller building situated behind the giants contained the company's information, logistical, and commercial divisions. The oldest building, a small, brick two-story constructed in 1854, was now used for *direction générale*. Another huge, modern, round-edged building, Monsieur Poitrenaud said, served as yeast stockage. As we stopped beside it, Monsieur Poitrenaud told me five thousand pallets of yeast can be housed in the building at any one time. The storage facility is completely automatic and managed via computer, according to the "first-in, first-out" method to assure customers the freshest product.

"In theory we produce three sorts of yeast, but in fact we have hundreds of references," Monsieur Poitrenaud said. "Each client has particular specifications—commercial and etiquette specifications. We adapt to each client in the world." Lesaffre works in over sixty languages, tailoring its product to the needs of all the countries it services. Most of the clients are distributors and agents who resell the yeast in their own countries.

While I was looking up at the stockage depot, a truck arrived and backed into the huge building to be packed with cartons of yeast. Another building, to the side and behind this one, I learned, was devoted to the vacuum-packing of a portion of the company's yeast. Yet another building, hidden behind the large ones, contained the research and development departments, and *"direction générale de la holding."* The company's baking research facility, Monsieur Poitrenaud said, was situated across the road in an old convent.

The hulking, immaculate warehouses of the plant reminded me more of a hospital complex than a place occupied with the slopping, frothing, fungal mess of life in my proofing bowl at home.

As we strolled, my obviously busy host set a leisurely pace and told me more about the company. "Altogether there must be five hundred people working for Lesaffre here in France, including the production, administration, research and development, and salespeople. The Lesaffre group must have three to five thousand worldwide. We don't know exactly."

It struck me as odd, here in the plant in Marcq-en-Baroeul, that despite the fact that the yeast company had a large number of employees, we had encountered almost no one as we walked along the factory's lanes. I had seen a man in a lab coat enter the storage warehouse, and there were drivers in the trucks, but these were the sum total of the human beings we'd come across during the leisurely tour.

"Lesaffre provides yeast for all types of bread—according to the preferences of each country," he said. "Our most important client is China."

Surprised that the French yeast company's largest client would be China, I asked what sort of bread that rice-eating culture ate so much of.

"There is a difference between North and South China," he said. "And of course the Chinese still mainly eat rice, but a lot of bread is consumed as well. There is one popular bread that is made without yeast and another made with yeast. If you consider the size of the population, they need a large volume of yeast for the bread-making process, even if bread is not the most important part of their diet."

We reversed directions to head back the way we'd come, and Monsieur Poitrenaud summarized Lesaffre's primary mission in crisp sentences. "Generally speaking, Lesaffre's objective is to provide a first-quality yeast at the best price, accompanied

by good service. In addition to our technical consultation service, we are also engaged in the development of new methods
of bread baking. Bread is always changing. It's a new civiliza-
tion we live in!"

We stood now at the entry to the huge compound, where
we could look back on it. I instructed my eyes to take it all in:
the giant white warehouses, the smaller brick office buildings,
the massive pipes, the clean, asphalt service lanes that cut between the mammoth edifices, the towering walls that rose up
to the gray French sky. This strange, enormous factory-king-
dom that helped produce the bread of a village baker.

"This yeast plant is the largest in the world," Monsieur Poitrenaud said again, following my gaze.

I was no longer in sleepy, rural France, and this was not a little chemistry lab, and I wasn't sure yet what to make of it.

ℰ

"Lesaffre is a good company to work for," Monsieur Poitrenaud
told me as we got into his car. "For instance, there are no fixed
work hours—a policy not uncommon in French companies. In
general, many people stay until seven, but it all depends on the
bread-baking or the clients."

My old envy of people-friendly European social policy woke
up and shuffled around for a second, distracting me. I would
love it if my husband could have more flexible work hours and
spend more time with me and our children in the evening.

Monsieur Poitrenaud told me he enjoys his work because it's
both technical and practical. "And because bread is *plus noble*.
Bread is more humane than meat or chickens. I couldn't work
in meat or chickens. And bread remains an art. There are still
some areas of bread baking that are mysterious, that we don't
understand—that remain to be explored. It's rich. We are always discovering new ways to make bread, and that's a *raison
d'être*. The fermentation of wheat goes deep to the roots of
humanity."

As Monsieur Poitrenaud spoke of the nobility of his work, I was reminded of Monsieur Choquet, the *paludiers,* and the millers' perspectives on their occupations. All four groups of men spoke of the richness their respective kinds of work brought to their lives. Work, these men made clear, is a central *raison d'être* for human beings. Ironically, in work-obsessed Washington, I sometimes forgot how basic to a good life work really is.

$\backsim$

Monsieur Poitrenaud drove me to the convent-cum-Baking Institut, a low brick building set across the street and down the block from the gate leading into the factory compound. He chuckled at the odd name of this facility as he opened the door for me, sharing the following story. "Over saucisson and Beaujolais—a lot of wine—we decided on the term 'Baking Institut'—because we thought the Franglais was appropriate."

The building had the spaciousness of a well-designed nursery school. Ushering me down a hall, Monsieur Poitrenaud asked if I would like *un café.* I followed him into a spotless, modern kitchen.

Soon after we were joined by Hubert Maitre, a man younger than Monsieur Poitrenaud, in his mid-forties or so, a baking researcher and worldwide baking advisor who holds an appointment in Lesaffre's Bakery Division.

They introduced me to a slice of French society I had not yet met in the course of my bread quest: the worldly-wise, cultivated, urbane French professional.

$\backsim$

Monsieur Poitrenaud filled our coffee cups and the two men offered me a history of baker's yeast.

Yeasts have been put to use by human beings ever since the beginning of the cultivation of grain. For centuries, household and village bakers used *levain* to raise their loaves. This soureddough method of bread making was effective, but it was a painstaking, unpredictable, and lengthy one, as the production of a *levain-chef,* a master leaven, takes close to a week, and the bread produced was of variable quality.

In 1665, a Parisian baker started using beer yeast to raise his bread, producing a product called *pain mollet.* The foamy "barm" from the surface of beer—used along with a base of *levain*—improved the taste of bread, increased its rising, and accelerated fermentation. The introduction of this new bread-making method caused a furor among Frenchmen. Many were enraged by this newfangled use of beer yeasts in bread, and a commission was formed to investigate and render an official verdict on the practice. Finally, on March 21, 1670, Parliament authorized bread made with yeast, and, from then on, until the nineteenth century, bakers made their way to the local brewery, captured the barm from the brewery beer, and toted it back to their bakeries, where they added it to their doughs to make their loaves rise.

The invention of the microscope in the early 1800s by Antonie van Leeuwenhoek, permitted the identification of microorganisms, including yeasts, which the scientist lumped together under the term "animalcules." In 1837, van Leeuwenhoek confirmed the existence of living organisms—which reproduced by budding and stimulated the production of alcohol—in beer. Louis Pasteur went on to prove that fermentation was caused by living organisms in 1860. Baron Max de Springer, from Vienna, founded Maisons-Alfort in 1872. This plant, the predecessor to Lesaffre, became the first French yeast factory.

Following the legalization of the use of yeast in French bread, liquid yeast, sold as "cream yeast," was mixed with *levain,* according to a process called *sur français* for many years. As time went on, bakers became concerned about the easy spoilage of cream yeast and its health threats, and about the amount of storage space required. As a result, a Dutchman invented an industrial process that eliminated the water in liquid yeast to produce compressed yeast. This compressed yeast was a great improvement as yeast could now easily be stored.

In 1840, an Austrian baker overturned the until then ubiquitous method of mixing yeast and *levain* by introducing to France the use of yeast alone. This style of baking, called *sur poolish,* and the *pain Viennois* it produced, was successful but limited to luxury breads due to the long preparation time. This lengthy method is the one Monsieur Choquet—concerned with quality first—uses for his *pain trois rivières.* Later, *le pain direct*—the immediate mixing of all ingredients—replaced the *sur poolish* method.

Both the United States and France benefited from the invention of compressed yeast, but the compressed yeasts of the two countries were quite different, hailing from different strains and possessing different speeds of fermentation—a distinction that holds to this day. The compressed yeast used by American industrial bakers has a different chemical composition from that used by the majority of bakers in France. American compressed yeast has a higher protein content and is much more active than that of France, multiplying more quickly because of its high protein levels. This is appropriate to the dominant, industrial, quick-rise bread baking process followed in the United States, the French yeast experts said. French yeast—Lesaffre yeast—on the other hand, goes primarily to "artisans," who represent 70 percent of the company's customers. While the more active compressed yeasts, like those of the Americans, are speedier, they are less stable too, and artisanal bakers need very dependable fermentation agents. Thus the French have veered toward yeasts that are slower and stabler than American yeasts. "An average French yeast can last four weeks, while in the United States it lasts about twelve days!" said Monsieur Poitrenaud.

The next key event in the evolution of yeast production, following the invention of compressed yeast, was the First World

War. "You still had to make bread during the war, and the Americans, who are very practical people, as you know, found that it was not possible to take the yeast to war and keep it alive. So they had the idea of drying the yeast—to preserve it without altering it, while maintaining it in an active state. That's what we call 'active dry yeast.'" This type of yeast—a granulated variety—needs only to be rehydrated in warm water.

The Lesaffre men explained that their company makes a different type of dry yeast from that developed by the Americans. Using a distinct drying process, they obtain active, dry yeast shaped in small dehydrated beads which can be kept in the open air and do not need to be wrapped in any special way, "not even in tins."

About twenty years ago, Lesaffre developed an "*instant* dry yeast." This yeast, in the shape of tiny vermicelli, may be added directly to flour without rehydration—an advantage in terms of efficiency and speed. It works like, and is just as active as, compressed yeast, but it is very sensitive to humidity and to the oxygen in the air, so it must be stored in protective packaging—depressurized vacuum packs such as those used for coffee. "This is the latest generation of yeast," Monsieur Poitrenaud said.

"The next upcoming invention will be cream yeast," my hosts told me. They explained that industries in the course of automatizing say, 'Yeast stocked in bags or in boxes that you have to open, is not interesting for us. We want cream yeast that we can pipe in like water.'

"This product," Monsieur Poitrenaud said, "is brand-new and at the same time, it is a return to the origins—to the bakers who came in with their buckets!"

Monsieur Maitre clarified that only the largest bread factories can make use of cream yeast, because only they can really justify deliveries of 23,000 liters of cream yeast by tank truck. "The reception installations required are impressive too. The cream yeast needs to be both agitated and refrigerated, so this kind of yeast is a lot of work. It exists everywhere, but we've had it in France for only the last two or three years."

Monsieur Poitrenaud cleaved to his stance of complete and balanced reporting. "In the United States, of course, it is very common. In France, we just don't have units big enough to allow this sort of installation."

℮

Back within the high walls of the plant, as Monsieur Poitrenaud leads me toward the enormous white yeast production facility, the *cuve de fermentation,* it strikes me as curious that such a gigantic installation is required to produce a microscopic fungus.

We halt for a moment on the access road across from the building to look at the molasses storage depot. Molasses is the primary food used by Lesaffre to nourish its growing yeast, and is thus required in huge quantities. A truck is delivering its molasses down a grate in the road. The molasses is green-black, bright and glistening, and smooth as honey. Gallons and gallons are flowing from the truck hose.

"This molasses comes from a canal boat," Monsieur Poitrenaud says. "From here, the molasses is conveyed, via piping, into the plant. Before using it for fermentation, though, we have to purify it. As you see, it's a brownish liquid which contains colloids in suspension—products that have to be eliminated. At the outset, the molasses is kept in big vats. In them, we blend nine lots we know the composition of, so that we can produce an average. We proceed this way because sometimes toxic elements remain in the molasses.

"Once the nine lots are mixed, we send the molasses into the clarifier, a centrifuge machine. It is then exposed for a few seconds to a very high temperature, 130 degrees Centigrade, under high pressure, and in this way all the germs are killed. The batch is then cooled to a temperature lower than four degrees Centigrade, and finally it is transported to underground tanks,

where it is stored until needed in the course of yeast production."

Lesaffre uses a mixture of cane and beet molasses, which
contain different nutrients. The molasses is used to feed and
grow the yeast strains carefully selected by the Lesaffre scientists, Monsieur Poitrenaud tells me, as we watch the dark,
sweet syrup flow down the opening in the road into its storage
cavern. "Molasses is very rich in microelements, vitamins, and
minerals, so it is very good for yeast. We also provide other mineral elements to meet the yeast's need for phosphorus and nitrogen to ensure that the yeast produces important proteins, vitamins, and minerals. It's very complicated. You cannot say,
'We'll just put all the ingredients together and let them boil.'
That will not make the cells multiply. As the process goes on,
we have to introduce more nutrients. And for each type of
yeast, there is a different way to add the nutrients. It is a very
complicated biotechnology, which cannot be used in any other
type of factory—also because each factory has its own know-
how.

"The plant also needs water in order to produce yeast," Monsieur Poitrenaud explains as he points toward the foot of the
hulking, white facade of the yeast production building across
the lane. "Wells under the factory tap the water table and yield
a very pure water.

"The other ingredient required by growing yeast is air," he
says, pointing high on the wall of the factory now. "Those grills
on the side of the production building suck millions of cubic
meters of air into the plant. As the air is full of microbes, dust,
and viruses, 'absolute filters' strain the air before it is circulated
through the vats of yeast."

In addition to the basic ingredients of air, water, sugar, and
nitrogen, the yeasts require "anti-bubble," Monsieur Poitrenaud explains. Antimousse, or antifoam, a soy oil, is used to

quell the bubbles—like those on a head of beer—which take up space in the tanks.

Monsieur Poitrenaud opens a door in the towering wall of the plant and we enter a completely bare, enclosed stairwell and walk up several high tiers of steps. I have the sense that I am ascending a tower of a hospital that conducts secret and important operations. At the end of our climb we are about six stories high. Monsieur Poitrenaud opens the only door and I step onto a kind of viewing balcony, or glass-encased bridge.

Huge stainless steel vats occupy the giant room below one side of the balcony. Across from my vantage point, in a narrow, glass-walled laboratory stretching the width of the building a floor below a lone man is working with beakers at a lab bench in a chamber full of small machines and dials. Beyond the lab is another enormous room set with equally enormous tanks and tubes four or five stories high.

"Here we are on top of the tanks," Monsieur Poitrenaud says. "At the outset the principle for making yeast is to start from a single culture, as I told you. The idea is to increase the population and to inseminate a growing mass until an industrial quantity is obtained. Prior to the multiplication phase, everything takes place in a laboratory."

Just forty-four hours after the initial sowing with ten kilos of "mother yeast," generated over seven days from one test tube of a carefully selected strain, and via a controlled process of rapid multiplication, the industrial cycle yields forty-eight tons, Monsieur Poitrenaud explained, pointing from one to the next of the enormous tanks.

But it is clear that, even now, like the proverbial housewife, Lesaffre's work is not done. Monsieur Poitrenaud takes a brief breath as we lean against the banister that fronts the glass overlook, and then goes on with yeast's many-stepped story. "At the last moment of the multiplication phase, at the end of the production of the last generation, we stabilize the yeast. This is a 'ripening' step, to ensure that the baker will have a very stable product to work with. Before this point the yeast couldn't be used in a bakery because it is not stable enough. Now we stop the yeast's growth because afterwards, it will be kept for some time.

The yeast cream is separated from the nutritious ambient liquid used to spur its growth by a centrifuge. Acid is then added to it to prevent the growth of bacteria. The molasses residues, meanwhile, are transformed into fertilizers and cattle food.

"The cream yeast is finally sent into a rotating vacuum filter where the water is expelled." In this essential phase, the cream yeast, made up of 22 to 23 percent dry material, is changed into a *gâteau de levure,* a sort of crumbly yeast cake or pudding of 32 to 33 percent dry material, which will be compressed into the pat that bakers find useful. The pressed yeast cake is cut into loaves of 500 grams, wrapped, and refrigerated. The yeast is kept at temperatures as low as minus 80 degrees Celsius throughout the process. "Refrigerated transport is essential; the chain of cold must not be broken."

Each production run is monitored to assure that the biochemical composition of the yeast conforms perfectly to norms, the yeast man tells me. Monsieur Poitrenaud's tweedy arm makes a sweeping motion toward the openness of the large building. He explains that there are other levels that I can't see from our position. These other sections of the building are kept in absolutely sterile condition. This means they are covered with special plastic to which air and dust cannot stick. Once a week they are cleaned manually, with a brush. People dressed for surgery scrub the floor inch by inch.

"There is a key word here: hygiene. Because we *must* avoid contamination. We have to be concerned with sanitation because yeast can be contaminated with bacteria. In the best cases yeast cannot be stored for a long time. In the worst, bad yeast will make people ill. Here we cannot risk that. That is the difference between us and some other countries. You don't find this concern in all countries. It's also why our yeast costs more—because when you make an investment in this type of factory, it costs a lot of money. To produce yeast with such high-quality standards is very expensive. This is why it's not always easy to be competitive on the market. But we are able to keep expanding our activities—because people recognize that we provide a high level of constant quality on which they can count.

"The only big problem we have is China," he notes. "They make imitations, counterfeits, as they do, you know, for watches, Vuitton handbags. They produce paper bags that are perfect copies of ours into which they insert poor-quality yeast which is not ours. That's a real problem, and we cannot solve it. And people don't know about it."

As I look out on the vast chambers of the factory, I decide I would buy any product that issued from this precision and perfection-obsessed company. I have never seen such a sanitary, spotless, automated space in my life. Even the bakery and the aquifer couldn't compare. The gigantic building is devoid of humans, save the lone scientist in the lab. The yeast production facility is a world of shiny, chrome vats and fresh-painted, cream-colored pipes and tanks set on floors the size of basketball courts. Pipes of enormous girths curve in and out and around. Enormous fans whirl. The one indication of human presence is the footbath set on the inside of each doorway—used by employees to sanitize their footwear before entering the stark yeast production chambers.

"Everything is under the control of computers," Monsieur Poitrenaud says, as if he's read my mind. "Did you see the number of people working here? Only three people are required to monitor the working of the plant."

"Only three people total?" I say.

"This factory, which is the biggest in the world, could function with just three people. There are more than three people,
in fact, because we want to keep a security margin, because we
conduct manual inspections. See this man?" I watch a man enter the tank chamber, slosh his white boots up and down in the
footbath, and walk across the spotless white floor with a clip-
board in a hand. "That's what he's going to do—manual inspection. . . . But everything could be done automatically. There are
more people working in the maintenance and the cleaning departments than in the processing unit."

"It's amazing," I say. "And everything is done by computer?"

"Yes, we actually asked an American firm to design our au-
tomatization system. They had previously designed the production system for the biggest Budweiser factory in the United
States. It turned out they couldn't help us because our process
is too complicated. So our own engineers in the end designed
the automated parts for us—because they are familiar with the
job," he adds graciously.

Monsieur Poitrenaud stops now to point out hefty pipes
looping through the large chamber. These contain the water
used to cool the vats. Much heat is produced by reproducing
yeast, he explains. The water that cools the tanks absorbs high
degrees of heat, so before returning it to the canal, it is cooled
to avoid thermal pollution.

I pause to take a last look around the gigantic facility—at
this strange and magnificent human creation that produces the
microscopic creatures that cause Monsieur Choquet's doughs
to puff into delicious loaves.

From the production building, we walk across the access
road to the Atelier de Séchage. Underground pipes transport
the yeast cream to this building where it is dried into active dry
and instant yeast. Monsieur Poitrenaud explains that we can't

enter the drying facility for two reasons: to prevent contamination and because the process is concealed from visitors. His eyes twinkle as he grins. "It's part of our particular *savoir faire.*"

೧

Later in the visit, Monsieur Maitre shows me several of the sorts of yeast produced in the Lesaffre *cuve de fermentation.* He hands me a block of fresh yeast about the size of a pound of butter. It looks like tofu, but is firmer, less moist, and buff-colored, and soft and smooth like plasticine. Before touching it, you think it's going to be sticky or wet or slimy, but it has a wonderful texture: giving a little to the finger, soft and satiny-smooth in the hands. It both crumbles and squeezes at the same time. A strange substance, it is smooth but breaks apart dryly, like a boiled egg white. It is marvelous stuff.

Fresh yeast, Monsieur Maitre tells me, has the greatest gassing power of all the yeasts. "A gram of compressed yeast—a pure strain of *Saccharomyces cerevisiae*—contains about ten thousand million living cells, each measuring only a few thousandths of a millimeter," he says. "Fresh yeast is seventy percent water."

Monsieur Maitre tells me the quality of a fresh yeast is evaluated through its color, its texture, and its neutral smell. "The color has to be neuter, ivory, or creamy. If you squeeze it in your hands it must crumble like that. If it's sticky, like pasta, it's not good. And it must have a fresh scent—a *sui generis,* a neuter scent. If it smells of alcohol or fermentation, it's a sign of putrefaction. These are the three parameters of a good yeast: color, smell, and texture."

Monsieur Maitre next pulls out a paper packet labeled "Saffre Levure/Levure Engranule/Active Dry Yeast," and pours its contents into his hand. His palm is a saucer for light brown spherules, or pellets—tiny hard beads like miniature marbles. They roll around freely like the skittery balls in a child's game.

A coating of dead cells creates a hard crust on this yeast that protects it from the air and the humidity.

"You never add the water to the yeast, but the yeast to the water. Then, to activate the fermentation, you add a pinch of sugar and you wait for ten minutes until the pellets absorb the water. After ten minutes, you stir it and then you add the yeast to the flour and you mix."

This yeast is familiar to me as the process used to activate it is similar to that for the Fleischman's I use at home.

"And this is instant dry yeast," Monsieur Maitre says, opening a small, buff-colored, air-sealed packet. "You can see the difference."

This yeast is a creamy, sandy color, and light and loose like very dry, light sand. Each tiny "vermicelli," as Monsieur Maitre calls them, is the size of a comma, or a couple of periods on a page. The yeast is so dry it doesn't stick to a sheet of paper, but trickles off as dry sand would. Something about its lightness makes it seem alive—or about to explode into multiplication. There is no carapace with this one; its particles are very thin and porous.

ᴄ⁓

Later, in a Tudor-style restaurant on a divided, four-lane road, a restaurant my dashing hosts called *"typique,"* I lunch on rich, pink pâté de fois gras, delicious, paper-thin salmon with lemon, and buttery noodles. For me, a casual American who usually grabs a yogurt and toast for lunch, the meal, at a white-clothed table, was a taste of the gracious past. By the way my French hosts dispatched their food, I could tell it was everyday.

As the courses arrived, I took the opportunity to pick the technical minds of my companions.

"What about the water for bread?" I asked. "Should it be of a certain type or quality?"

The water for bread dough must be potable, my lunch partners told me, but spring water was not indispensable. Water used in doughs should be sufficiently hard because the minerals in solution reinforce the gluten. "Soft water may give slack, sticky doughs, but hard water will strengthen the dough. What is not good is a water with too much chlorine in it. Because ferments, like yeast, are killed by chlorine."

The amount of chlorine in a baker's water supply can mean the difference between voluminous, well-risen, or flat bread, Monsieur Poitrenaud said. If chlorine levels are high, fermentation is slowed. This is why, in the United States where chlorine levels are high, bread factories are equipped with filters that lower the chlorine level in their water supply. "If you want to completely stop the fermentation, you need to put a lot of chlorine into the water." On the other hand, if there is no chlorine, the same amount of yeast produces a faster fermentation. "So, if you can manage to use a water free from chlorine, it is better," Monsieur Maitre concluded.

Monsieur Poitrenaud's mind was still immersed. ". . . And the water must not contain too much salt, either. A pure and standard water has no impact on taste," he said. It is fermentation that brings taste. The influence that water may have is on the structure of the bread. The amount of water a baker uses can determine whether he produces a firm dough or a softer one.

"It's the same thing with salt," Monsieur Maitre, the baking expert, said. "The kind of salt makes little difference. You hear a lot about the salt from Guérande. For me, Guérande salt is just a matter of marketing and commerce. Between ordinary salt, other sea salt, and salt from Guérande, there is little difference.

"Maybe if you ask another baker, he'll tell you that the salt from Guérande is the very best, that bread made with another salt doesn't taste the same. As I say, Bernard and I are technicians and we have a technician's viewpoint. I am ready to acknowledge that the salt from Guérande has specific characteristics, but it has yet to be proven to me. I want to have the proof: let's make one loaf with ordinary salt and one with salt from Guérande and then let's establish which has the best taste. If the one made with salt from Guérande has some particular taste or property, okay. But for me, Guérande salt is mainly marketing and publicity. That's how I see things. There comes a point when a technician has to say, 'There. It's true or it isn't.'"

As for the acclaimed trace mineral content of Guérande salt, the Lesaffre scientists had a skepticism similar to that they held with regard to whole wheat bread. "Whole wheat is a kind of unrefined wheat, so it contains dirty parts. What is important to know is that the bran, or epidermis, in wheat concentrates all the bacterias, all the pesticides. So if you are not eating a whole wheat bread grown through organic agriculture—a nonpolluted, noncontaminated wheat—you will be swallowing bacterias, which are far from clean, as well as significant quantities of pesticides and chemical fertilizers. In the same way, the sea is polluted, so the salt taken from it will concentrate pollution."

Paludier Michel Evain, too, had said that salt made through the crystallization of sea water contained not only sodium chloride, but other salts, and other extraneous matter as well. While Monsieur Evain and the other Guérande paludiers see the salts and minerals as adding to their salt's special quality, the yeast company men view those special qualities as pollutants. "In the salt of Guérande, all this dirty, extraneous matter gets concentrated along with the sodium chloride. An ordinary salt, on the other hand, is cleared of all that. In the process of refining salt, the salt is put back into clear water and everything that rises to the surface is cleaned away, 'because it's dirt.' In the end, you get a purified product."

It appeared that the quality of my pure and natural Guérande salt, like everything else in the world, was subject to debate. Dismaying as it was to a mind inclined to romanticization, I now had to bow to the truth. Everything in the world is composed of gray crystals, like the salt of Guérande.

℮

As we finished our *plats*, at my hosts' urging I ordered a rich and creamy crème brûlée.

"The big problem in France now is that the consumption of bread has gone way down," Monsieur Poitrenaud said, shaking his head, as we awaited our desserts. The two men retraced the history of French bread I had heard before—the standard, hearty, large, round loaves of prewar France; the dark, heavy, untasty, mixed-grain bread of the war years; the delight in the white loaves available after the war; the baker in Vendee who discovered a way to whiten and lighten dough and the rapid switch by bakers to production of lighter, whiter loaves; and the dominance of the baguette over the last twenty or thirty years.

A part of the evolution to lighter loaves, aside from the postwar Frenchman's preference for white bread, the men explained, was that, starting at the end of the war, the price of bread was frozen, so bakers made the larger but lighter loaves in order to increase their revenues.

"Simultaneous with all this," Monsieur Poitrenaud said, "was a very significant drop in the consumption of bread." The men attributed this to two main factors: the new sociocultural habits—common to all industrialized countries—featuring less physically demanding work and lower needs for high caloric intake, and the availability of other, richer foods; and an anti-bread propaganda campaign—now reversed—led by postwar doctors seeking to curb the obesity that spiked after the war.

Now the men got to the kernel of the matter. "There are sociocultural reasons for the drop in bread consumption, but there is also another factor: the quality of the bread itself," Monsieur Poitrenaud said.

The men pointed now to the twin problems of reduced flavor and rapid staling. "With such voluminous loaves like these, and intense kneading, the bread gets stale very quickly. Your bread comes out of the oven and it looks very nice. It is crispy. It smells nice. You eat it, it's OK. Three hours later, however, it's like cardboard. It dries, it flakes. It's no longer good to eat! But this is the predominant bread-baking approach that still exists today in France—what we call 'the white bread method.'"

Monsieur Maitre explained now that one reason the white bread method was so dominant was that the professional baking centers no longer taught the older, more traditional methods. "Bakers trained over the past few decades have not known how to make anything besides white bread—the baguette."

I realized now that while I rolled my eyes at American "white bread," the French had their own version of bland "white bread."

Monsieur Maitre said, "The baguette stales because of its shape—its extensive crust and its lack of crumb—and also because of the definition of the product. Do you agree, Bernard?"

"Yes, but depending on the method used to make the baguette it will stale more or less quickly," Monsieur Poitrenaud said. "If you buy bread made in the old way, say, in the morning, it will keep until the evening. But if your bread is made via the white bread method, by noon it will be completely dry."

I thought of the many loaves of *pain trois rivières* that I had so blithely consumed. They stayed crunchy and retained their full, slightly sour flavor until at least the third day. Once again I was impressed with how unusual Monsieur Choquet's fine baguettes were, even in the land of bread.

Now these two savvy men directed me toward the essence of French loaves.

"French bread dough contains very few ingredients: just flour, water, yeast, and salt. It is easy to make bread tastier if you begin adding sugar, butter, or margarine such as the Americans do. But it is difficult to give an 'identity' of its own to such a simple product made of just four ingredients. That's why fermentation is so important. It is fermentation, through yeast, that gives a loaf its aromas, so if there's no fermentation, there's no taste!" I heard Monsieur Choquet's calm, deliberate voice in my mind now, uttering these same words.

"If you make a 'no-time' bread, and skip the fermentation, it is very difficult to obtain anything tasty. Even we French sometimes forget these notions. But a dough with few ingredients is the law here. There are regulations about that," Monsieur Maitre said. "You must understand—French dough is a 'poor dough,' thus it is more difficult to give it an identity as far as taste is concerned."

"That is the beauty of French bread," his colleague jumped in, "I would say it's something like the difference between color and black-and-white pictures. With color it is easy to achieve a product that is immediately pleasing. You can make artistic pictures with black and white, but it's difficult because you have to play with the light. Baking French bread is like making photographs in black and white. With French bread, you don't have the color, by which I mean that you don't have the other ingredients such as fat or sugar. You do have light, which is the fermentation."

Monsieur Poitrenaud's words confirmed my sense that good French bread is a work of art. A baker in France is a painter with a four-color palette. At his board his challenge is to make something beautiful of severely limited materials.

The men described an encouraging recent "backward movement" toward more traditional methods and the production of higher quality, tastier bread: the Coté Retour.

"There are many people, like us, who don't hesitate to make a big detour to buy their bread where it is good," Monsieur Poitrenaud said, "but for many people, bread is just something to help you eat, to soak up the sauce on the plate."

"It is also a question of generation," Monsieur Maitre said. "People born in the fifties know a certain type of bread. They have been used to white bread from the time they were young and they don't want to change. If you make them try another type of bread that you consider the best, they will say that it's not good! Because their tastes and habits are different."

"Europe" now rose up like a great beast from the lake of the conversation. With vehemence in his voice, Monsieur Poitrenaud explained that under the regulations of Europe flour classifications and bread content standards would not be as rigorous as those written into French law. Under Europe's regulations, any country in the community would be permitted to sell any type of loaf made of any type of flour and call it bread.

"We have adapted the regulations made by the European Union to the French regulations. In particular, the French wanted to maintain a *pain au levain* 'of the French tradition,'" Monsieur Poitrenaud explained.

"The European legislation is very complicated," Monsieur Maitre said. "I think today, baking professionals feel somehow lost. Nobody can keep track of it all. The names are not clear. The set of rules has been written and modified by non professionals . . ."

". . . And under pressure from professionals who have committed errors and have wanted to protect their domain." On the same urgent train of thought, the men finished each other's sentences.

"For instance, the confederation of the French bakers wanted to protect itself from the industrial bakeries in particular, the people who made frozen doughs and those sort of things. So, they strengthened the regulations about what bread can be called by what name. The result is that now, technically, there are certain problems—for example, with regard to what we call 'retarded dough.' This is dough made in the afternoon and kept for several hours at a lowered temperature in a fermentation chamber. Via this method, the baker is able to sleep while his dough rises, and then bake it in time for early morning sales. For this type of technique, there is an additive which is called ascorbic acid, which is technically necessary but doesn't change the taste. It helps the baker to maintain constancy in his dough quality but has no influence on the dough. In fact, it contains vitamin C. The regulators have forbidden that although it is absolutely necessary. So there have been technical misunderstandings on the part of the European regulators."

"The rules are written by technocrats, people who are not professionals, who don't know the techniques of bread making. So, they have changed the law without knowing critical things.

"And in the end, who has reaped advantage from this? The super and hypermarkets, and not the independent bakers."

"There are also certain categories of bread which are made of special types of flour. Under French law, each type of flour has a specified type and quantity of enzymes and mineral content level. All this is settled by a law."

"With the new European regulations applied in the fall of this year, it's not the same. The French have managed to keep the names of their breads, but from now on, any country belonging to the community will be able to sell any type of bread made of any type of flour and the name will just be 'bread.' So the market is open now."

A horrifying thought occurred. Under the new, loose regulations, maybe American sandwich bread would take over Europe, or all the European breads would meld together into a uniform, bland, tasteless loaf. That would be like losing summer lemonade in Maryland or rice in China. This was what Monsieur Choquet and the National Confederation of Bakers were fighting to prevent.

When I expressed dismay at this potentially devastating blow to French bread, Monsieur Poitrenaud reassured me with his customary, optimistic calm. "I think each country will keep some of its unique products. We have reason to hope."

e͜

Lingering over a second cup of coffee, I put to my thoughtful hosts a fundamental question. "What *is* good bread? Why do some bakers and some countries make good bread while others do not?" I expect them to wax eloquent on the reasons that French bread is the best in the world.

"You are right in the heart of the subject!" Monsieur Poitrenaud says. "That's where everything begins. The definition of good bread depends on the culture. There is no 'good bread,' in the absolute. Good bread is the one you like. For instance, I could tell you what a good and nice American bread is, even if it's not the one I like best.

"What bread is defined as good depends on what final product you want to obtain. Do you want a bread with a certain taste or a good storage capacity? Some breads are very light while others have a close-grained crumb, a creamy color, a different pattern of alveoles, a different structure. You have to know what you want. As a baker, what you want is to sell to your client what he wants."

Monsieur Maitre adds, "This is important to say because French people tend to be very chauvinistic about bread. They tend to say: Our bread is the best bread in the world and that American bread is, pardon me, 'disgusting'! Yikes! I'm being recorded." He laughs, looking at my tape recorder.

Later, leafing through one of Lesaffre's glossy promotional brochures, I see that these broad-minded bread men's views are closely aligned with those of their company. The description of the Baking Institut in Marcq-en-Baroeul is set off with the heading "Yeast: an international ambassador."

Monsieur Poitrenaud and Monsieur Maitre clip back and forth now, over a topic that intrigues them.

"For a given culture, there is a given quality of bread," Monsieur Maitre says. "For example, take pita bread. All the Arab world eats it. It's their bread. It may be the most common bread in the world.

"And the Chinese eat a lot of steamed bread—stuffed with meat and other things. They also eat a lot of American-style sandwich bread. They are very fond of its sweet taste."

"The Chinese like sweet bread," observes Monsieur Poitrenaud, "but there is also the U.S. wheat association which promotes American wheat everywhere in the world, and especially in Asia."

"Their potential is very high."

"They go so far as to provide fully equipped factories where people learn to make American sandwich bread."

Monsieur Maitre surmises that the Chinese fondness for soft and sweet things may or may not come from the Americans. What *is* established is that they don't like hard crusts—one reason for the prevalence of steamed breads in China.

"There may also be physiological reasons for the preference for soft breads, like a certain tenderness of the gums," Monsieur Poitrenaud suggests. "For example, in Western Africa, Senegal, or Ivory Coast, the people don't like hard-crusted breads because they hurt their gums. You have to give them softer breads."

Monsieur Maitre says, "It's really very specific. For example, if you bake French bread in China and give it its normal golden color, they will say, 'Oh, no, it's overcooked, it's nearly burned!' Whereas for us, it's just its characteristic color." As they say this I remember the steamed buns I ate as a child in Taiwan. They were tacky, and the color of white rice.

Aside from texture, countries vary in their taste for sourness in bread, and have adapted their bread-baking methods accordingly, my hosts explain.

"The Germans and people from the eastern countries of Europe make rye bread," Monsieur Poitrenaud says, "and for this they need a lot of acidity. They have developed lactic bacteria which produce lactic and acetic acids. The biochemical conditions for rye bread must be acid so those countries want acidity. French, Spaniards, and Italians, on the other hand, make their bread with wheat flour. They don't want acidity. They want to leaven the dough and to produce aromas. They encourage the growth of yeast as opposed to bacteria. For the Germans, it is the opposite. The Germans add yeast at a later stage in the process—though yeast is always absolutely necessary since rye doesn't contain as much gluten as wheat."

"You have chosen a good topic. Everybody talks passionately about bread. And it also has a religious and political meaning," Monsieur Maitre says.

Monsieur Poitrenaud jumps on this. "Yes, a political one too. Lesaffre was summoned for a consult to the Iraqi government, for instance, to help the Iraqis improve their bread and their installations. The Iraqi government said, 'We are going to build automatic factories to show the grandeur of the regime, and we'll have a better bread, cheaper than the bread made by our bakers.' But this didn't work at all. The village bakers still made better bread than our factory bread. And in Libya, it was the same thing."

As for American sandwich bread, Monsieur Maitre had this to say: "American sandwich bread is made of flour, water, salt, and yeast like French bread, but as we said before, it also contains sugar and fat—that's the base. Often the fat is soy oil because that is the least expensive. Because the Americans are practical people, they discovered that if they added fat to bread, it would remain soft longer. And if they added sugar, it could be kept even longer. In addition, many American breads contain a different type of flour—oat flour, for example. Then they add seeds and additives. Among these additives, you'll find emulsifiers, which add softness to the crumb, diminish the staling process, and enhance shelf life. You'll also find oxidants to strengthen the gluten—in particular, potassium borate. Then there are ammonium salts, also called 'yeast food,' which are used to stimulate the growth of the yeast and of the dough. This practice is an old habit which, in my opinion, can be dated back to the beginning of this century. American bakers are conservative people, so they still use that!"

"You also must take into consideration the most commonly used American 'sponge and dough' method," his partner says. "There are two steps in this bread-making process. In one step, which is called the sponge, seventy percent of the total amount of flour is allowed to ferment for three and a half to four hours. Then there is a second stage, called the dough stage, in which you add the rest of the flour, the water, and all the other ingredients. The big difference is that the dough is baked in a mold. This way the bread has very little crust and a lot of crumb.

"What is important in the making of American sandwich bread is to have a very tight dough structure. Very tight and very regular, so that the food you put on it doesn't go through. You don't want to have ketchup on your shirt! In France, we have an ad for hamburgers. They show an ordinary hamburger. A man takes a bite of it, the ketchup goes on his shirt and the man says, 'My dry cleaner is rich.' This refers to a sentence everybody knows in France that comes from an English lesson we've all had in which the first sentence you learn is 'My tailor is rich.'

"What the American baker wants to have is a fine and regular crumb. He also wants to have softness, because American people love what is soft and sweet—marshmallows, for example! It's like with chocolate. For the French market, the Swiss sell a black and sour chocolate. For the Americans, they sell a very sweet one."

"In my opinion sandwich bread developed in the United States due to the English influence," Monsieur Poitrenaud says. "Sandwich bread is from the English tradition. Americans added the sugar and fat. That is its specificity.

"At the beginning of its history, the United States did not make purely white bread. The pioneers who went from the East Coast to the West Coast took with them the yeast they had cultivated. This yeast was finally set in San Francisco. And nowadays, there is San Francisco sourdough bread, which is a very specific kind of bread. It is linked to the microorganisms that reside in that part of California due to the humidity and air temperature of the area."

"Yes, it's true," Monsieur Maitre says of the good California bread to which his colleague referred. "But in general American bread is a different bread, which corresponds with a different way of life."

"For instance, you cannot eat American bread just like that, alone," his compatriot adds. "You have to eat it with something else. With a good French baguette, when you buy it and head for home, you realize halfway, 'I should have taken two!' because you have already eaten three-quarters of it just like that, on your way home! I think that is the difference!"

"You need to take into consideration the American context, the way people eat," Monsieur Poitrenaud says. "I personally am fond of American bread for making sandwiches. I lived for two and a half months in Minneapolis and we ate sandwich bread every day. A worse thing is the cheese. Red and yellow cheddar!" I can tell Monsieur Poitrenaud has a good rail in him about that.

"My impression is that even in the United States, there is a trend in favor of French bread," Monsieur Maitre suggests.

"Yes, but it's French bread in the American way. The baguette with sugar and fat is an adaptation of a French idea to the American taste," his colleague says. "The American is pragmatic, unlike the Japanese who is respectful. For example, when the United States wanted to import croissants from France, the French bakers who went there and made croissants the French way didn't succeed. Croissants sold in the United States, among other characteristics, have to be bigger, less darkly baked, and have a pale color. And as long as you're making them, you add some colored green and pink stuff on top, or melt Swiss cheese on them."

I am a little embarrassed at the truth of all that the men are saying. We Americans seem to have a propensity for gilding the lily, for going overboard, for adding glitter to something lovely in its simplicity.

Sandwich bread is taking over the world, the two men imply. "There is something about people's choice of sandwich bread nowadays which seems to be linked with urbanization," Monsieur Poitrenaud says. "You see the same trend toward sandwich bread in India. Now in India, people traditionally eat *chapatis*, a sort of pancake made with unrisen wheat dough, or *nan*, a sort of bread cooked in small ovens at home, but consumption of Western-style bread has increased at a rate of maybe ten percent a year there, for a long time. Why is that so? It's linked with the fact that today in big cities like Bombay or Calcutta or Delhi, many people work in offices and can no longer cook their noon *chapatis*. And in India, factories were built on the English model, so the sandwich came as a help. The sandwich is an easy way to eat away from home—in offices, in the street. My impression is that in China, we have the same evolution. The demand for American bread meets the Chinese taste and is also linked with urbanization."

"The general decrease in bread consumption is linked to way of life," Monsieur Maitre adds. "In France what we call *sandwicheries* have popped up everywhere, shops which make fast food. In Paris, at noon, almost nobody goes home to have lunch nowadays. People who live in the suburbs and work in

Paris leave their offices for thirty to forty-five minutes to grab lunch at McDonald's or some sandwich shop. Many bakeries now include a take-away department that opens on the street. Have you noticed that? Have a closer look at these places. There is a little counter where someone can make you a variety of sandwiches with ham, *saucisson,* cheese, salad."

I know the sort of place.

The yeast men's comments depress me. I consider my country responsible for the wrecking of the easier-going, more humane European lifestyle, the ransacking of the leisurely lunch hour and the more family-friendly work policies. But perhaps this is an arrogant attitude in itself, an overestimation of my country's influence. Probably the world would be headed in the direction of maximum production, rush, and overwork even if the United States did not exist. The yeast men do not blame the United States, and the United States lunch practices *are,* it seems, hitting some sort of practical nail on the head.

Lifestyles, as well as products, it is clear, are being globalized and exchanged every which way. Madame Eslan, the wife of the director of tourism in Blain, told me she saw great advantage in the abbreviated English lunch hour as compared to the longer French repast. "You can eat quickly and be done with it, and get home earlier in the evening." Meanwhile, my friends and I long for those long, leisurely, three-hour French lunches. The acceptance of *sandwicheries* by these men loosens me up. Other cultures give us a mix of ingredients, emotions, perspectives, and new adaptations to human problems that would not otherwise be at our disposal. American-style sandwich lunches are part of the mix. A waning of vehement nationalism may result, but perhaps that is not the worst outcome. And the truth is, everyone is free to choose between options. As Monsieur Pautrot suggested at the water plant, it is wonderful to be able to choose one day to have a Big Mac and the next, coq au vin.

Monsieur Maitre is wending on with the story of the breads

of different cultures. "We had an old teacher, Monsieur Calvel. He was a well-known teacher at the French school of milling. Now he is retired. He must be eighty-five or eighty-six years old. He was devoted to the promotion of French bread, especially in Japan. He came back with stories about the Japanese. For the Japanese, French bread is a special bread. They sell it at a much higher price, so they can take time to make it. When you see baguettes on the Japanese shelves, there is not a single loaf out of line."

"If you teach the Japanese something," Monsieur Maitre says, "if you give them a formula, they are very respectful. They won't alter anything. Whereas French people, if you give them a piece of advice or a formula, a week later, they already have altered it. It's their type, it's a Latin thing!"

Monsieur Poitrenaud now delivers the most startling comment I've yet heard in my bread journey. "The truth is, the French bread the Japanese make is much better than the average French!"

My romantic bubble about French bread now bursts. I am flabbergasted. Can I really accept that I ought to go to Japan for the best French bread? I know it could be true, but the earth shakes.

⁓

We are now in the baking center, Monsieur Maitre's bailiwick, the last stop on my tour of Lesaffre. The Baking Institut as a whole is responsible for the commercial side of Lesaffre: training, investigations of yeast's application to baking, the development of new techniques, and communications. It is also a professional school, offering courses around the globe on the practice and theory of baking *pain français.*

The baking lab where we are now standing is a large, efficient, white-walled kitchen with an oven at one wall and several long tables in the middle of the room. Monsieur Maitre tells me that this week a group of Poles and a Turkish group have come to the center for consultations and lessons in bread making.

He shows me an experiment the lab is conducting on behalf of the Turkish group. Three different bakers are in the process of baking three different *"essais"* of *pain français*. He picks up a very blond loaf and hands it to me. It is as light in weight as it is in color. "This is the bread made in Turkey," he says. "It is highly kneaded. See the color of the crumb? It's very white. It's a rather light bread in weight," he says, judiciously. "When a loaf is too light it is not a sign of quality. The lighter the bread is, the more quickly it will dry. So, the conservation time for this bread will be very short. Now smell the loaf. Its smell is not very agreeable. It contains a lot of yeast and you can smell the yeast."

I hold the loaf to my nose. The smell of the bread is strong and the crumb is spongy and moist. To my taste, it's soggy and unappealing. I wouldn't want to eat it.

I ask whether the Turks came seeking to learn or incorporate French bread-baking techniques.

Monsieur Maitre says, "Yes, they are interested in the baguette. But they like their Turkish bread. That's how they want their bread to be. It's just like if we French tried to say to the Americans, 'Forget about white bread or sandwich bread. It's no good. Just stop everything.' It would be a revolution. They'd tell us, 'It's none of your business. This is the kind of bread we like, and that's that!' It's very difficult to change a country's habits."

Throughout our conversation about the breads of different cultures, it has struck me that Monsieur Poitrenaud and Monsieur Maitre, like rural Monsieur Cruaud, are a new breed. Open to and accepting of the different tastes of people from other cultures, rather than cleaving to nationalistic, patriotic, ethnocentric views, they are, in a sense, new-minted citizens of the world.

A further aspect of these men strikes me. While obeying the commands of business—Monsieurs Maitre and Poitrenaud are nothing if not savvy publicists for their company and it's their *job* to understand the points of view of people from other cultures—these are men of standards. They are ready to speak up on behalf of their own preferred breads, but they don't consider themselves or their own table bread inherently superior. Wide-minded, they are unable to just say, "This is the best bread in the world," since they know all too well that judgment is relative. Theirs is the anthropologist's outlook. If you look closely enough there is an intelligence behind each country's bread, just as there is behind each country's child-rearing practices or code of manners. The United States, under this lens, is no better or worse than any other country. It strikes me that the yeast men together represent the resident of the globalized world at his best—a fair and open person able to take a stand in the face of an array of possibilities, but without judging the perspectives of others, a new kind of human being respectful of others' cultures and individual preferences without being threatened by perspectives different from their own. If more people had this kind of loyalty—I wax large now—world conflict might be significantly diminished.

e

On the way back to the station in his zippy Renault, Monsieur Maitre told me he has served as an advisor to McDonald's, among scores of other companies, bakeries, and institutes around the globe. As a liaison between the client and the product, he offers clients the technology and know-how to use yeast correctly, and counsels people about their baking problems.

He told me he is from Besançon, of Swiss and French heritage. His parents were dairy farmers. "It was a hard, demanding life, as my parents had to be there twice a day for the cows." His parents never had vacations. "My mother didn't know the sea until she was sixty-eight! I would have become a farmer—it's a good life, in nature—but my mother advised me not to." No one ended up taking over the farm.

"Are you glad you didn't do it?" I asked.

"Today you can hire someone to take the farm so that you can have vacation. It's bit easier now," he said, a thread of wistfulness running through his words.

It occurred to me then that here beside me was a kindred spirit. Like me, this urban Frenchman had a romantic vision of farm life. Both he and I needed reassurance that rural calm exists. It suddenly dawned on me that the French long for *la France Profonde* as much as I. They, too, need rural vistas and good bread. They, too, long for the France of Millet. And all of the efforts to preserve *gîtes,* all of the regulations concerning bread composition, wheat and yeast production were also an effort to preserve and confirm what was essentially French.

e⁓

Just before I left the baking lab at the Lesaffre Baking Institut, Monsieur Maitre had wanted me to see one more loaf.

"Now this one," he said, taking me to a smaller table, upon which sat a nicely browned saucepan-shaped loaf, "favors conservation because there is more crumb inside. It is made for *pain surprise.*

"Xavier!" he called. Referring to the man walking toward us, he said, "He will show you how we cut the crumb out."

The tall, dark-eyed man in a short lab coat came up to the table, sliced the top off the loaf, and began to cut around the inside edge, scooping out the inner crumb, and turning the loaf into a bowl. He commented that the bread was a little too hot, really, for easy cutting. Normally it should be completely cool. "The goal is to take out all the crumb and keep only the crust, as a container," he explained. "Then to put some butter, some cheese, some *saucisson* inside it and replace the top, for a nice presentation. It's a surprise bread—for cocktail parties and special occasions."

It struck me now that this was what my exploration of a French loaf had been like—a surprise bread. Once I cut into it, I discovered all kinds of odd and unexpected tidbits hidden inside.

The first set of surprises was the ingredients themselves. *Pain trois rivières*, I learned, is made of four miraculous ingredients: salt raked from the sea by an ancient, mystical process; glowing, green wheat from a lowly sloping field; clear water from deep among the rocks of the earth; and invisible but powerful yeasts born and nourished in industrial vats of up-to-the-minute sophistication. Each ingredient, in the end, seemed to me both solid and earthy, and magical, romantic, a jewel.

Another surprise was the people who produce the elements of the loaf. The *paludiers*: dike-dancing, erudite Michel Evain, salty Lucien Gaspard. The wheat farmer: somber, thoughtful Joseph Orieux. The millers: hassled but ardent Christophe Giraudineau, his businesslike mother, and his reverent father. The water men: sleek, fast-talking Marc Pautrot and comfortable, earnest Jean-Marc Cruaud. The tweedy yeast men: dashing Bernard Poitrenaud and kind-eyed, thoughtful Hubert Maitre. And, most important of all, solid, smart Jean-Claude Choquet and the various members of his bakery: early-rising, hardworking, cheerful Marie-Madeleine; the handsome apprentices; athletic Pa-Paul Breher, Jean-Claude's partner; and his sweet parents. My French loaf draws from the wisdom of many different kinds of people: a practical, worldly-wise younger generation, and an older generation bringing their steadiness, richness, and solidity to the loaf. The old and young, the traditional and the new are kneaded into *pain trois rivières*. The last line of the Gibran poem, "Your Children," in the Choquet's kitchen was:

> *For even as He loves the arrow that flies*
> *So He loves also the bow that is stable.*

Beyond the loaf's basic ingredients and their producers, I discovered in the heart of my loaf sundry, seemingly contradictory truths resting side by side. I came upon strange and odd surprises about the bread of France: French bread, the symbol of nourishment and the good life for the world, is often of poor quality; North Dakota wheat is nestled inside of many French baguettes; the best French bread in the world may be found in Japan.

To hold a loaf of *pain trois rivières* in my palm now, toward the end of the story, is to look at the multicolored, mixed-up nature of the world.

As I examine my favorite French loaf, it looks a little less French to me, and more a product of a particular Monsieur Choquet and of our creative, protean world. On the one hand, nationalism now appears foolish to me. If the "Frenchness" of a loaf is relative, how many other things are? Why shouldn't anyone, anywhere, enjoy and take advantage of the richness, wisdom, and technical expertise of other peoples?

On the other hand, though the loaf has given me a sense of the world as one organism, I find myself also struck, ironically and contradictorily, by the importance of nationalism—the broader iteration of individualism and the local and the idiosyncratic. Although difference and national identity may at times not promote cross-cultural humanity or compassion, they do result in the flowering of exciting and divergent works of creativity, innovation, and artistry. Obviously—as the cheese makers of Roquefort, France, will shout at you—if we lost all idiosyncrasy and local tradition to big money and McDonald's, our freedom would be nil. Without strong regional affiliation, French loaves might no longer be produced in a certain French village. Monsieur Choquet's exceptionally fine loaf is fundamentally and profoundly *French*.

As for my own nationalism, I set out for France with a disdain for the United States and its loaves. Strangely, the French gave me a greater appreciation of my own country. American influence abroad, these generous Frenchmen have made me understand, is not all bad. Frenchmen may eat *noisettes d'agneau* one day and a burger and fries the next, and like them both. American sandwich bread has its place in the world, even in France. The survival of wonderful, local, handmade, high-quality natural products may sometimes depend upon sophisticated, U.S.-conceived, internationally relevant marketing strategies. I'm not going to take up going to McDonald's, but I feel less condemnatory toward it.

What of the questions that propelled me to France: my longing for community and my tussle with Time? Monsieur Choquet, the *paludiers,* and the water men clearly had a sense of community in the old-fashioned sense of being deeply tied to neighbors and a particular geography. So community does exist in rural France. At the same time, my visit made clear that community can be very differently defined from place to place. Jean-Marc Cruaud, for instance, wouldn't view community as requiring people to throw open their doors: he likes his French fences. And perhaps the men at the urban yeast company have as viable and satisfying a community as Monsieur Orieux, the wheat farmer.

Time is precious. It was so at the beginning of my quest, and it remains so at the end. Fermentation is the answer to Time that I've found here in France. Compulsive overwork is not quality work. As so many I've met during this exploration have noted, the baker in Vendée who speeded up the kneading time for bread did not enhance the quality of his product. Just as fermentation—deciding to take the extra time for it—allows a loaf to take on taste and depth, allowance for fermentation time at work contributes to an excellent life. All excellence requires it.

Did I find my romance? Does romance fade when reality creeps in? The truth is, I now see that French bread is not pure in the way I'd originally imagined it, but I still love to eat *pain trois rivières*. I have given up my romantic picture of a loaf and received something real, a loaf with peculiarities, like those of the human beings who helped create it. Initial disillusionment took me to a sturdier magic than that rooted in ignorance and wishful fantasy—one grounded in real salt, wheat, water, and yeast. I see my loaf with its oddities and necessities now, but, as in mature love, as opposed to new love, I have accepted them, and come to appreciate it more deeply.

As I set out for a loaf of bread, I assumed I would find something as simple as a round, red apple. Instead, I found myself sitting down to a rich, five-course French meal. Knowledge is difficult. Knowing more about the world can breed discontent. It is tough to cope with the inexorability of modern life and historical currents. In the final analysis, though, romance based on ignorance and fantasy and unconscious prejudice is not as satisfying or rich as romance grounded in the truth. Maybe one can include fairy tales in the range of possibilities, and consciously choose to be romantic sometimes and just stick to the opinion that you are eating the world's most glorious loaf of bread.

The ideal, perhaps, in the end, is to stand, as Jean-Claude Choquet and the others do: planted in one particular place but looking outward toward the world.

❧

A deep sense of relief pours into me during the hour's ride back to Paris. I have done it. Something is resolved. A flecked crumb is the most delicious now, gray the truest color.

Out the train windows I see trees in the shapes of lollipops across the farm fields.

Epilogue

A LOAF IN
MY ARMS

The best smell is bread, the best savour salt,
the best love that of children.

Graham Greene
The Power and the Glory

With bread and wine one walks the road.

Spanish proverb

IN APRIL, THE MONTH I ARRIVED IN FRANCE FOR MY second visit, the Loire-Atlantique earth was parched white, but in wild bloom. The dirt everywhere was pale and dusty, but sprinkled with flowers, as if the soil couldn't help but shout and fruit.

Home is the place, as a wise person once said, that you miss even when you're there. My whole being ached as I looked out over the land. That first day back in the French countryside, it hit me that the charm of France resides, most deeply, in its beautiful, nourishing terrain. I couldn't rest if I thought those odd-shaped fields were to vanish from the earth.

Arriving in Blain I felt like a sailor returning home after a long sea voyage. My heart skipped a beat as I walked toward the Boulangerie Choquet. From way up the street, I could see the maroon awnings bearing the familiar white lettering.

Madame Choquet was minding the shop when I arrived. We exchanged happy grins and the many obligatory French air-kisses. I asked for the family news. The children were doing well, she said. Sarah was in Lyon. She and her fiancé were now working engineers and were going to be married at the Blain "Castle of the Crow," the town's château, in August. The other daughter was in her second year of physical therapy school. Jerome was thriving in the bakery.

Then, in one breath, she told me that Jean-Claude's father, Rogatien, had died a month and a half before, and two weeks later, she and Jean-Claude had become grandparents. As I exclaimed both my sadness and pleasure, joy and worry wrestled across her vivid face.

Madame Choquet ushered me back into the cozy family kitchen, where Monsieur Choquet materialized out of nowhere, like a wizard, just the way he had on the first day I met him.

Handsome Monsieur Choquet greeted me with warmth, but he looked tired and drawn. The sparkle still played in his soft eyes, but seemed to flicker a little like a light in heavy weather. Grief, like streaks of rain down a window, had marked his face.

"And how do things go for you?" I asked.

"Very well," he said, dismissive, going immediately to topics closest to heart. "I have lost my father. On the other hand, I have a grandson. *C'est la vie,*" he said, standing very still.

At this moment, Jean-Claude's mother came into the room. She was wearing a long, sheltering coat around her thin frame. We exchanged greetings and then she immediately broke into tears.

"He has left me," she explained, wiping her cheeks.

The older Madame Choquet stood close to her son, as if drawing strength from him. She spoke slowly, after a few seconds, gathering herself together, her words sluggish with sorrow.

"But we have gotten a *grand supplémentaire,*" she said then, smiling through her wet eyes. "Have you told her?" she said, turning to her son.

"*Oui, oui.*"

"*Oui,* he is a grandfather!"

"One month old," Monsieur Choquet said. "Fifty-five centimeters." He laughed.

"One is well content," his mother said. "One has left and then comes the replacement." Very quietly, tearfully, she said, "*C'est la vie.*"

Seeing the mother's and son's heads bent toward one another, Millet's painting *L'Angelus,* came into my mind. It portrays a man and a woman in a field praying over a basket while the faraway church bell rings for mass. Even within the Choquets' sorrow, as in the painting, there seemed to exist a kind of wholeness. A sense that life *is* what it is—life comes with gifts and retrievals.

Grief, however, had not slowed Monsieur Choquet's schedule. He was taking the train to Paris at 11:30 for a meeting of the National Confederation of Bakers. On his return, he would go directly to a meeting in Nantes and return home at about nine at night from there. Then he would be up at two A.M. "It's a busy week," he said, in vast understatement. "The *pâtisserie* apprentice is on vacation and we have a very full weekend ahead, with marriages requiring pastries for over a thousand people."

We chatted for a few moments about the fast pace of life nowadays, each of us complaining about the same things—me about life in Washington and the Choquets about life in a small French town. Madame Choquet asked her husband if he would eat at home before leaving. He replied that he would grab a sandwich on the fly. The baker of *pain trois rivières,* like any busy turn-of-the-century man, was going to have the lunch equivalent of supermarket bread.

Monsieur Choquet looked toward me with apology in his eyes. He explained that he, like a lot of Frenchmen, had stopped going to restaurants for lunch, and now just grabbed "a sandwich, some cheese, a dessert, and a coffee to make it quick," at a *sandwicherie.* "People work far from home now and no longer return home for lunch. This pattern has increased a lot in the last ten years. It is truly a loss for French families."

Aware of time passing, and Monsieur Choquet's imminent departure, I cut to the chase. "What do you think are the most important things in life?" I asked, seeking a final bit of wisdom from the baker of my favorite loaf.

After a pause, he folded his hands in front of him, and said, slowly, thinking his answer through as he spoke, "Life is complicated in itself. It is not something you can rejoice at since every day we come closer to death, but still, it is worth living. The important thing, in my view, is that work should serve to make a man blossom. A man's *métier* should permit him to stand straight, to be truly himself—rather than just require him to serve his *métier*. And, I think, a man should not run after money, with the 'always more' mentality. We see that we are not any happier now than we were fifty years ago, though we are able to buy more things. . . . What is important to me is that every morning, when I get up, I am happy to go to work. After that, I am happy to enjoy myself. But to me, to have the luck to be able to do what I like to do, and to be happy just doing my job—that is the essential thing."

How strange, I thought, to have first set out for France disillusioned with the Washington work-orientation only to be told by a French baker that good work was the key to a satisfying life.

‹͜

At the end of the story, Monsieur Choquet and his family do fit into a glowing Millet painting of small-town, rural French life. They pass their days anchored in local geography, a thickly peopled community, committed work, and a reliable and strong family, keeping traditions alive—to the extent that a life led close to the earth is possible these days in France. For even in the mid-1800s, when Millet and the other Barbizon painters worked, the rural life they were documenting was fast disappearing. The Choquets feathered my dream, but at the same time the Choquets are real: producing good, simple bread rather than just frosted cakes. As is the loaf, so is the man.

As I watched the Choquets go about the business of their lives, my dream of a pure *pain au levain* and my idealized preconceptions of the unhurried lives of French villagers melted away, but the French baking family gave me another and greater gift. They have lent me—obvious, perhaps to others—

a clear picture of life as it is: hard, meaningful work and a thread of connection made up of family and friends make the warp and woof of a good life, no matter where you live—and no place is more richly endowed with these than any other.

My last night at the *chambre d'hôte* in beautiful, ordinary Pays Trois Rivières, I just sat and took in the sight and fragrance of Monsieur Choquet's loaf of *pain trois rivières* for a while, reflecting on my journey. I now had the crumb as well as the crust of my loaf. I saw it clearly now, and still, this plain, simple bread before me made me feel like dancing a jig.

Bread seems to me now a quotidian treasure hailing from somewhere outside of culture, beyond the flurries of human predicament and struggle—a signal of the way to live.

"Bread may not always nourish us," Thoreau wrote, "but it always does us good, it even takes stiffness out of our joints, and makes us supple and buoyant, when we knew not what ailed us, to recognize any generosity in man or Nature, to share any unmixed and heroic joy."

ᘒ

Here now in Washington, as I go to bed each evening it is a sustaining and abiding comfort to know that, daily, in the misty, dawn fields of Blain, across the sea, the crew at Boulangerie Choquet is shaping simple, honest rounds of dough.

Acknowledgments

First and foremost, I must thank the people who shared their stories, and gave of their time to enrich my understanding of a simple French loaf. They include Jean-Claude Choquet, Marie-Madeleine Choquet, Rogatien and Marie Choquet, Michel Evain, the couple I call Lucien and Madeleine Gaspard, Christophe Giraudineau, Marie-Thérèse and Daniel Giraudineau, Joseph Orieux, Jean-Claude Cruaud, Marc Pautrot, Bernard Poitrenaud, Hubert Maitre, and Carol, Carl, and Jerome Choquet.

Next, I thank Juliette, Jac, and Madeleine Fournot, for they, in large measure inspired this wonderful journey and set me on the road to my loaf. Jac's help with books, ideas, and contacts was invaluable in the early stages of the project.

Without Madeleine Cardona's generosity, wisdom, and practical help with translation and transcription, this book could never have come to fruition. I thank her, and her family, for this great gift.

William Strachan gave welcome support to the book early on. Blandine Trouille at the French Embassy in Washington and Christabelle Salmon of the French Lycée in Washington offered their help right when I needed them. Art Norton, Karen Noyce, Wade Miller, Val Giddings, and Orvin Voth served as consultants for the water, yeast, and wheat chapters.

I wish also to thank bakers Jean-Paul and Valerie Evain of Herbignac, Brittany, and the organic bakers at Guenouvry, Loire-Atlantique. The miller J. Taupin of Saint Omer de Blain gave me a fascinating tour of his mill, and he and his wife, their hospitality. Yves Alix, Loire-Atlantique hydrologist, sent information on the geological composition of the Nort-sur-Erdre aquifer. Monsieur Eslan, director of tourism for Blain, gave me a wonderfully informative tour of the Pays Trois Rivières region.

Writer friends read and advised at various points along the way. These include Jon Luoma, Kate Phillips, Jesse-Lee Kercheval, William O'Sullivan, Susan Land, Mary Stucky, Wendy Pollock, and Maggie Sheen. Catherine Mayo and Patricia Hampl stood by faithfully. A few friends, among so many who aided and abetted during the writing of this book, must be specially thanked. The Troyansky family offered rich hospitality and sound advice in their tiny Paris apartment, and Amy's drawing of the loaf is perfect. I cannot imagine a better companion in crime than Valerie Hanlon. Renée Burgard and Merrill Carrington knew the right poems when they saw them.

I must thank my agent Sloan Harris and his assistant Teri Steinberg for their good work on behalf of this loaf. Teri's prompt and friendly notes were an unfailing delight. Erin Clermont's copyediting was expert. Tisha Hooks has been a wonderful editor. She knew just what to do. I cannot thank her enough.

Finally, with all my heart, I thank my parents, Charles and Lois Taber, who taught me to love foreign cultures and hearty bread, and who gave me a thousand kinds of help on this journey, as they have on so many others.

With Peter, Maud, and Forrest, and a fresh loaf, I need nothing more.

The following books served as resources:
Le Livre du Boulanger, by Jean-Yves Guinard and Pierre Lesjean.
Le blé, la farine, le pain, published by EPI, Espace Pain Information.
Folklore du Boulanger, by Christian Bouyer.
Guide de l'Amateur de Pain, by Lionel Poilane.
On Food and Cooking, by Harold McGee.
The Breads of France and How to Bake Them in Your Own Kitchen, by Bernard Clayton, Jr.
English Bread and Yeast Cookery, by Elizabeth David.
World Sourdoughs from Antiquity, by Ed Wood.

CREDITS